IN PURSUIT OF A VISION

Two Centuries of Collecting

at the American Antiquarian Society

AMERICAN ANTIQUARIAN SOCIETY

Worcester, Massachusetts

2012

Library of Congress Cataloging-in-Publication Data

American Antiquarian Society. Library.
In pursuit of a vision : two centuries of collecting at the American Antiquarian Society : a bicentennial exhibition at the Grolier Club, New York.
    pages cm
Catalog of an exhibition drawn from the collections of the American Antiquarian Society held at the Grolier Club in New York from September 12 through November 17, 2012.
Exhibition curated by David R. Whitesell; catalog essays and entries by Lauren B. Hewes (co-editor), Thomas G. Knoles (co-editor), David R. Whitesell, Laura E. Wasowicz, and Vincent Golden; preface by Ellen S. Dunlap; exhibition conservation by Babette Gehnrich and Laura Oxley; photography by Stephanie Richardson; digital coordination by Jaclyn Penny; and editorial management and design by Abigail P. Hutchinson.
Includes bibliographical references.
ISBN 978-1-929545-68-1 (hardbound) -- ISBN 978-1-929545-69-8 (softcover) 1. American Antiquarian Society. Library--History--Exhibitions. 2. Research libraries--Acquisitions--Massachusetts--Worcester--History--Exhibitions. 3. Book collecting--United States--History--Exhibitions. 4. United States--History--Bibliography--Exhibitions. 5. United States--Imprints--Exhibitions. I. Whitesell, David R. (David Rhodes), 1954- curator. II. Hewes, Lauren B. III. Knoles, Thomas. IV. Grolier Club, host institution. V. Title.
Z733.A465A44 2012
025.2'18770747471--dc23
                          2012024968

The paper used in this publication meets the minimum requirements of the American National Standard for Information Sciences—Permanence of Paper for Printed Library Materials.
ANSI Z39.48.1992

Table of Contents

Preface

In the early days of the American Antiquarian Society, our founder Isaiah Thomas would write to new members whom he had recruited from every part of the Union, admonishing them to send materials for preservation in the Society's library and cabinet in Worcester. He wrote, "We cannot obtain a knowledge of those who are to come after us, nor are we certain what will be the events of future times; as it is in our power, so it should be our duty to bestow on posterity that which they cannot give to us, but which they may enlarge and improve and transmit to those who shall succeed them. It is but paying a debt we owe to our forefathers." Over the course of two subsequent centuries, eight generations of the Society's members and staff have heeded Thomas's admonition. The story of how they did has been told by Philip F. Gura in *The American Antiquarian Society, 1812-2012: A Bicentennial History* (Worcester, 2012).

In the present volume – and the Grolier Club exhibition it accompanies – we have attempted to tell the collateral story of what they collected and preserved. It is a story that could be told in many different ways. We could have followed the example of AAS librarian Clarence S. Brigham in his 1958 book *Fifty Years of Collecting Americana...* and explored the Society's extensive collections, genre by genre: almanacs, annuals, atlases, auction catalogs, bibles, bibliographies, bindings,... and on to United States views, western Americana, and yearbooks. Alternatively, we might have focused on the rarest items in the collection – the "firsts" and the "only knowns" – as was the case with our 1969 Grolier Club exhibition, *A Society's Chief Joys*. In 1976, we celebrated the bicentennial of the nation with an exhibition called *Wellsprings of a Nation*, featuring only items dating before 1801, an area of collecting in which the Society remains without peer. Or, we might have chosen to shine a light solely on the nineteenth-century collections, demonstrating an astonishing depth and breadth built up largely over the past fifty years. The story of AAS collections could also have been told through an exploration of the projects of the Society's past research fellows – some 900 graduate students, scholars, writers, artists, and performers who have come to the Society over the past forty years – displaying not only the publications and works of art which resulted, but also a sampling of the primary source materials that fueled their research and discoveries. Instead, we have presented *In Pursuit of a Vision* as a celebration of the generosity and farsightedness of a few of the many collectors, dealers, librarians, and others who have, each in his or her own way, contributed to the greatness of the Society's library by sending collections our way. As we continue our vigorous pursuit of new acquisitions today, we are "but paying a debt we owe" to them.

In Pursuit of a Vision has been a truly collaborative undertaking. Early on, former AAS curator David R. Whitesell did the lion's share of organizing the exhibition and wrote many of the catalog essays and entries, and to him we offer our heartfelt thanks. With his departure for a new position at the University of Virginia, the reins for the project were taken into the capable hands of curator Lauren Hewes, who along with curators Thomas Knoles, Vincent Golden, and Laura Wasowicz, had also contributed essays and entries, each according to his or her own area of curatorial expertise. Hewes supervised the work of staff photographer Stephanie Richardson and digital coordinator Jaclyn Penny, put in hours of editing along with Thomas Knoles and bicentennial coordinator Abigail Hutchinson, and worked closely with conservators Babette Gehnrich and Laura Oxley to see to the myriad of details concerning preparation, transportation, and installation. To these colleagues, and many others unnamed, I extend on behalf of the Society special thanks for a job very well done.

Ellen S. Dunlap
President

Introduction

In the two centuries since its founding in 1812, the American Antiquarian Society in Worcester, Massachusetts, has become a principal research center for the study of American history and culture. In support of that mission AAS has gathered one of the world's foremost collections of books, pamphlets, newspapers, broadsides, and ephemera printed in early America: preeminent for the period up through 1820 and exceptionally strong for the years 1821-1876. Supplemented by an outstanding assemblage of secondary source materials, the Society's library presently contains nearly 750,000 volumes, over two million newspaper issues, and substantial holdings of periodicals, graphic arts, children's literature and manuscripts.

The story of how the Society's collections were formed is the subject of this bicentennial exhibition. In the years after the American Revolution, patriot printer Isaiah Thomas gradually built in Worcester, Massachusetts, one of the most successful printing and publishing businesses in the new nation while simultaneously forming one of its best contemporary private libraries. Thomas's principal objective was to document the output of the American press, a mission that led him, in 1810, to publish his path-breaking two-volume *The History of Printing in America,* still an essential source for the history of the book in the colonial and early national periods. It was primarily to preserve his collections, to augment these with complementary materials, and to ensure their productive use that Thomas formed the American Antiquarian Society.

In the words of AAS bicentennial historian Philip F. Gura, Thomas's vision for the Society was that it would "collect all things that pertained to American history, no matter how slight or insignificant they might seem at the time of their acquisition." Thomas's interest in American imprints extended beyond 1812 to encompass the entire contemporary output of the American press, an ambitious goal which the Society eventually capped by setting a terminal date of 1876 for much of its collecting. That endeavor has been spectacularly successful: it is estimated that AAS presently owns over half of all books and pamphlets published in what is now the United States prior to 1821.

AAS curators well know that each item added to the collection comes with its own story. Because it is impossible here to tell, or even to summarize, several million individual stories, this exhibition adopts an alternative strategy. It traces the development of the Society's collections through the exemplary generosity of some of the committed donors who have embraced Isaiah Thomas's ambitious vision over the ensuing two centuries. The narrative begins with Thomas's own gift of his personal library, soon augmented by the important collection of Mather family books and manuscripts acquired from Hannah Mather Crocker, and a remarkable bequest from the book collector and diarist William Bentley. During the early 1830s, with few funds at his disposal, AAS librarian Christopher Columbus Baldwin greatly expanded the Society's library through his inspired resourcefulness and tireless pursuit of books and manuscripts. Acutely aware of the historic events to which they were witness, sisters Lucy and Sarah Chase documented the Civil War by collecting contemporary publications and materials, which they later gave to AAS for preservation. In the late nineteenth century, the Society was the grateful beneficiary of two very generous bequests from George Brinley and Joseph J. Cooke; with these funds, AAS acquired wisely and well at the Brinley and Cooke auction sales, considerably strengthening its already distinguished holdings of rare Americana. Other significant gifts came from members of the Society who themselves collected Americana in a serious way, including three prominent Worcester residents: Stephen Salisbury III, Nathaniel Paine, and George F. Hoar.

AAS initiated its second century by reassessing its mission and realigning its acquisitions policy more closely with Isaiah Thomas's original vision. And in a profound stroke of good fortune, the Society found the ideal person to implement that strategy. In his fifty-four years as AAS librarian, director, and president (1909-1963), Clarence S. Brigham increased the Society's holdings of early American imprints and secondary sources more than six-fold. Critical to his success were the close and enduring relationships Brigham formed with collectors, bibliographers, booksellers, and fellow librarians, who helped him transform AAS into the leading repository of America's early printed heritage. Among the people who assisted in the building of the collections was Charles Henry Taylor, whose many gifts served especially to shape the Society's graphic arts and newspaper collections. Taylor joined with AAS members Herbert E. Lombard, Matt B. Jones, and Frank Brewer Bemis to help Brigham form, in a relatively short time, an outstanding gathering of American literature and poetry. From the superb private libraries of Boston collectors Frederick L. Gay, John W. Farwell, James F. Hunnewell, and his son James M. Hunnewell, Brigham obtained remarkable early American imprints, maps, Hawaiiana, and illustrated Americana.

Brigham also saw to it that the Society's membership ranks included many of the day's foremost collectors in specialized fields, a number of whom chose AAS as the permanent home for their carefully assembled holdings. Among them were Edward Larocque Tinker (Louisiana imprints), Samuel L. Munson (almanacs), Frank J. Metcalf (hymnals), Thomas O. Mabbott (flash press newspapers), Waldo Lincoln (Caribbean newspapers and cookbooks), and Charles L. Nichols (Worcester imprints and children's literature). Brigham's friends in the antiquarian book trade were no less dedicated in building the AAS library—partly for profit, to be sure, but also because they, too, embraced Thomas's vision for AAS and understood their responsibility to place rare imprints and primary source materials in an appropriate home. Several of the donors who steered invaluable research material on the American book trades to AAS were booksellers, including Arthur Swann and William J. Campbell (annotated auction catalogs), and Michael Papantonio (bookbindings).

Near the end of his tenure Brigham published *Fifty Years of Collecting Americana for the Library of the American Antiquarian Society, 1908-1958*, a guidebook describing the dozens of specialized collections he had successfully developed for AAS through gift, exchange, and purchase. Brigham's lead was capably taken up by his successors R.W.G. Vail, then Clifford K. Shipton and Marcus A. McCorison, all of whom continued Brigham's successful cultivation of donors. Special emphasis was placed on expanding the Society's coverage of the Midwest, South, and West, and of America's relentless westward expansion. Two members in particular supported that initiative in extremely generous fashion: Donald McKay Frost for western Americana, and Thomas W. Streeter for material on early American canals, railroads, and much else besides. Streeter's benefactions were crowned by a bequest which, in Brinleyesque fashion, enabled AAS to acquire many rarities at the celebrated Streeter auction sales. Also largely built in recent decades has been AAS's outstanding collection of early American children's literature, which has benefited immensely from the sustained interest of collectors such as Wilbur Macey Stone, d'Alté A. Welch, Ruth E. Adomeit, Elisabeth Ball, Herbert Hosmer, and book scout Benjamin Tighe.

In entrusting his collections to AAS, and in encouraging others to do the same, Isaiah Thomas envisioned a Society whose members and staff would work intensively with its holdings in order to vastly expand our knowledge of American history. His original vision for AAS entailed more than collecting and preservation. A principal objective was to define the universe of early American printing. Thomas made a concerted effort to list all pre-1776 American imprints known to him, but his checklist remained unfinished at his death in 1831. A generation later Thomas's extensive notes were reworked and substantially expanded by Samuel F. Haven, Jr., son of librarian Samuel F. Haven. His checklist—the first comprehensive early American imprint bibliography—was published posthumously by the Society in 1874. Twenty years later Charles Evans began his singular quest to update Haven's work with a far more comprehensive checklist extending through the year 1820. Without the Society's committed assistance over five decades, Evans's monumental *American Bibliography* probably would never have been finished. Evans's opus was one of many bibliographical projects actively encouraged by Brigham and his successors, and the 118 volumes of *Proceedings* and dozens of bibliographical monographs published by AAS have contributed greatly to the study of American printing and publishing history. Among these were Brigham's own works on pre-1821 American newspapers and Paul Revere's engravings.

During the second half of the twentieth century, it became increasingly clear to Clifford K. Shipton and Marcus A. McCorison that, in order to more fully realize Thomas's vision for AAS, the Society needed to expand its range of activities. If the universe of early American imprints was now well defined, it was imperative to make these resources more accessible to all who needed them. Consequently, in 1954 AAS formed a successful and enduring partnership with Readex Microprint Corporation to make as many pre-1801 American imprints available via microform as possible—including those not owned by the Society. The AAS-Readex collaboration has since been expanded to include all pre-1820 imprints as well as vast selections of pre-1877 newspapers and ephemera, all now available digitally with full-text search capabilities.

AAS has had a long-standing practice of aiding scholarship by creating a supportive and collaborative research environment. In 1967 the Society and Clark University partnered to undertake a new critical edition of the writings of James Fenimore Cooper, now nearing completion. AAS's contribution has been to build the best extant collection of Cooper's works in pre-1877 editions and to make these available to the project's editorial teams. And in 1983 the Society established its Program in the History of the Book in American Culture which, through conferences, intensive summer seminars, lectures, and publications—most notably the five-volume *A History of the Book in America* (2000-2010)—has nurtured a thriving scholarly interest in American book history.

These programmatic initiatives, as well as a more comprehensive acquisitions program, have been made possible by extremely generous funding provided by government agencies, foundations, and especially the many members and supporters who have embraced Isaiah Thomas's vision as their own. Over the past half century the Society has been the grateful recipient of many important gifts which have established new programs, created dozens of endowed acquisitions funds, and expanded AAS's physical plant. The Society's curators now have the resources to collect more systematically and in areas, such as children's literature, in which its holdings had previously been uneven. And like their predecessors, AAS curators continue to seek out innovative collecting fields which, if presently little known or under-appreciated, hold much promise for future generations of researchers. To offer just a few examples: periodical issues in original printed wrappers; nineteenth-century imprints illustrated with original mounted photographs; fine and unusual examples of bespoke and publishers' bindings; examples of "transatlantic" publishing, that is, items reflecting a transatlantic collaboration among author, printer, publisher, illustrator, binder, and/or distributor; newspapers and other publications issued from "amateur" presses; periodicals issued in manuscript; and partly printed volumes prepared for customized record-keeping of all kinds.

As the Society has approached its third century, it has continued to pursue and to broaden Isaiah Thomas's original vision. A host of new fellowships has expanded the vibrant intellectual community nurtured by AAS, as has the recently established Center for Historic American Visual Culture. A state-of-the-art stacks addition has provided much-needed room for collection growth and ideal storage conditions for the Society's irreplaceable holdings. New digital partnerships have enabled the Society to offer convenient online access to over twenty million pages of AAS library materials to researchers worldwide. But as this exhibition seeks to make clear, the Society's success in pursuing that vision is truly a collective achievement shared by all of the individuals and institutions whose commitment and generosity over the past two centuries have made it a reality. To them the Society offers its most heartfelt thanks; and to all extends an invitation to pursue that vision into the third century of this noble institution.

ABCDE

HIJKLM

J

Two   Line   Englifh.

ABCDEFG

JKLMNO

Two   Line   Pica.

ABCDEFGH

LMNOPQRS

Isaiah Thomas as Printer, Collector, Historian, and Benefactor

The American Antiquarian Society owes its existence to Isaiah Thomas, printer, journalist, publisher, historian of printing, and philanthropist. The Society was Thomas's vision, and from the time of its founding in 1812 until his death in 1831, he was its principal benefactor. Thomas gave AAS its founding library, its first building, and funds for the support of its first librarians.

Isaiah Thomas was born on January 19, 1749, the child of Moses Thomas and Fidelity Grant. Shortly after Isaiah's birth, Moses Thomas left his family; he died in North Carolina in 1752. Left with three children in Boston, Fidelity kept a small shop. In 1755 the Overseers of the Poor in Boston placed the six-year-old Isaiah with a Boston printer, Zechariah Fowle, and the boy was apprenticed to Fowle the following year. In later life Thomas described Fowle as "a Printer and seller of ballads and pedlar's small books," "an indifferent hand at the press, and much worse in the case. He was never in the printing house when he could find an excuse to be absent." By Thomas's account, Fowle made little effort to educate his apprentice and Thomas's learning, both of the printing trade and of things more generally, was done through his own efforts.

In 1765 Thomas left Fowle after an argument and went to Halifax, Nova Scotia, with a plan to go on to England to learn more of the printing trade. Instead, he spent several years moving, working in Portsmouth, New Hampshire, and Charleston, South Carolina. In 1770 Thomas returned to Boston and began publication of the *Massachusetts Spy* in partnership with Fowle, buying Fowle out after just three months. The *Spy* increasingly became a strong proponent of liberty, and on more than one occasion Thomas was brought before the British authorities. Finally, in April 1775, Thomas removed his press to Worcester, some forty miles west of Boston, where he continued publication of the *Spy*.

In the years following the Revolution Thomas's business empire grew. He formed partnerships with printers (many of them former apprentices) throughout New England. By the 1790s his business was matched in size only by that of Mathew Carey in Philadelphia. After 1800 Thomas gradually reduced his active involvement in the printing and publishing business, and he turned his attention to gathering information on the history of printing and publishing in America from their origins up to the Revolution. This process included the active collection of books, pamphlets, and newspa-

FIG. 1

pers. Thomas wrote, "Few persons would form an idea of the cost which has attended the collection of the information I have found it necessary to procure, from various parts of the continent.... The purchase of volumes of old newspapers alone, has required a sum amounting to upwards of a thousand dollars. It is true, however, that these volumes are valuable; and, together with the collection previously owned by the author, probably, constitute the largest library of ancient public journals, printed in America, which can be found in the United States." The first fruit of this research and collecting was *The History of Printing in America, with a Biography of Printers, and an Account of Newspapers...* (Cat. 9) which appeared in two volumes in 1810. Thomas's work is a singular source for its subject, containing much that would otherwise be unrecoverable. The second fruit of this activity was the American Antiquarian Society.

The earliest record of Thomas's plan to found the Society is an entry in his diary early in 1812 noting that he had proposed the organization to two other Worcester men. A few months later Thomas and a group of hopeful incorporators sent a petition to the Massachusetts Legislature, and the Society was created by law on October 24, 1812. Thomas conceived of AAS as a learned society similar to the Society of Antiquaries of London. His hope was that the Society would "enlarge the sphere of human knowledge, aid the progress of science, . . . perpetuate the history of moral and political events, and . . . improve and interest posterity." "The chief objects of the inquiries and researches of this society will be American Antiquities, natural, artificial, and literary; not, however, excluding those of other countries."

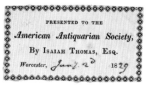

FIG. 2

In keeping with the Society's national ambitions, men from all over the country were elected to membership and plans were made to have at least one councilor in each state who would be able to receive gifts and forward them to Worcester. The initial library of AAS was a collection of books which Thomas listed in a catalog he completed in July of 1812 (Cat. 11). The catalog listing Thomas's initial gift contains 2,650 titles which Thomas conservatively valued at $4,000. Almost immediately Thomas began listing additional gifts he made to the Society in its donation books, and by the time of his death in 1831 he had made 116 additional gifts of printed works, manuscripts, and items for the Society's cabinet, all of which he valued at a total of over $6,000. By 1827 the library contained 7,000 volumes and some 15,000 pamphlets.

In the early years the Society's books and cabinet were housed in Thomas's Worcester mansion. Construction of the first Antiquarian Hall began in 1819; Thomas supplied the land, $2,000, and 150,000 bricks toward the building. In addition to his own benefactions, Thomas also sought gifts on behalf of AAS, cultivating collectors and others who could supply books. These early donors included Hannah Mather Crocker, the daughter of Samuel Mather; William Bentley, a Salem minister; Mathew Carey; and William Buell Sprague of Albany, who would in later life author *Annals of the American Pulpit.*

Thomas was also the initiator of the Society's publication program. In 1820 AAS published the first volume of *Archaeologia Americana: Transactions and Collections of the American Antiquarian Society.* The primary work in this volume was Caleb Atwater's "Description of the Antiquities Discovered in Ohio and Other Western States." This was the first of a number of nineteenth-century publications dealing with Native American archaeology, ethnography, and languages. Over the next ninety years eleven more volumes of the *Transactions* appeared, including Isaiah Thomas's own diary, published in two volumes in 1909.

Thomas was careful to provide for the continued health of the Society after his death in 1831. His total bequest to AAS amounted to more than $30,000, which included the land, building, and collection materials he had already given to the Society, as well as $12,000, the interest of which was to pay a librarian's salary. This support allowed AAS to enter its third decade as a healthy, active organization.

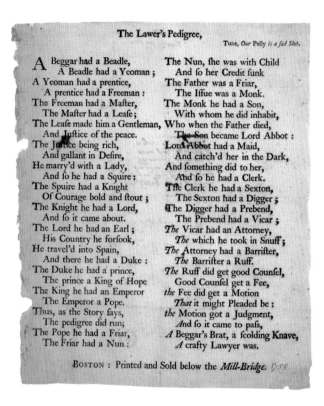

CAT. 1. *The Lawer's Pedigree*, 1755.

1. *The Lawer's Pedigree.* Boston: Zechariah Fowle, 1755.

BEQUEST OF ISAIAH THOMAS, 1831.

As a child, Isaiah Thomas received only six weeks of schooling before his mother allowed Boston's Overseers of the Poor to place him with printer Zechariah Fowle. The precocious six-year-old Thomas performed chores, sold ballads on the street, and soon was put to the job of setting type. Thomas's first composition was *The Lawer's* [i.e., Lawyer's] *Pedigree*, a humorous broadside ballad about the making of a lawyer, sung to the tune "Our Polly is a Sad Slut." Pleased with young Isaiah's industry, Fowle took him on as an apprentice in 1756, and Thomas's life course was set.

Thomas took great pains to preserve two copies of his first effort, eventually bequeathing them to AAS to ensure their permanent preservation; these are the only copies to have survived. Thomas inscribed one copy: "This is a copy from the first types that I set for the press. It was in the summer of 1755." Thomas also told the story of this broadside in the autobiographical essay he published in *The History of Printing in America*.

AAS Chief Joys 4; Evans 7446.

2. *Tom Thumb's Play-Book; to Teach Children Their Letters as Soon as They Can Speak.* Boston: Printed by Isaiah Thomas and sold by A. Barclay, 1764.

GIFT OF ISAIAH THOMAS, 1812.

Isaiah Thomas's manuscript notation— "Printed by I. Thomas, when a 'prentice in 1764, for A. Barclay"—shows that this rare miniature chapbook was one of the earliest pieces that he printed. With its evenly spaced lines, consistently centered ornaments, and elegant use of white space, it is quite a neat production for a fifteen-year-old apprentice. The text features alphabet rhymes which had been earlier printed in *The Child's New Play-Thing*

15

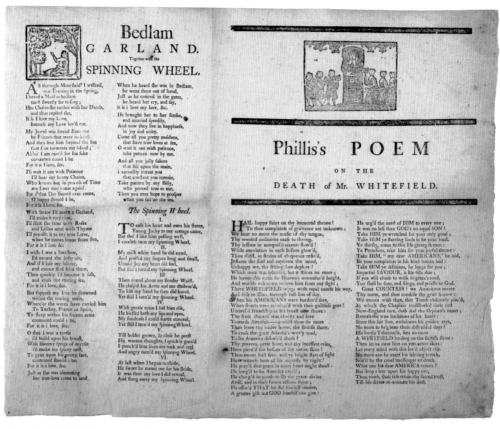

CAT. 3. Phillis Wheatley, *Phillis's Poem on the Death of Mr. Whitefield*, 1770.

(London: T. Cooper, 1743; Boston: John Draper for Joseph Edwards, 1750). In some respects, *Tom Thumb's Play-Book* provides a more light-hearted and secular alternative to *The New England Primer*. Instead of featuring events from the Bible, the alphabet letters in *Tom Thumb's Play-Book* allude to earthy, even humorous scenes such as, "A was an archer and shot at a frog," and "D was a drunkard and had a red face." But like *The New England Primer*, the text concludes with a catechism—albeit much more simply worded than the Westminster Assembly's *Shorter Catechism*, which is frequently found in *The New England Primer*—and various short prayers. The back cover features a wood engraving of boys playing with marbles and hoops and offers the modern viewer a glimpse into the eighteenth-century world of children at leisure.

Bradbury B5; Evans 10189; Welch 1318.1.

3. Phillis Wheatley. *Phillis's Poem on the Death of Mr. Whitefield.* On a sheet with *Bedlam Garland. Together with the Spinning Wheel.* Boston: Isaiah Thomas, 1770.

BEQUEST OF ISAIAH THOMAS, 1831.

Phillis Wheatley, the first African-American to compose a book of poems, was brought to Boston on a slave ship in 1761 and sold into slavery to the family of wealthy merchant John Wheatley. Unusually, she was educated and encouraged in her literary efforts. Her poem on the 1770 death of George Whitefield, the prominent English clergyman who prompted the Great Awakening and founded multiple American schools and orphanages, was Wheatley's first published work, written when she was just seventeen years old. Isaiah Thomas's

16

broadside printing was one of several contemporary editions. The poem mentions the Countess of Huntingdon, who in 1773 would assist Wheatley with the publication in London of her verse collection, *Poems on Various Subjects*.

Wheatley's poem was printed with a second broadside containing two unrelated ballads, *Bedlam Garland* and *The Spinning Wheel*. After printing, the sheet was intended to be cut so that each broadside could be sold separately. The frugal use of expensive paper demonstrates how Thomas, like his fellow printers, carefully controlled printing shop costs.

Wheatley: Evans 42198; Bedlam: Wegelin 425.

4. *A Monumental Inscription on the Fifth of March. Together with a Few Lines on the Enlargement of Ebenezer Richardson, Convicted of Murder.* Boston: Isaiah Thomas, 1772.

BEQUEST OF ISAIAH THOMAS, 1831.

This rare broadside, bearing a woodcut reinterpretation by Paul Revere of his famous copperplate engraving of the Boston Massacre, exemplifies the patriotic nature of much of Isaiah Thomas's printing work. The founder of AAS actively participated in events leading up to and during the American Revolution, and Thomas's newspapers, broadside, and ballad printings often reflected his political views.

This 1772 broadside marking the second anniversary of the Boston Massacre of March 5, 1770, recalls the violent events and glowers over the injustice of legal foot-dragging on the part of British authorities in general. It draws a parallel between the acquittal of British officers on murder charges after the Boston Massacre and the perceived British favoritism that accompanied the trial and sentencing of a locally despised customs official, Ebenezer Richardson, for murder. Richardson, who in February of 1770, fired a musket into a mob of rowdy youths, wounding one and killing a second, was tried and found guilty but never formerly sentenced by the British authorities (and in fact a pardon eventually arrived from Lon-

don early in 1772). His release from prison in March 1772 impelled Thomas to express his outrage via this broadside, which calls Richardson an "Informer, and tool to Ministerial hirelings." Thomas annotated the sheet in the lower margin, providing a key to the identity of the judges referenced in the poem—"Bridge of Tories," for example, stood for Judge Edmund Trowbridge.

AAS Wellsprings 102; Evans 12302; Wegelin 646.

5. *A Narrative, of the Excursion and Ravages of the King's Troops under the Command of General Gage, on the Nineteenth of April, 1775 … Worcester: Isaiah Thomas, 1775.*

GIFT OF ISAIAH THOMAS, 1812.

During the early 1770s, Isaiah Thomas ran one of Boston's most successful printing businesses. His achievements included a popular almanac, an innovative monthly magazine, and an influential newspaper, *The Massachusetts Spy*, with a circulation exceeding 3,500. When war seemed imminent in April 1775, Thomas quietly slipped his printing equipment out of Boston, sending it forty miles inland to Worcester, where he could print for the patriot cause without British interference. Two nights later Thomas helped to pass the alarm through Middlesex County, then hastened to Lexington in time to join the fighting before following his press to Worcester.

On May 3, 1775, Thomas published the first Worcester edition of *The Massachusetts Spy*, filling that issue with news of Lexington and Concord. Three weeks later, the Massachusetts Provincial Congress commissioned Thomas to print this pamphlet, with its official account of the battles. The twenty-three-page document, which Thomas completed by July 1775, published depositions collected from various eyewitnesses as well as a list of the Minutemen killed, wounded, and missing, arranged by town of residence. This is Thomas's own copy, annotated by him on the title page, "First Book printed in Worcester."

AAS Chief Joys 35; AAS Wellsprings 149; Evans 14269.

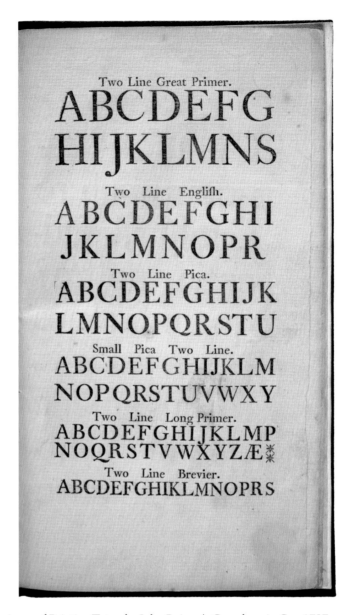

CAT. 6. *A Specimen of Printing Types by John Baine & Grandson in Co., 1787.*

6. John Baine & Grandson. *A Specimen of Printing Types by John Baine & Grandson in Co., Letter-Founders.* Edinburgh: John Baine & Grandson in Co., 1787.

GIFT OF ISAIAH THOMAS, 1812.

While developing his printing business following the Revolution, Isaiah Thomas invested heavily in equipment and new printing types ordered from England, which he showcased in an elaborate type specimen book issued in 1785. Thomas preserved the type-founders' specimen books from which he ordered these and later types, donating over twenty to AAS in 1812 as part of his initial gift (Cat. 11). Hence the Society possesses an important collection of late eighteenth-century English type specimen books, several of them unique, from such type founders as John Baskerville, William Caslon, Thomas Cottrell, Alexander Wilson, Joseph Fry, and others.

Perhaps the most significant is this copy of

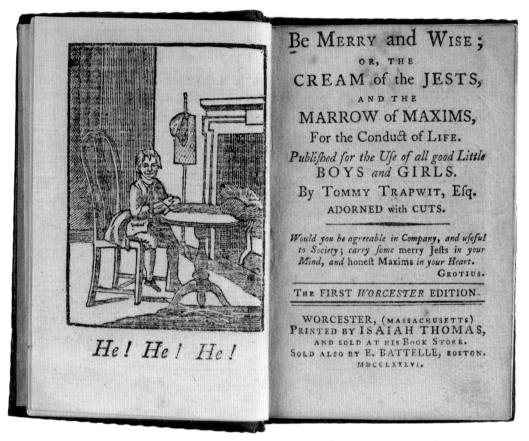

CAT. 7. *Be Merry and Wise*, 1786.

John Baine & Grandson's 1787 specimen book, the only copy known to survive. Baine had long been a successful Edinburgh type founder before emigrating to Philadelphia in the summer of 1787. There he proved equally prosperous, establishing the first commercially viable American type foundry. Although printed in Edinburgh, Baine's 1787 volume displayed the range of types and ornaments he was now able to cast in Philadelphia for American printers. Baine's types apparently influenced noted American type founders Archibald Binny and James Ronaldson, who cut several similar faces a decade or so later. This copy bears manuscript price annotations, possibly in the hand of Philadelphia publisher Mathew Carey, as well as Thomas's title-page note: "This Foundry was brought to America by the Grandson, about 1791 [sic], and established at Philadelphia. John Baine came over not long after his Grandson."

AAS Chief Joys 247; Mosley 5.

7. Tommy Trapwit. *Be Merry and Wise; or, the Cream of the Jests, and Marrow of Maxims, for the Conduct of Life. Published for the Use of all Good Little Boys and Girls.* First Worcester edition. Worcester: Isaiah Thomas and E. Battelle, 1786.

GIFT OF ISAIAH THOMAS, 1812.

This joke book is part of the *Youth's Library,* an eleven-volume set of children's books published by Isaiah Thomas; this copy was exquisitely bound in gilt leather for Thomas's private library. AAS has ten of the eleven volumes—the only children's books, of the many that Thomas published, included in his initial 1812 gift to AAS. In an age when primers and catechisms dominated children's book publishing, *Be Merry and Wise* is quite

CAT. 8. William M.S. Doyle, *Isaiah Thomas,* ca. 1805.

unusual for its focus on humor, and for the wood engraving of a smiling boy reading what appears to be this very book at his parlor table. The caption title, "Jests for the Entertainment of Youth," seems to be a more accurate title, as the book is filled with references to flat beer, college students, and prostitutes.

Evans 20028; Rosenbach 106; Welch 1331.2.

8. William M. S. Doyle. *Isaiah Thomas.* Watercolor on ivory, ca. 1805.

GIFT OF ISAAC RAND THOMAS, 1947.

In his diary for November 25, 1805, Isaiah Thomas recorded sitting for this miniature when he was fifty-six years of age. The receipt for Boston miniaturist William M. S. Doyle (1769-1828) is preserved in Thomas's business papers at AAS. At the time the portrait was made, Thomas had been retired from the printing business for several years and was working on the manuscript for *The History of Printing in America,* which would be published five years later (Cat. 9).

Doyle, who began working as a miniature painter and silhouette cutter in Boston around 1803, depicted the bewigged Thomas in dark coat and vest, with the hint of a smile. Thomas, an active consumer of portraiture (he had multiple likenesses taken throughout his life in oil, pastel, and watercolor), considered Doyle's portrait an accurate depiction. He allowed the miniature to be engraved for the 1811 issue of *Freemason's Magazine,* which contained Thomas's farewell speech to the Grand Lodge of Massachusetts, delivered on the occasion of his retirement as Grand Master.

9. Isaiah Thomas. *The History of Printing in America. With a Biography of Printers, and an Account of Newspapers ...* Worcester: Isaiah Thomas, Jr., 1810.

GIFT OF ISAIAH THOMAS, 1812.

In 1810 Isaiah Thomas published his masterwork, a two-volume history of printing in British North America to 1775, with extended digressions on the history of printing in Europe and elsewhere. It is conceivable that his purchase at auction in 1784 of a copy of Joseph Ames's *Typographical Antiquities* (London, 1749) inspired Thomas to undertake an American equivalent. As time permitted, he assiduously gathered the primary evidence he

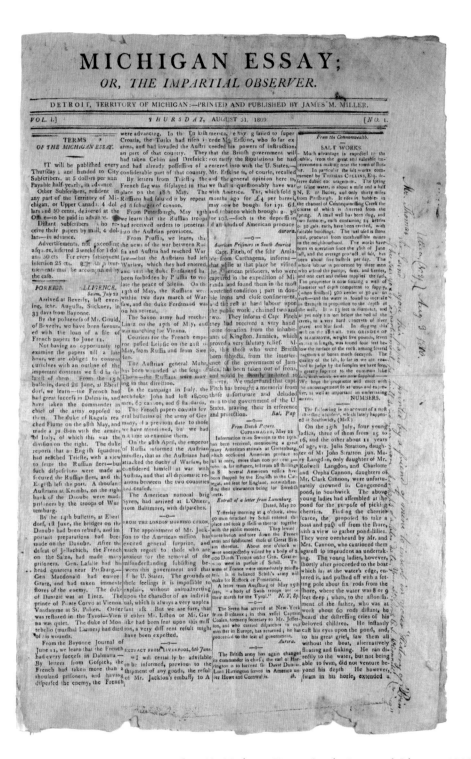

CAT. 10. *Michigan Essay; Or, the Impartial Observer*, 1809.

would need, collecting early American imprints for his library, delving into public archives, and seeking information on his book trade contemporaries through correspondence and conversation. The extraordinary result was a comprehensive series of printer biographies, newspaper and periodical histories, and invaluable appendices on booksellers, paper mills, and related topics; though for reasons of length Thomas omitted a planned checklist of pre-1776 American imprints (Cat. 155). The first history of its kind, Thomas's work has never been entirely superseded, not even by the AAS-sponsored *A History of the Book in America* (2000-2010; Cat. 185).

This is one of two copies at AAS formerly owned by Thomas. Both sets are in contemporary gold-tooled tree calf bindings by John Roulstone (1777?-1826), then generally acknowledged as Boston's most accomplished bookbinder. This copy bears Roulstone's distinctive Greek key and feather roll on each cover.

Shaw & Shoemaker 21483.

10. *Michigan Essay; or, The Impartial Observer.* Detroit, Michigan, August 31, 1809.

GIFT OF ISAIAH THOMAS, 1812.

Isaiah Thomas devoted substantial space in *The History of Printing in America* (Cat. 9) to a history of American serial publications, closing with an eight-page census of newspapers "Published in the United States in the beginning of the year 1810." Thomas sought help in its compilation in March 1810 by placing a widely reprinted notice in *The Massachusetts Spy*, requesting publishers "to forward one or two of their papers ... that the right titles of their several Newspapers, may be correctly inserted." Many responded, and the newspaper issues sent to Thomas were later donated to AAS.

This example—the first and only extant issue of the first Michigan newspaper—arrived too late for inclusion in Thomas's checklist. The manuscript notation on the side reads, "Utica, (N.Y.) Aug. 3d 1810. Mr. Thomas, Sir I send you this paper printed by a friend of mine to insert in your 'History of Printing.' If he sees

your advertisement, he will send more, perhaps of a later date. Your obt. Servt. C.S. McConnell." *The Michigan Essay* was printed by James M. Miller on Michigan's first press, brought to Detroit from Baltimore in 1809 by Father Gabriel Richard. Most of the text is in English, but a few articles and advertisements are in French.

AAS Chief Joys 96.

11. Isaiah Thomas. "Catalogue of The Private Library of Isaiah Thomas, Senior, of Worcester, Massachusetts." March-July 1812.

GIFT OF ISAIAH THOMAS, 1812.

At the front of this manuscript volume Thomas wrote, "The following Catalogue of Books is presented to the American Antiquarian Society, to be the exclusive property of said Society to all intents and purposes so long as it shall continue as a body corporate, pursuant to the provisions of the act of incorporation of said Society. By Isaiah Thomas. Worcester, July 12, 1812."

The catalog's 2,650 titles are arranged topically under headings such as ancient and modern books, works in the Indian language, Masonic works, printing, periodicals, newspapers (a twenty-page checklist), and works printed by Thomas and his son, Isaiah Thomas, Jr. Its contents reflect both Thomas's diverse collecting interests and his efforts to assemble materials for *The History of Printing in America* (Cat. 9). The 1812 gift represented about nine-tenths of Thomas's personal library and included "most of his choicest and best Books."

Isaiah Thomas Papers.

12. "Songs, Ballads, &c. In Three Volumes. Purchased from a Ballad Printer and Seller in Boston." Volume 1 of 3. Boston: Various printers, 1811-1814.

GIFT OF ISAIAH THOMAS, 1814.

Shortly after founding AAS in October

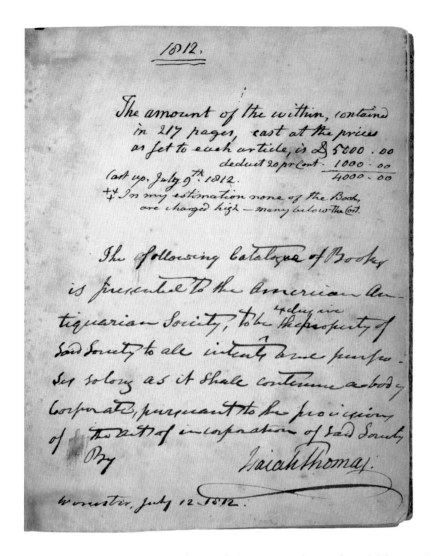

CAT. 11. "Catalogue of The Private Library of Isaiah Thomas, Senior, of Worcester, Massachusetts," 1812.

1812, Isaiah Thomas presciently resolved to collect for its library the popular street literature of the day. Having printed broadside ballads and chapbooks as an apprentice (Cats. 1, 7), Thomas well understood the significance of these ephemeral publications which few considered worth preserving. At Thomas's request, Boston publisher Nathaniel Coverly gathered broadside ballads from local shops for a year before selling him the 326-sheet hoard in June 1814 for $4.50. To these, Thomas added sixteen others from his own collection before binding the group in three volumes, "to shew

what articles of this kind are in vogue with the Vulgar at this time."

Volume one of the ballads set is displayed here. The collection is a diverse mix of handbills and sheet poems, such as the lament over a theater fire in Richmond, Virginia, on December 26, 1811, as well as popular ballads about executions, political events, and bawdy songs like "Meg of Wapping." Over half of the broadsides are Coverly imprints. As a record of early nineteenth-century American popular song, Thomas's collection is of inestimable value.

Hannah Mather Crocker
and the Mather Family Library

Hannah Mather Crocker (1752-1829) was the granddaughter of New England divine Cotton Mather (1663-1728). The wife of Boston minister Joseph Crocker and mother to ten children, she took up the pen after her children were grown and began a career as an author. She wrote several unpublished poems and essays, preserved in the Mather Family Papers at AAS. Her pamphlet *A Series of Letters on Free Masonry,* a defense of male and female involvement in Freemasonry, appeared in 1815. However, Crocker is best known for her book *Observations on the Real Rights of Women, with Their Appropriate Duties, Agreeable to Scripture, Reason and Common Sense* (1818) which argued for the intellectual equality of women and is considered to be the first book on the rights of woman written by an American.

Crocker made gifts to the American Antiquarian Society of books, manuscripts, and artifacts on fourteen occasions and, after Thomas himself, was the most frequent donor to the Society in its first decades. She made her first gift to AAS in 1813 after Isaiah Thomas visited her home in Boston. In 1814 she sent Thomas the Mather family arms (Cat. 16) as well as a whetstone used by Increase, Cotton, and Samuel Mather to sharpen their pen-knives, adding in a note, "with an ardent wish, if yet a spark remains in it, the fire of the flint may be communicated to every member of the Society."

FIG. 3

Soon after this she wrote to Thomas, "Please inform the members; I early imbibed an interest for such a Society, having in my possession, a number of valuable documents respecting the rise, and progress, of literature in America, I formed an ardent wish they might be preserved and transmitted by the vigilance and care of the Antiquarian Society to the latest posterity." In December 1814, Crocker and Thomas concluded a bargain which brought one of its most significant collections to Worcester—the portion of the Mather Library that was in her hands. This included some 900 printed volumes as well as the manuscript material that today forms the core of AAS's Mather Family Papers. Thomas paid her $200 for the library. In the donation book he listed the value (rather than cost) of his gift at $500, plus another $300 as a portion of the library given by Crocker, for a total value of $800.

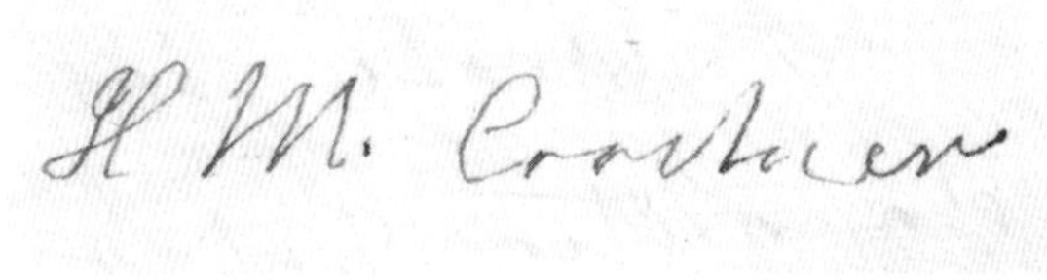

In 1815 Hannah Mather Crocker made another important gift to the Society. This consisted of a group of early painted portraits of Richard, Increase, Cotton, and Samuel Mather, as well as a child's high chair made in New England in the seventeenth century that had descended in the family. Like the arms and the Mather Library, Crocker's gift of these portraits and the high chair are an indication of her continued confidence in both Thomas and AAS as appropriate guardians of her illustrious family's relics.

CAT. 13. "Donors and Donations to the Amer. Antiquarian Society," Vol. 1, 1813-1829.

13. "Donors and Donations to the Amer. Antiquarian Society." Vol. 1, 1813-1829.

The first entry in this manuscript record of donations is for Isaiah Thomas's 1812 gift of his personal library. Following this are entries which form a detailed and fascinating picture of the early growth of the Society's collections, revealing their eclectic nature. Alongside books and manuscripts, one finds a diverse array of objects, including coins, Native American artifacts, geological specimens, and such curiosities as "a Lady's Silver Trinket, made in the year 1111, or 1121, consisting of a Tooth, Ear, and Nail Picker" (given by Thomas), the "jawbone and tusk of a wild hog," and a piece of a tent used by George Washington during the Revolutionary War. Catalog entries are in Thomas's hand until June 1829, when AAS librarian and cabinet-keeper Christopher Columbus Baldwin took over the job of recording gifts, likely because of Thomas's failing health.

AAS Archives.

14. Richard Mather. "A Platforme of Church-discipline, Gathered out of ye Word of God, and Agreed upon by ye Elders and Messen-

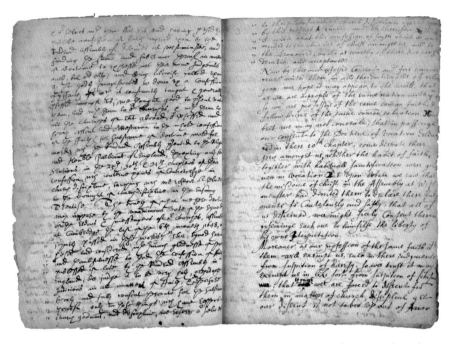

CAT. 14. "A Platforme of Church-discipline," 1648.

gers of ye Churches, Assembled in the Synod at Cambridge in New England, ye 6th month, 1648."

GIFT OF ISAIAH THOMAS AND HANNAH MATHER CROCKER, 1814.

Having been suspended from his church in Toxteth Park near Liverpool because of theological disagreements with his Church of England superiors, the Puritan minister Richard Mather (1596-1669) emigrated with his family to Boston in 1635. Soon after his arrival in the Massachusetts Bay Colony, Mather was called to the pulpit in Dorchester, a post he held until his death.

One of the primary reasons the Puritans had come to New England was to escape the secular authority imposed on them in England. However, New England's Congregational churches soon found that they lacked a mechanism for ensuring doctrinal consistency from church to church. In 1646 a synod was convened in Cambridge to discuss the issue. There Mather took a leading part in drafting "A Platforme of Church-discipline," which limited the role of secular authority in governing churches. This 1648 manuscript of the Cambridge Plat-

form is in Mather's hand. The following year the text was printed at the Cambridge press of Samuel Green. AAS's copy of the first edition, which bears Increase Mather's signature on the title page, is listed in the catalog of the Mather Family Library made by Isaiah Thomas.

Mather Family Papers.

15. Letter, Cotton Mather to Increase Mather, May 17, 1690.

GIFT OF ISAIAH THOMAS AND HANNAH MATHER CROCKER, 1814.

Increase Mather was born in Dorchester, Massachusetts, four years after his father Richard's arrival in Boston. After graduating from Harvard College, Increase studied at Trinity College, Dublin, before becoming the minister at Boston's Second (or North) Church. Mather subsequently became a leader among New England Puritans, president of Harvard College, and author of dozens of books.

In 1686, amid growing concerns about the degree of independence being displayed by the Massachusetts Bay Colony, the charter of 1629 was revoked and a new government, the "Do-

CAT. 16. *Mather Family Coat of Arms*, before 1767.

minion of New England in America," was established. Its governor-general, Sir Edmund Andros, showed little respect for long-established systems of self-government. In 1688 Increase Mather went to England as an advocate for the Colony, remaining there for four years.

In this draft letter from the extensive Mather Family archive, Increase's son Cotton chides his father:

> Tis not a little Trouble unto mee, to find your so speedy and sudden an Inclination in you, to such a Dishonourable Thing, as, Your not Returning to N.E. Where you have such measures of Respect and Esteem, as no person in this part of America, ever had before you…. have you indeed come to Resolutions of seeing N.E. no more? I am sorry for ye countrey, ye Colledge, your own Church, all of which languish &c for want of you…. I am sorry for myself, who am left alone, in ye midst of more cares, Fears, Anxieties, than, I believe, any other person in these Territories.

Increase Mather did return to Massachusetts two years later, in 1692, arriving in the midst of the Salem witchcraft trials.

Mather Family Papers.

16. Thomas Johnston, attributed. *Mather Family Coat of Arms.* Watercolor and ink on paper, before 1767.

GIFT OF HANNAH MATHER CROCKER, 1814.

Hannah Mather Crocker preserved this family coat of arms along with the family library and manuscripts. The artist and engraver Thomas Johnston (1708-1767) was likely its creator, as he was one of the few heraldic painters at work in Boston in the mid-eighteenth century. Family crests in America follow English heraldic traditions and often appear on bookplates, silver, and in needlework. The American Mathers traced their coat of arms back to 1602 and William Mather of Shropshire (abbreviated here as Salop), England. They adopted his crest design of a knight's helmet and a seated golden lion, which represent courage, magnanimity, and strength. The same qualities are reflected in the Latin motto adapted from Virgil's Aeneid—"Sunt fortia nobis pectora"—which loosely translates as "Our hearts are strong." In the American colonies, a painted and framed crest symbolized

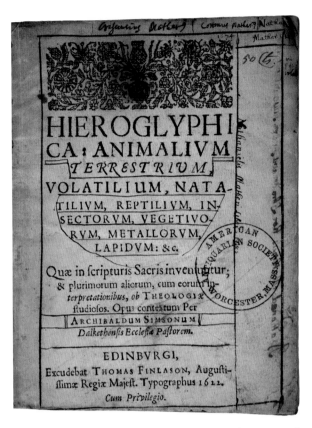

CAT. 17. Archibald Simson, *Hieroglyphica Animalium ...*, 1622 [1624].

connection to nobility and the well born, and the piece was probably displayed prominently in the Mather family's home.

17. Archibald Simson. *Hieroglyphica Animalium Terrestrium, Natatilium, Reptilium, Insectorum … quæ in Scripturis Sacris Inveniuntur … Edinburgh: Thomas Finlayson, 1622 [i.e. 1624].*

GIFT OF ISAIAH THOMAS AND HANNAH MATHER CROCKER, 1814.

The surviving portion of the Mather Family Library in the possession of Hannah Mather Crocker came to AAS in 1814, a combination of purchase by Isaiah Thomas and Crocker's gift. Assiduously built by five generations of passionate family bibliophiles, the library was said to number some 7,000 volumes at Cotton Mather's death in 1728—then the largest collection, institutional or private, in the American colonies. In succeeding generations the library

was split among descendants and by 1814 only some 1,500 titles in 900 volumes remained with Crocker. Even so, as the largest surviving portion of a seventeenth- and early eighteenth-century American library, the Mather books at AAS are an incomparable resource for American intellectual history. Most volumes are in their original or contemporary bindings, and many are signed and annotated by one or more of the Mathers, often heavily.

Few of the books more evocatively convey the Mathers' special, almost sacred, relationship with the printed word than this volume. Simson's work, which describes all of the animals mentioned in the Bible, bears on the title page the ownership signature of Increase ("Crescentius") Mather. Per the adjacent inscription in Cotton Mather's hand, Increase gave the book in 1674 to his eleven-year-old son, perhaps on the occasion of his entering Harvard College that year. In 1681 Cotton gave the volume to his brother Nathanael, who that year began his Harvard studies.

Mather Family Library.

STC 22567.

29

HOMERUS. B.C. 850.

Opera Omnia.

Chalcondylis. Florent. Fol. 1488. Gr.

Aldus. Venet. 12mo. 1504..17..24. Gr.

Martinus. Lovan. 4to. 1523. Gr. 2 vo.

Cephaleus. Argent. 8vo. 1525..34..42.

Rescius. Lovan. 4to. 1535. Gr. 2 vols.

Hervagius. Basil. Fol. 1535..41..51.

Francini. Venet. 8vo. 1535. Gr. 2 vo.

Farraeus. Venet. 8vo. 1542. Gr. 2 vols.

Nicol. de Sabio. Venet. 8vo. 1551. Gr.

Crispinus. Genev. 12mo. 1559..67. Gr.

Castalionis. Basil. Fol. 1561..67.

H. Stephanus. Paris. Fol. 1566.

Idem. . . . . Ibid. 8vo. 1588. Gr.

Morell et Libert. ———. 4to. 1620. Gr.

William Bentley and His Library

The Reverend William Bentley's substantial bequest to AAS on his death in 1819 was the first of many which have enriched the collections and added to its resources. Today Bentley is best known for the detailed diary he kept over a period of thirty- five years, a rich record of New England life in the early years of the Republic.

William Bentley was the son of Joshua Bentley, a Boston boatbuilder, although he was raised in the household of his grandfather William Paine in order to be educated. After graduating from Harvard College in 1777 Bentley taught school for several years before becoming a tutor at Harvard, working also as an assistant in the college library. In 1783 he was called to the East Church in Salem, Massachusetts, where he remained for the rest of his life.

An avid book collector, Bentley eventually accumulated a library totaling more than 4,000 volumes. Many of these were gifts from his parishioners and from the German geographer Christoph Daniel Ebeling, but Bentley also purchased books in shops and at auctions. In later life, he enlisted the aid of his nephew and namesake, William Bentley Fowle, a young bookseller, in buying books at sales in Boston. Bentley also collected prints, as well as objects for his cabinet.

Bentley was elected a member of the Massachusetts Historical Society in 1796 and made several gifts of newspapers, books, and objects there. He contributed a history of Salem to that Society's *Historical Collections* in 1800, but he became disgruntled when, the following year, the *Collections* contained criticism (which Bentley believed had been written by Charlestown minister and geographer Jedidiah Morse) of Bentley's scholarship. In 1808 he was incensed to receive a letter from the Society's treasurer demanding twelve years' worth of dues and threatening a lawsuit. "So much for the Historical Society," he wrote in his diary.

Bentley had become acquainted with Isaiah Thomas as least as early as 1793, when he visited Thomas's printing establishment while in Worcester. When Thomas was working on his *History of Printing in America* (Cat. 9), the two men exchanged a number of letters on various aspects of printing history. In 1809, at Thomas's request, Bentley sent him his copy of the 1640 *Whole Booke of Psalmes*, the first book printed in what is now the United States. This copy is still at AAS. Bentley was nominated for membership to the American Antiquarian Society at one of its first meetings, and he was elected and made a councilor in 1813. After the election Thomas wrote to Bentley, "I know of no one whom I think can make a better [member] of this Society than yourself—and hope you will not be dissatisfied with our choice." Although Bentley was soon concerned to find his old adversary Morse potentially exerting even more influence at AAS than at MHS, he nonetheless offered the Society his "literary and curious treasures." He and Thomas kept in touch in the years that followed, and the gift finally came upon Bentley's death. His will left his books printed in New England, his German books (which had come from Ebeling), his paintings and engravings, and his cabinet to the American Antiquarian Society. The bequest amounted to about 1,100 of the 4,000 volumes in Bentley's library, although some seven hundred of these were in German. Thomas was somewhat disappointed, writing "the New England printed books were much fewer in number than I had expected, and there were no old public journals...the German books were much more numerous than I had expected....However, the Legacies...to the Amn. Ann. Society, are very valuable."

However, this is not the end of the story. Bentley had left his own manuscripts, including his diary, to his nephew Fowle with the recommendation that they be destroyed, but fortunately Fowle preserved them. He died in 1866, leaving Bentley's sermons to the fledging Tufts College in Medford, and the rest of the manuscripts, including the diaries, to the American Antiquarian Society. In 1918 the German books, which were out of scope for AAS, were sold to Harvard, which had acquired Ebeling's library a century earlier, and the proceeds were used to acquire materials more directly useful to AAS.

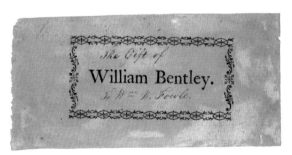

FIG. 4

18. William Bentley Fowle. Inventory of the Library of William Bentley, 1820.

GIFT OF THE ESTATE OF WILLIAM BENTLEY, 1820.

In a will made seven months before his death in 1819, William Bentley designated as his executor his nephew and namesake William Bentley Fowle, then a young bookseller in Boston. Chief among Bentley's concerns was the disposition of his large library. In the will, he directed that his New England imprints, his books in the German language, manuscripts other than his own, and his cabinet, should go to AAS. The recently founded Allegheny College in Meadville, Pennsylvania, was another legatee, receiving Bentley's "classical and theological books, dictionaries, lexicons and bibles." The college's founder and president Timothy Alden had approached Bentley for help a few years earlier. The remainder of the library went to Fowle.

Fowle proceeded to draft this inventory in preparation for the library's distribution. Items marked with an "A" were to be sent to Meadville, while items marked with a "T" (for "Thomas") were destined for AAS. Although Bentley kept his own partial library catalog and made other notes on items he acquired, this inventory is of particular significance because it shows the library's actual contents at the time of Bentley's death as well as the portion bequeathed to AAS.

William Bentley Papers.

19. William Bentley. Diary, October 9, 1815-March 15, 1818.

BEQUEST OF WILLIAM BENTLEY FOWLE, 1866.

William Bentley is perhaps best known today for the voluminous diaries he kept between 1785 and his death in 1819. They contain rich details about events in Salem, Massachusetts, and its environs. Bentley also frequently commented on national and international affairs, although much of this non-local material was omitted when the diaries were published, in four volumes, between 1905 and 1914. In addition to the diaries, the Bentley papers now at AAS include correspondence, notes on his reading, commentaries on scripture, and accounts concerning his book collecting.

Bentley did not leave his own manuscripts to AAS, and in fact he recommended to his nephew and executor William Bentley Fowle that they be destroyed. Fowle, however, chose to preserve them, promising AAS librarian Christopher Columbus Baldwin in 1834 that one day they would come to the Society. Although Fowle gave various theological manuscripts to Tufts College and meteorological records to Harvard, upon his death in 1865 he honored his promise by bequeathing the bulk of Bentley's papers to AAS.

Bentley's diary entry for August 15, 1817, includes an account of the sea monster, called by Bentley "A Norway Kraken," that a number of people reported sighting off the Massachusetts coast over a several-month period. Bentley writes: "The general representation is that his head is like a horse & that he raises it several feet out of water. That his body when out of water looks like the buoys of a net, or a row of kegs, or a row of large casks."

William Bentley Papers.

20. William Bentley Fowle. "An Abridgement of Dibdin's Classics to which are Added Useful Notes and Remarks," ca. 1813.

PURCHASE, HARRY G. STODDARD MEMORIAL FUND, 1992.

In 1810, when he was fifteen, William Bentley Fowle was apprenticed to the Boston bookseller Caleb Bingham. Three years later Fowle began to use his book trade knowledge and connections to help his uncle, William Bentley, acquire books—particularly foreign ones—for his library. Fowle sent Bentley catalogs and attended sales on his behalf; in return, Fowle received much advice on how he might best serve his uncle, including the suggestion that he study Thomas Frognall Dibdin's *An Introduction to the Knowledge of Rare and Valuable Editions of the Greek and Latin Classics.*

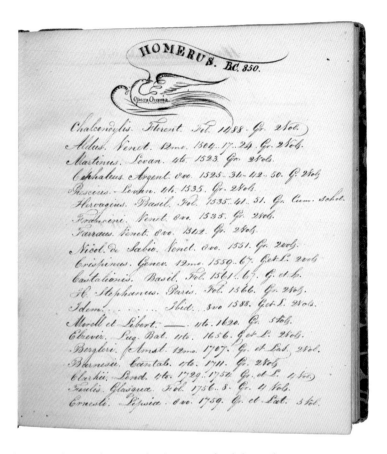

CAT. 20. William Bentley Fowle, "An Abridgement of Dibdin's Classics," ca. 1813.

Fowle located a copy of the third edition (London, 1808) and transcribed the names of Dibdin's authors and editions in a blank book. As a preface Fowle wrote:

> While I was an apprentice, during the war with England, no books could be imported fr[om] England, and, as valuable works were scarce, & no Bookseller acquainted with them, I abridged Dibdin's work, of which I found a copy that I could not buy, that I might learn to trade in rare books, and be useful to my uncle, Rev. Wm Bentley of Salem, whose Library, at that time, was the best private library in the U. States, Jefferson's having been the best until it was sold to the U. States Congress, after the Capitol was burnt by the British.

This volume came up for public auction in 1992 and AAS purchased it because of the evidence it contains regarding Fowle's activities in aid of his uncle's collecting.

William Bentley Fowle Papers.

21. John Foster. *Mr. Richard Mather.* Woodcut, second state, ca. 1670.

BEQUEST OF WILLIAM BENTLEY, 1819.

The first woodcut and first portrait print produced in America, this important portrait is attributed to John Foster (1648-1681), the earliest engraver and printer in Boston. After graduating from Harvard in 1667, Foster taught school in Dorchester before opening Boston's first printing establishment in 1675. He published nearly a hundred books, almanacs, broadsides, and maps before his death.

This portrait was printed to accompany *The Life and Death of That Reverend Man of God, Mr. Richard Mather,* authored by Mather's son Increase and published in 1670 at the Cambridge, Massachusetts, press of Samuel Green and Marmaduke Johnson. One of only five recorded copies, this impression was owned by William Bentley. Richard Mather, one of the translators of *The Whole Booke of Psalmes* (1640) and patriarch of the

34

CAT. 21. John Foster, *Mr. Richard Mather*, ca. 1670.

Mather dynasty of New England ministers, was admired by Bentley as a preacher and religious scholar. The Foster woodcut was an unusual acquisition for Bentley, who typically commissioned contemporary artists to copy or reproduce likenesses owned by institutions or private individuals. In 1804, Bentley carried this print from Salem to Boston to compare it with a painted portrait of Mather owned by the family (and now at AAS). While he bemoaned the painting's faded condition, he also noted in his diary that "It agrees as well as possible with my block print."

AAS Chief Joys 10; AAS Wellsprings 3.

22. Samuel McIntire. *John Winthrop.* Carved and painted pine, 1798.

BEQUEST OF WILLIAM BENTLEY, 1819.

This bust of John Winthrop (1588-1649) was made nearly one hundred fifty years after the revered Massachusetts governor's death. It was commissioned in 1798 by Bentley for his cabinet of portraits. Bentley also owned a painted miniature of Winthrop, which he loaned to Salem artist and architect Samuel McIntire (1757-1811) to use as a reference for the carving. Bentley was very familiar with McIntire and his work: not only had he been ordering frames from the carver's shop since 1796, but the McIntire family was active in Salem's East Church, where Bentley preached.

Bentley carefully recorded the transactions relating to the Winthrop bust in his diary (Cat. 19): "Mr. MacIntire is engaged to make my bust of Winthrop & spent the day in examining my collections in this way." Nine days later, the work was complete and McIntire delivered the bust to his patron, who noted, "Mr. MacIntire returned to me my Winthrop. I cannot say that he has expressed in the bust anything which agrees with the Governour." Although not happy with the likeness, Bentley paid McIntire $8.00 for the work. He continued to patronize McIntire for frames and woodworking, commissioning a second bust, of Voltaire, in 1802.

AAS Chief Joys 271; Hewes 155; Weis 149.

23. Samuel Harris. *Portrait of Elisha Cooke, the Son.* Red chalk on paper, ca. 1805-1807.

BEQUEST OF WILLIAM BENTLEY, 1819.

William Bentley met the young Boston engraver and artist Samuel Harris (1783-1810) in 1805. Knowing of the Salem minister's growing collection of likenesses of prominent Massachusetts clergymen and politicians, Harris sent Bentley a small chalk portrait of the Rev. Jeremy Belknap and a painting of the Protestant martyr John Rogers. Bentley approved of the artist's work and commissioned several portraits for his cabinet collection, including this arresting drawing of Elisha Cooke, Jr., the Boston doctor and politician who famously argued with royal officials over New England's colonial rights of representation. Harris probably copied the likeness from a painting or print of Cooke, who died in 1737, but he used a dramatic, closely cropped composition and let the chalk exuberantly render the curls of Cooke's wig.

Bentley closely followed Harris's career, encouraging him to enter Harvard College to study languages, and sharing documents in Arabic and Hebrew with the young artist. Tragically, Harris drowned in the summer of 1810. Bentley was greatly saddened by the event and noted in his diary: "This day proved the melancholy day of the exit of my young friend Samuel Harris. He drowned while bathing in the Charles near the Colleges ... He has furnished me with my best paintings & engravings ... He was a modest, inquisitive, indefatigable man ... In a moment our thoughts perish."

Weis 38.

CAT. 23. Samuel Harris, *Portrait of Elisha Cooke, the Son,* ca. 1805-1807.

A COPY OF
The Church-Covenants

which have been uſed in the
Church of

SALEM

Both formerly, and in their late Renewing of
their Covenant on the day of the publick Faſt,
April 15. 1680.

As a Direction pointing to that Covenant of
Gods Grace in Chriſt made with his
Church and People in the holy Scripture.

---

*Gather my People unto me which have made a Covenant with
  me by Sacrifice,* Pſal.50.ʒ.
Jeſus the Mediator of the New Covenant, Heb.12 24.
The Blood of the Covenant, Heb.10.29.
The Blood of the everlaſting Covenant, Heb,13.20.
Who is this that engageth his heart to approach unto me, and y
  ſhall be my People, and I will be your God, Jer.30.21,22
They ſhall goe and ſeek the Lord their God, they ſhall ask th
  way to Zion with their faces thitherward, ſaying, Com
  let us joyn our ſelves to the Lord, in a perpetual Covenant
  that ſhall not be forgotten, Jer.50.4,5.

Christopher Columbus Baldwin Collects for AAS

In just a few years as the Society's librarian, Christopher Columbus Baldwin accomplished a remarkable amount, acquiring vast quantities of material for the library and preparing most of the first catalog of the AAS collections. His surviving diaries and correspondence reveal both his zeal in working on behalf of the Society and his sense of humor.

Baldwin was born in 1800 in Templeton, Massachusetts, a hill town twenty-five miles northwest of Worcester. His father owned a sawmill, lumber yard, and brick yard. After attending Leicester Academy he entered Harvard College but was rusticated along with thirty-four of his classmates shortly before graduation as a result of the "great rebellion" of the class of 1823. He studied law in Worcester and practiced briefly, but his historical interests quickly outpaced his interest in the law. He was one of the publishers of the *Worcester Magazine and Historical Journal* in 1825-26, and was elected a member of AAS in 1827. Upon his election Baldwin was also made temporary librarian and cabinet keeper. Isaiah Thomas's will made provision for a salaried librarian, and in 1832, the year after Thomas's death, Baldwin was given this position. He conducted his duties with great energy, begging for books and other materials from historically-minded people across the United States. In 1833 he wrote to Edward Everett:

> As the institution is general and not local, I have believed that I ought to adopt some course that shall invite the cooperation of persons from all parts of the country. I know of no way to accomplish this except by directing my labors to the collection of all the productions of American writers. This rule will include every thing, and thus far I have found it advantageous…. We cannot tell what is valuable until it shall be called for. Who could have calculated 20 years ago that the subjects of intemperance, slavery and Free Masonry would have occupied so much of the public attention as they do now? And these revolutions in public sentiment are constantly returning. I procure everything in relation to them that I can find.....I am well aware that by my plan I shall procure a great deal of what may be called trash. It will not answer, however, for beggars to show themselves to be epicures. I reject no book or tract that may be offered. For it often happens, that a bad book is wanted merely for its badness.

Baldwin's most notable acquisition was a collection of more than two tons of books, pamphlets, and manuscripts belonging to Thomas Wallcut that Baldwin removed from the attic of a whale oil warehouse in Boston over the course of several very hot summer days in 1834. In his diary, he wrote that on the second day of his labors "One of the first

FIG. 5

things that gladdened my eyes was the forty-first year of the Diary of the never to be forgotten Cotton Mather. It was perfect and in good condition and the first pages contain an account of a young lady's having asked him to marry her! After several fasts, and plenty of prayers for divine direction in such an embarrassment, he wrote her a letter declining her suit!" Even in the midst of this major effort in a sweltering and odorous garret, Baldwin was unable to resist stopping to read the diary.

For some years Baldwin suffered from occasional attacks of inflammation in his joints, but this became more severe at the end of 1834. The AAS Council, believing that his illness was due to overwork, sent him west to inspect the Native American mounds in Ohio. (In fact, modern opinion is that he was probably suffering from tuberculous arthritis.) On August 19, 1835, after less than four years as full-time librarian, Baldwin was killed near Zanesville when the coach in which he was riding overturned. Baldwin's friend and AAS member William Lincoln wrote in 1836 that Baldwin was, "an associate so valued and a friend so loved... his memory will continue in the hearts of those who knew his worth, and the ardor of his enthusiasm in those pursuits to which our institution has been dedicated."

FIG. 6

CAT. 24. Sarah Goodridge, *Christopher Columbus Baldwin*, 1835.

24. Sarah Goodridge. *Christopher Columbus Baldwin.* Watercolor on ivory, 1835.

GIFT OF ADELAIDE R. SAWYER, 1907.

This miniature, commissioned by Baldwin's father, was taken shortly before his departure for Ohio in 1835. Baldwin sat for the painter Sarah Goodridge, who worked in Boston and in Worcester County. Goodridge's younger sister, Eliza, also a miniature painter, knew Baldwin socially and wrote to him saying, "I hope an opportunity will appear for me to do ample justice to that Proteus face of yours & if all the varieties cannot be represented in one picture, I will endeavor to remember the 'majestic and sensible looking countenance' supposing you consider that of the goodly sort." But it was Sarah, the more experienced artist, who ultimately received the commission.

Goodridge has been called America's finest woman miniaturist, and her sitters included Gilbert Stuart, Daniel Webster, and an elderly Dolley Madison. Her work, which she steadily executed at the rate of two miniatures a week, is distinctive for its directness and lifelike quality and, in her own day, was highly regarded for its accuracy.

Hewes 2; Weis 4.

25. Christopher Columbus Baldwin. Diary, September 15, 1833 - July 15, 1835.

GIFT OF LEVI LINCOLN, 1856.

Christopher Columbus Baldwin began to keep a regular diary on January 1, 1829. It is a highly engaging account of life in central Massachusetts, whether Baldwin is describing his first view of a locomotive, a house being raised "without using any ardent spirit: believed to be the first instance of the kind in New England," or the massive flocks of passenger pigeons seen in the spring of 1832. First printed in somewhat abridged form in 1901, the complete text of Baldwin's diary was republished by the Society in 2010 in a newly edited and heavily illustrated edition.

Central to Baldwin's life were his activities

as AAS librarian. His enthusiasm in acquiring books for the Society pervades his diary and letters. At one point he wrote: "some philosopher has said that his unhappiest moments were those spent in settling his tavern bills. But the happiest moments of my life are those employed in opening packages of books presented to the Library of the American Antiquarian Society. It gives me real, substantial, and unadulterated comfort."

A particularly memorable passage concerns the massive gift from Boston antiquarian Thomas Wallcut (Cats. 28, 29). In July 1834, Baldwin obtained permission from Wallcut's nephews to take what he liked from the portion of Wallcut's collection then housed in a fourth-floor garret of a Boston oil store. Baldwin set out for Boston on August 1, 1834, and the next day he began gathering material for AAS, working under a slate roof "in a heat and dust and stench of oil that would have been intolerable in any other circumstances." Baldwin nonetheless felt that he had "never seen such happy moments. Every thing I opened discovered to my eyes some unexpected treasure." After five days' toil in temperatures above ninety degrees, Baldwin had assembled 4,476 pounds of pamphlets, manuscripts, books, and newspapers for carting back to Worcester. "I cannot but think," he wrote, "that it is the most valuable collection of the early productions of New England authors in the country."

After Baldwin's death, his papers went to his good friend William Lincoln, who died in 1843. William's brother Levi then took possession of the Baldwin papers, later presenting them to AAS.

Christopher Columbus Baldwin Papers.

26. Christopher Columbus Baldwin, "Catalogue of Pamphlets Received of the Boston Atheneum [sic] by the American Antiquarian Society." January 23, 1834.

During his relatively brief tenure as AAS librarian, Christopher Columbus Baldwin distinguished himself as a master acquisitor. With few funds at his disposal, Baldwin relied heavily on his formidable powers of persuasion.

In December 1831, for example, he visited the Boston Athenæum and convinced librarian Seth Bass to promise the Society its pick of the Athenæum's duplicate pamphlets, free of charge. In Bass, however, Baldwin did not find a kindred spirit: "The Librarian, Dr. Bass, has more love for shells and objects of Natural History than for Black Letter or anything appertaining to the typographic art. But what right has a Librarian to have any affection but for books and Mss?"

It was not until January 1834, however, that Bass invited Baldwin to make his selection. Within a few days Baldwin was in Boston and at work on the pamphlets. In the end he brought away some 466 pamphlets for the Society. These he promptly inventoried in this catalog, which he sent to Bass, who fortunately identified only half a dozen as not being true duplicates. Having found a productive source, Baldwin returned to the Athenæum the following January, selecting "between three and four Thousand" more pamphlets from among its duplicates.

AAS Archives.

27. *The Sons of Africans: An Essay on Freedom, with Observations on the Origin of Slavery.* Boston: African Society, 1808.

GIFT OF THE BOSTON ATHENAEUM, 1834.

Christopher Columbus Baldwin's selection of pamphlets from the Boston Athenæum duplicates ranged in date from the early eighteenth century up to the 1830s. Among these were a few English pamphlets, though the vast majority were American, with a preponderance of Boston imprints; virtually all related in some way to American history. If not considered of special significance in 1834, today some of these pamphlets are acknowledged as rare and important.

One example is this pamphlet, written by an unidentified member of Boston's African Society and published by that Society for its members. Founded in 1796 by the leaders of Boston's tightly-knit free African-American community, the African Society used its mem-

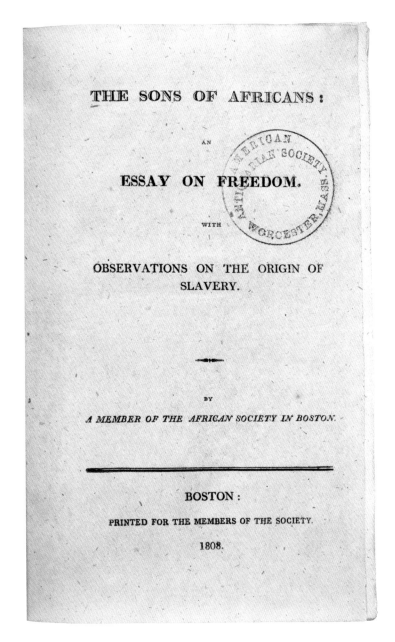

CAT. 27. *The Sons of Africans*, 1808.

bership dues to fund social welfare services in the Beacon Hill neighborhood where most of Boston's African-Americans then lived. In 1808 the Society issued *The Sons of Africans*, its first formal statement in support of abolition. Framing its argument in terms of the American Revolution's political ideals, and drawing from the Bible, the text presents an impassioned but reasoned case for granting freedom to all, regardless of race.

Shaw & Shoemaker 16217.

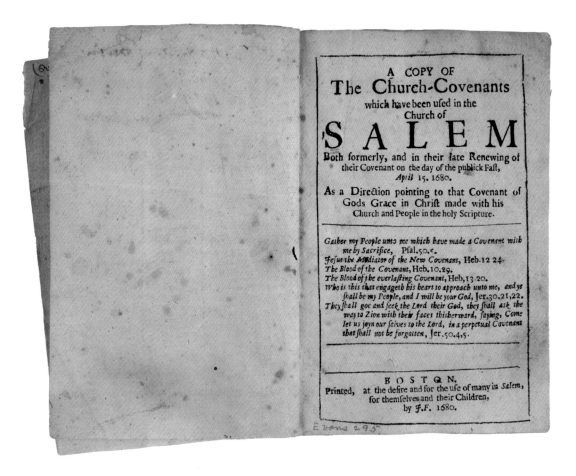

A COPY OF
The Church-Covenants
which have been used in the
Church of
SALEM
Both formerly, and in their late Renewing of
their Covenant on the day of the publick Fast,
April 15. 1680.

As a Direction pointing to that Covenant of
Gods Grace in Christ made with his
Church and People in the holy Scripture.

*Gather my People unto me which have made a Covenant with
me by Sacrifice,* Psal.50.5.
Jesus the Mediator of the New Covenant, Heb.12 24.
The Blood of the Covenant, Heb.10.29.
The Blood of the everlasting Covenant, Heb.13.20.
Who is this that engageth his heart to approach unto me, *and ye
shall be my People, and I will be your God,* Jer.30,21,22.
*They shall goe and seek the Lord their God, they shall ask the
way to Zion with their faces thitherward, saying, Come
let us joyn our selves to the Lord, in a perpetual Covenant
that shall not be forgotten,* Jer.50.4,5.

BOSTON,
Printed, at the desire and for the use of many in *Salem*,
for themselves and their Children,
by *J.F.* 1680.

CAT. 28. *A Copy of the Church-Covenants*, 1680.

28. First Church, Salem, Massachusetts. *A Copy of the Church-Covenants Which Have Been Used in the Church of Salem …* Boston: John Foster, 1680.

GIFT OF THOMAS WALLCUT, 1834.

We owe to Thomas Wallcut's decades of collecting the existence of many early American imprints which otherwise would not have survived. One is this unique copy of the earliest separately printed American church covenant—the document by which Puritan congregations bound themselves to God's word, and to each other, when establishing a church.

Preceded only by the congregation at Plymouth, the First Church of Salem, Massachusetts, was founded in 1629. This pamphlet prints the text of the church's 1636 covenant, followed by the revised covenant approved on

April 15, 1680. The revision was a response to the Reforming Synod, convened at Boston in 1679-1680, which addressed widespread fears of spiritual decline and the subsequent signs of divine wrath. Although church members renewed their vows "to keep our selves pure from the sins of the Times," Salem's social fabric remained subject to great strain. In 1689, residents of nearby Salem Village broke away to form their own church, only to find themselves tormented by accusations of witchcraft in 1692. The First Church was also deeply affected, excommunicating Rebecca Nurse and Giles Corey following their convictions in the Salem witch trials presided over by magistrates (and church members) John Hawthorne and Jonathan Corwin. This copy is believed to have belonged to Corwin.

Evans 295.

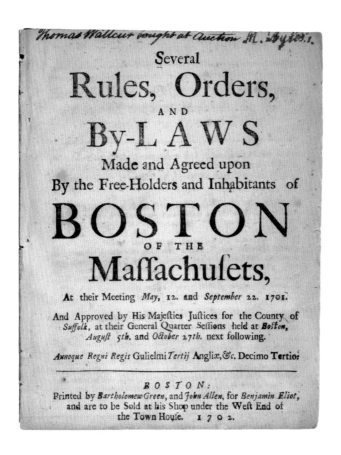

CAT. 29. *Several Rules, Orders, and By-Laws ...*, 1702.

29. *Several Rules, Orders, and By-Laws ... Made and Agreed upon ... May, 12. and September 22. 1701...* Boston: Bartholomew Green and John Allen, for Benjamin Eliot, 1702.

GIFT OF THOMAS WALLCUT, 1834.

This pamphlet constitutes a mere half ounce of the 4,476 pounds of books and manuscripts that Baldwin brought from the Thomas Wallcut hoard to AAS in August 1834. Yet it is representative of Wallcut's careful selection over several decades from the offerings of Boston bookshops and auctions. As the title-page inscription indicates, it was one of many items obtained by Wallcut at the posthumous auction of the Mather Byles library. Byles (1707-1788), a famed Boston minister and poet

who was, in his latter years, notorious for his Loyalist sympathies, possessed a substantial 2,500-volume collection. Much of it consisted of the quarter portion of the celebrated Mather Family Library which Byles inherited from his uncle, Increase Mather.

This rare pamphlet is the earliest extant separate publication documenting the deliberations of that quintessential New England institution, the town meeting. All residents were welcome to attend these democratic gatherings, where town officers were elected and ordinances enacted, though only freemen could vote. New laws enacted in Boston in 1701 included: "For preventing danger by persons Riding or driving a-gallop in the Streets," "Against Dogs doing damage to Gardens," "For preventing danger by Foot-balls, Squibs and Snowballs," and "For Regulating Town-Meetings." Boston's town meeting persisted until 1822.

AAS Chief Joys 17; AAS Wellsprings 25; Evans 1040.

Sale June 30th 1847

Omohundro	+	1 Boy Charles	Ck	pd	585	+ JW Ritche
Jolly & Matthias	+	1 Girl Susan	Ck	pd	470	+ JH Mac
do	+	1 Girl Kelly	Ck	pd	450	+ JW R
do	0	1 Girl Sarah		0	~~~~	JH Jor
H x Brokes C	+	1 Girl Eliza	Cash	pd	550	+ JW Ke
G W Nixon	0	1 Girl Selina		0	~~~~	JH Gray
J G Murphy	+	1 man Abram	Ck	pd	760	+ E Fountle
Nixon	+	1 Girl Virginia	Ck	pd	630	+ JH Warr
J M Covington	+	1 Man Albert	Ck	pd	760	+ JW Ritche
Nixon	+	1 man Jerry	Ck	pd	680	+ do
J W Redmon	+	1 Girl Eliza	Ck	pd	500	+ JH Warr
do	+	1 woman Ann & 3 chil. Wm Peter, Peggy ex	pd	95	+ JH Ritch
do	+	1 woman Letty & chil Eliza an sol	pd	575	+ J S Camp
Jno S Townsend	+	1 woman Harriett & child	cash 75	pd	600	+ Thos William
Wyatt Maye	+	1 woman Margarett & 3 chil Robert, Cora & Ammert	pd	1.150	+ do do
Warren & R	+	1 Boy Charles bysaw	0	pd	600	+ do do
Conrad						

Lucy and Sarah Chase Collect Contemporary History

The coming of the American Civil War quickly led to a widespread appreciation of the historical significance of current events, and these feelings were shared at AAS. The earliest references to the war occur in the minutes of the October 1861 meeting. The Council report recognized a new opportunity:

> ...[I]t has seemed to the Council to be advisable to call the attention of the Society, and of its individual members, to the expediency of adopting vigorous and systematic measures, to obtain, as far as possible, complete files of periodical publications in the several States which are attempting to withdraw from the government of the United States; and also all books, pamphlets, and whatever else may tend to explain or establish their claims and pretensions, or to assist in ascertaining the truth concerning military operations, and the proceedings of public bodies or private associations, of which they purport to give an account.

At the same meeting, librarian Samuel Foster Haven wrote "If there ever was a time when Historical Associations should be busy in their vocation, it is now, when documents are to be gathered and preserved which may yield a true solution to the exciting questions that agitate the land, illustrate the real condition of public sentiment, and secure to posterity an accurate account of the measures and exploits of a great revolution."

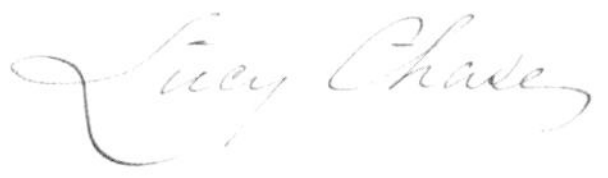

FIG. 7

A year later Haven was able to list twenty four individuals and organizations that had sent war-related publications to the Society. Gifts continued to arrive during and after the war. Among the most interesting were materials collected in the South by two Worcester sisters, Lucy Chase (1822-1909) and Sarah E. Chase (1836-1919). Born into a Quaker family, the Chase sisters went to Virginia in 1863 to

FIG. 8

teach in freedmen's schools. While in the South the Chases were able to collect a variety of materials including business records of a Richmond slave dealer, papers from Jefferson Davis's office, and also souvenirs from General Grant's headquarters at City Point. The Chase sisters' correspondence during this period is now also at AAS and reflects their interest in preserving material as evidence of the historic events that were happening around them. In this way, the sisters parallel the actions of Society founder Isaiah Thomas who preserved broadsides, newspapers, and books documenting the actions of the American Revolution and the challenges of building a new nation.

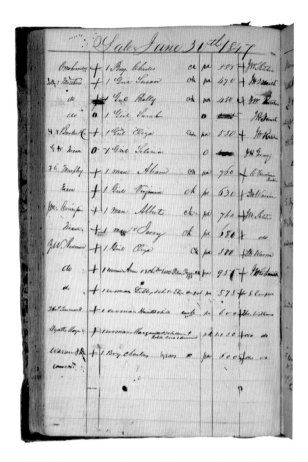

CAT. 30. Dickinson, Hill & Co. Account Book of Slave Auctions, 1846 to 1849.

30. Dickinson, Hill & Co. Account Book of Slave Auctions, Richmond, Virginia, 1846 to 1849.

GIFT OF THOMAS HOVEY GAGE, 1941.

Within days after Union troops captured Richmond, Virginia, in 1865, the Chase sisters entered the city. They went into the just-abandoned auction house of R.H. Dickinson and Brother and took account books and correspondence documenting the sale of enslaved people. Sarah appropriated one of the account books for use as a diary, writing in it that just a few days earlier, on "March 31 Slaves were sold. I read the mem. of sale in the Day book. A Heavy line was drawn beneath it and "April 1st" was written—but, thank God—no more was written or ever will be written in that bloody Register."

The Dickinsons were major dealers, con- ducting auctions of enslaved people who were sent to them in Richmond on consignment. The company grossed more than $2,000,000 in 1856. The records preserved by the Chase sisters span the period from 1846 to 1862 and document the sale of hundreds of individuals and families throughout the region. These volumes and the company's correspondence were preserved in the Chase family until donated by descendants in the twentieth century.

Slavery in the United States Collection.

31. Coffee beans removed from General U.S. Grant's headquarters at City Point, Virginia, April 1865.

GIFT OF LUCY CHASE, 1879.

In 1863 the Boston Educational Commission, a freedmen's aid organization, sent Lucy and Sarah Chase south to Craney Island, Vir-

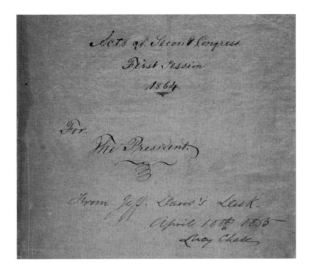

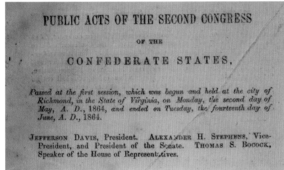

CAT. 32. *Public Laws of the Confederate States of America,* cover and title page (details), 1864.

ginia, where they began teaching former slaves. These beans were collected at the Union headquarters on April 9, 1865, days after Grant's departure. In her diary Sarah Chase wrote "I was most desirous to be with the colored people in worship on their first Sabbath of Freedom – but unfortunately and unnecessarily we staid most of the day at the Point – and made the most of it going all abt. the Point, ransacking Genl. Grants Head Qtrs. a one story log house of two rooms." In addition to the beans, the sisters' "ransacking" included papers that Grant's staff had left behind.

Chase Family Papers.

32. Confederate States of America.

Public Laws of the Confederate States of America, Passed at the First Session of the Second

Congress; 1864 ... Richmond: R.M. Smith, 1864.

GIFT OF LUCY CHASE, 1879.

On April 10, 1865, one week after Davis and the Confederate government fled Richmond, and a day after Lee's surrender at Appomattox, Lucy and Sarah Chase visited Davis's office and removed several pamphlets, a group of muster rolls, and other Confederate documents. Among the pamphlets was this copy of the final Confederate session laws to be published, covering the May-June 1864 session. Specially bound "For The President" of the Confederacy in brown wrapping paper reflecting wartime shortages, this advance copy for legislators lacks the title page, contents list, and section of "private laws" found in the public version issued shortly afterward.

Parrish & Willingham 34.

OULD

Mountaynes forest

Masons bushe

Waldens oake

L:D: Lenox rocks

Mangoack Richmonds

VIR

GI

Howa

Cawruuock

Pananaioc

Stuards reac

NI

Añadales chase

A

Nustoc

Secota

Setuoc

Purc

Mecopen

Cotan

Cecils Harbor

Tama

Davers Ile

Paquinip

Abigails Iles

L

feare

La

Ynys Uygod

Romeiock

Salvage Ile

P. Box

Da ssamopog

Gordens Ile

Ile Hatton

P. Vaughan

Abbots

Ile

Greenevills rode

The Brinley and Cooke Sales

For four decades following the Civil War, the AAS library continued to grow steadily but unevenly, showing some signs of being more an accumulation than a purpose-built collection. Librarian Samuel Foster Haven and his successor Edmund Mills Barton labored under several handicaps, perhaps the most significant being a rather unfocused and too broadly defined mission. Isaiah Thomas's original donation, Christopher Columbus Baldwin's inspired collecting, and numerous gifts had endowed AAS with enviable holdings of early American imprints and primary sources for American history. But these materials shared increasingly crowded shelves with a hodgepodge of miscellaneous publications ranging from incunabula to modern reference works. This *omnium gatherum* approach was reflected in the adjoining exhibition area, which displayed the Society's substantial and multifarious assemblage of cabinet artifacts. Unable to define its collecting policy in clear and manageable terms, AAS was further handicapped by a perennially small acquisitions budget. As did many of its peers, the Society supplemented its purchasing by exchanging its publications and duplicates for those of other institutions, and by participating in a network of libraries receiving and exchanging federal documents. But gifts remained the primary engine of collection growth, and AAS had few means of filling the many holes in a collection being built largely by happenstance. Twice, however, the Society found itself the unexpected beneficiary of substantial and inspired bequests: from George Brinley in 1879 and Joseph J. Cooke in 1883. Each benefactor left $5,000 to AAS, the funds to be expended in purchasing books at the auction of that collector's private library. In both instances, AAS bid wisely and to good effect, acquiring several thousand desirable items in a range of subject areas, but which primarily enhanced its existing strengths in early Americana.

The son of a well-to-do Boston merchant, George Brinley (1817-1875) moved with his parents to Hartford in 1836. There he helped manage the family's investments, which included substantial real estate holdings in Hartford, Boston, and Worcester. Much free time remained, however, for Brinley to pursue an interest in book collecting. The origins of Brinley's library are obscure—perhaps he simply adopted his father's interest in books—though by 1845 Brinley's collecting had blossomed into full-blown bibliomania. When in that year Boston bookseller Samuel G. Drake announced plans to auction a 1,517-lot collection on Native Americans, Brinley swooped in to purchase the library *en bloc*. Shortly afterward Brinley became acquainted with AAS, initiating a thirty-year correspondence with Samuel Foster Haven that reveals much about his collecting. Brinley's promise as an antiquarian was immediately apparent, and in October 1846 he was elected to membership in the Society.

In many ways Brinley's collecting reflected the Society's own acquisitions policy, as implemented, resources permitting, during the nineteenth century and as formally defined in the early twentieth century. Although not uninterested in the European Americana prized by his contemporaries James Lenox and John Carter Brown, Brinley was far more eager

FIG. 9

to acquire early American imprints. And, like AAS, he wanted everything. If today the Society can boast of having the finest extant collection of early American printing, it was Brinley who, after three decades of determined collecting, could make the same boast in 1875. Possessed of an excellent memory, admirable tenacity, and resourcefulness worthy of Christopher Columbus Baldwin, Brinley built his library in inspired ways. In addition to working with dealers, for instance, Brinley was famous for traveling New England's back roads, calling at residences in search of old books and pamphlets, and bargaining skillfully for the treasures he spotted. During the Civil War, when waste paper was in high demand at paper mills, Brinley frequented the mills to rescue early imprints before they were pulped. And as his library grew in importance and his chief competitors receded from the scene, Brinley eventually turned to London, where American expatriate bookseller Henry Stevens helped supply many of the finest rarities gracing Brinley's collection.

Another useful source was AAS, which profitably exchanged duplicates with Brinley for nearly three decades. Defective and fragmentary volumes were also of interest to Brinley since he owned many rare but imperfect books that he was eager to perfect with leaves from other copies. In this Brinley was simply following what many perceived at that time to be a best practice, and it was also one he encouraged for the Society. Seeing the shabby state of the 1685 second edition of the Eliot Indian Bible which had been given to AAS in 1858, Brinley offered to pay for its restoration. Off it went to Francis Bedford in London, returning three long years later, in 1874, after having been washed, resized, and rebound in appropriate gilt-tooled morocco, the missing leaves expertly supplied in facsimile. In his report to the AAS membership, librarian Samuel Foster Haven exulted on its arrival: "It is a subject of serious congratulation, the possession of a perfect copy, in durable and beautiful state, of this distinctive and peculiar monument." Most of Brinley's frequent benefactions, however, consisted of very generous gifts, including a copy of Herodotus (Rome, 1475) presented in 1851, and a nearly complete set of de Bry's *Voyages* (Frankfurt, 1590-1619) given in 1860. In his letter of transmittal for the latter, Brinley wrote to Haven: "There is nothing in my library too good for [AAS] and I hereby present you with the freedom of it in a gold box; barring a pleasant fiction about the box."

Brinley died intestate in 1875, but nearly four years later his executors were ready to begin the dispersal of his extraordinary library containing upwards of 50,000 volumes. The plan, devised from hints left in Brinley's papers, was to sell the entire collection at auction. Given Brinley's fears of fire and institutional neglect, it was decided not to place the collection in a single favored institution by selling the entire collection intact. Instead, the books would be offered to those individuals and institutions that truly wanted them; and to help institutions compete with collectors, Brinley's solution was to distribute a credit of $25,000 among five deserving libraries. AAS's share was $5,000 which, over the course of the five Brinley auction sales (1879-1891), was expended on 1,151 books and 1,544 pamphlets, plus "many early broadsides, proclamations and newspapers of great interest and value." Fully aware of the singular opportunity it had been handed, AAS wisely chose to build on strength, purchasing as many Mather family tracts and early New England imprints as possible, with the acquisitions including some 700 early almanacs. Librarian Edmund Mills Barton reported to the Society's membership in 1893: "The fact remains that we have secured for all time, rarities which would have been added to this great library of American history in no other way." The same could be said for several of the other great institutional Americana collections, for the Brinley sales proved a watershed in the development of American research libraries.

Shortly after the third Brinley sale in 1881, prominent book collector Joseph J. Cooke died. Born in Providence, Rhode Island, Cooke (1813-1881) entered his father's mercantile business before establishing his own in New York City. The business flourished during the California gold rush by supplying goods to California's burgeoning population, and Cooke himself spent some time in San Francisco. His savviest investment, however, was the purchase of a large parcel of land on the outskirts of Providence, which became the foundation of his considerable fortune. In his later years Cooke divided his time between Providence and Newport. The origins of his book collecting are unknown—apparently Cooke rapidly accumulated his library during the 1870s, buying heavily at auction. After his death, nearly 25,000 volumes were found stockpiled in Cooke's homes and offices. Cooke's collection is memorialized in the three-part auction catalog prepared by Leavitt & Co. in 1883. Like many collectors of his day, Cooke's tastes were eclectic, but books and manuscripts concerning American history, the Revolutionary War, and George Washington took pride of place. And if the condition of Cooke's volumes was not always perfect, it was fully acceptable to contemporary collectors.

Apparently Cooke was impressed not only by the magnificence of George Brinley's library, but also by its method of dispersal, for he ultimately decided to follow suit. In his will Cooke bestowed upon ten southern New England libraries credits totaling $50,000, to be expended at auction on items from his collection. Among these institutions was AAS, even though Cooke was never a member; perhaps it was the growing reputation of the Society's library collections, or Brinley's explicit endorsement, that attracted Cooke's attention. In any event, the Cooke sales proved ideal for AAS's needs. Most of the lots consisted of a miscellany of relatively inexpensive books, which enabled the Society to fill many gaps in its then very broadly based collections while selecting more carefully from among the rare materials. AAS's purchases amounted to 1,667 volumes costing $4,917.25. Among the more expensive acquisitions were notable examples of fine printing to complement those originally donated by Isaiah Thomas, some English literature and local history, and various notable illustrated works suitable for a general reference collection. For the majority of its purchases, however, the Society followed its Brinley sale strategy of strengthening its American history and imprint holdings. Much of the rare Americana was acquired in the third and final sale, with AAS selecting important European Americana and early imprints which had eluded it in the Brinley sales and some volumes distinguished for their bindings and provenance.

33. Letter, George P. Brinley and J. Hammond Trumbull to Stephen Salisbury II, February 24, 1879.

Few letters have proven as momentous for the AAS collections as this one. George Brinley died intestate in 1875, as did his wife shortly thereafter, leaving their son George and bibliographical advisor J. Hammond Trumbull (librarian of Hartford's Watkinson Library) to decide the fate of Brinley's library. They resolved to sell the collection at auction; and, so that five favored libraries could acquire what they most wanted, they followed Brinley's novel idea to distribute $25,000 in sale credit. This letter notified the Society of its share, half of which could be spent in the first Brinley sale, to be held in New York a mere two weeks hence.

AAS treasurer Nathaniel Paine and assistant librarian Edmund M. Barton represented the Society at the sale, securing 227 books and 459 pamphlets. Following the fifth and final Brinley sale in 1891, AAS found that its total expenditures for 1,151 books and 1,544 pamphlets of choice early Americana amounted to $5,065.36. The sale credits eventually dispersed by the Brinley estate accounted for nearly twenty percent of the $127,138 auction proceeds.

AAS Archives.

34. Richard Mather. *A Defence of the Answer and Arguments of the Synod Met in Boston in the Year 1662 ...* Cambridge, Massachusetts: S. Green and M. Johnson for Hezekiah Usher, 1664.

PURCHASED WITH FUNDS BEQUEATHED BY GEORGE BRINLEY, 1879.

The George Brinley bequest offered AAS an ideal opportunity to add depth and definition to two emerging collecting strengths: early Americana, and especially its collection of Mather family publications. The first Brinley sale included a remarkable group of some 400 Mather family titles. Of these, AAS acquired over sixty.

Among them was this rare imprint, un-signed but largely written by prominent Puritan minister Richard Mather (Cat. 14, portrait, Cat. 21). This is known because Mather presented this copy to Thomas Shepard II (1635-1677), minister at Cambridge, who recorded the gift (and Mather's authorship) on the title page before proceeding to fill the pages with marginalia. The 1662 Boston Synod attempted to resolve a serious doctrinal dispute over infant baptism. Mather led those (including Shepard) who argued for a "half-way covenant," in which the grandchildren as well as children of New England's "visible saints" could be baptized and admitted to full church membership. A vocal minority, including Mather's son Increase, argued for more restrictive church membership. Richard Mather won, and he sought to explain his position more fully in this work. Later this copy passed through the hands of Benjamin Wadsworth (1670-1737), eighth president of Harvard College.

Brinley Sale I, 936; Evans 89;

Holmes, *Minor Mathers*, Richard Mather 39.

35. Increase Mather. *Wo to Drunkards. Two Sermons Testifying against the Sin of Drunkenness...* Cambridge, Massachusetts: Marmaduke Johnson for Edmund Ranger, 1673.

PURCHASED WITH FUNDS BEQUEATHED BY GEORGE BRINLEY, 1879.

Among the most noteworthy of the many Mather family works purchased by AAS at the Brinley sales was this presentation copy of Increase Mather's first published sermon. One of six sons of Richard Mather, Increase (1639-1723) was born in Dorchester, Massachusetts, receiving degrees from Harvard and Trinity College, Dublin, before settling in Boston's North End as minister of the North Church. Chief among his parishioners' sins, Mather found, were pride and drunkenness. "Time was," he thundered from the pulpit, "when there was not need for Ministers to preach much against [drunkenness] in New-England; Oh that it were so now!"

Shortly after publication in late 1673, Mather inscribed this copy on the final blank

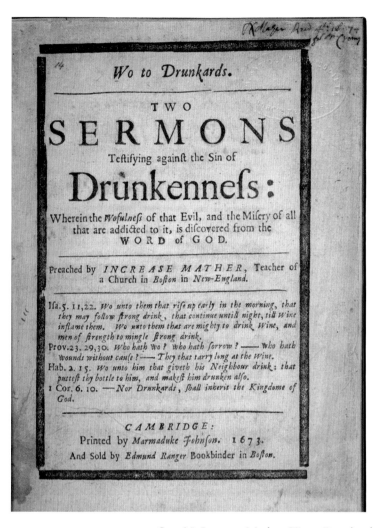

CAT. 35. Increase Mather, *Wo to Drunkards*, 1673.

page: "For Mr. Nath. Mather In Dublin." He then dispatched it to Ireland, where Increase's older brother Nathaniel noted on the title page: "N. Mather Rec'd 4th. 18. [16]74." *Wo to Drunkards* is notable, not only for its early use of Greek and Hebrew types in colonial American printing, but for being one of four known works published by Edmund Ranger in Boston; copies of all four are at AAS.

Brinley Sale I, 1048; Evans 179;
Holmes, *Increase Mather* 175-A.

36. James Janeway. *A Token for Children. … to Which is Added, A Token for the Children of New England.* Boston: Nicholas

Boone and Benjamin Eliot for Timothy Green, 1700.

PURCHASED WITH FUNDS BEQUEATHED BY GEORGE BRINLEY, 1879.

James Janeway (1636?-1674) wrote *A Token for Children* to provide youngsters with real life examples of pious individuals who died young. This is the earliest known American edition to contain both Janeway's *Token* and the supplement, *Token for the Children of New England*, by American divine Cotton Mather (1663-1728). Puritan children already had Jesus, the apostles, and the subjects of John Foxe's *Book of Martyrs* as examples of Christian life as willing sacrifice. The *Tokens* took it a step further by showing how children living in everyday circumstances could heroically face

M. T. CICERO's

CATO MAJOR,

OR HIS

DISCOURSE

OF

OLD-AGE:

With Explanatory NOTES.

PHILADELPHIA:

Printed and Sold by B. FRANKLIN,

MDCCXLIV.

CAT. 37. *M. T Cicero's Cato Major,* 1744.

death and find eternal life through Jesus Christ. The biographies follow a standard format: the child's conversion to Christ, his or her descent into fatal illness, and finally a resolute deathbed declaration of Jesus as savior. The text includes Mather's biography of his younger brother Nathanael (1669-1688), a promising scholar who died at age nineteen.

With dangerous diseases like cholera, tuberculosis, and smallpox common in this era, death was very real to youth of the Atlantic world. The *Tokens'* examples of fatally stricken children as Christian heroes aspiring to Heaven resonated in American culture; the English and American *Tokens* would continue to be published together well into the nineteenth century.

Brinley Sale I, 1249; Evans 914;
Holmes, *Cotton Mather* 403-A; Welch 665.1.

37. Marcus Tullius Cicero. *M. T. Cicero's Cato Major, or his Discourse of Old-Age: with Explanatory Notes.* Philadelphia: Benjamin Franklin, 1744.

PURCHASED WITH FUNDS BEQUEATHED BY GEORGE BRINLEY, 1880.

At the second Brinley sale, held in March 1880, AAS obtained this interesting association copy of what is often considered the finest Benjamin Franklin imprint. The English translation and extensive notes were by James Logan (1674-1751), the accomplished Philadelphia book collector who had recently joined with Franklin and others to found the Library Company of Philadelphia (Cat. 78). One thousand copies were issued of this elegantly printed edition, set in an old-age friendly Caslon great primer (i.e., 18-point) font. In his preface, Franklin expressed the wish that this work would "be a happy Omen, that Philadelphia shall become the Seat of the American Muses."

Some copies were evidently shipped to Boston bookseller Charles Harrison. At Franklin's direction, this copy was finely bound in paneled calf in Harrison's bindery for presentation to Thomas Clap, who recorded the gift on the front flyleaf. President of Yale College since 1740, Clap (1703-1767) was as renowned for his mathematical, scientific, and astronom-

ical knowledge as for his stubborn religious orthodoxy. Among Clap's accomplishments was the first printed catalog of the Yale College Library (1743) and, with Franklin's help, the establishment of a press at New Haven, Connecticut, in 1755.

AAS Wellsprings 39; Brinley Sale II, 3281; Evans 5361.

38. Roger Williams. *The Bloudy Tenent, of Persecution, for Cause of Conscience, Discussed, in a Conference between Truth and Peace ...* London, 1644.

PURCHASED WITH FUNDS BEQUEATHED BY JOSEPH J. COOKE, 1883.

It was not until the 1878 auction of New York collector Almon W. Griswold's early Americana that Joseph J. Cooke succeeded in obtaining this key work by Roger Williams. Five years later that copy was acquired by AAS in the third Cooke sale.

Having alienated Massachusetts authorities with his controversial religious and political beliefs, Roger Williams (1604?-1683) fled southward in 1636 to found the new settlement of Providence Plantations. While in England from 1643-1644 to secure a colonial charter, Williams found time to explicate his views in several publications, chief among these being *The Bloudy Tenent*. Here Williams forcefully advocated for the twelve key points enumerated in the book's opening pages, which call for the strict separation of church and state and the guarantee of religious freedom for all. So incendiary were these concepts—now, of course, enshrined in the United States Constitution—that a pamphlet war ensued and Parliament ordered that Williams's book be burned. Nonetheless, protections for religious freedom were granted to Rhode Island in its royal charter, and the colony became a haven for the persecuted.

AAS Wellsprings 11; Cooke Sale III, 2741; Wing W2758.

39. John Smith. *The Generall Historie of Virginia, New-England, and the Summer Isles ...*

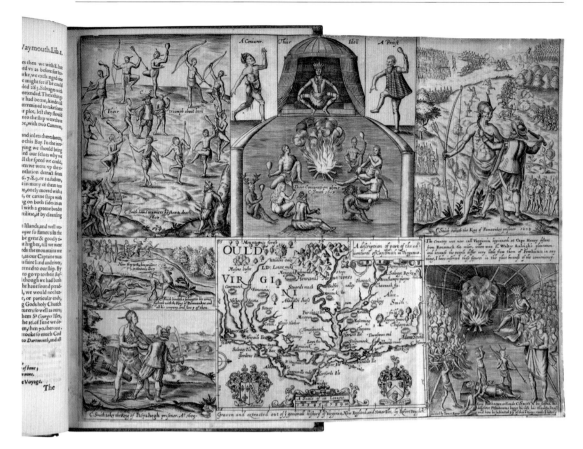

CAT. 39. *The Generall Historie of Virginia*, 1632.

London: John Dawson and John Haviland for Edward Blackmore, 1632.

PURCHASED WITH FUNDS BEQUEATHED BY JOSEPH J. COOKE, 1883.

AAS made its most expensive purchase of the Cooke sales in the third sale, paying $85 for this copy of Captain John Smith's classic account of England's early North American settlements. First published in 1624, this is the sixth and final reissue, with minor modifications to the engraved title and plates, but with the letterpress text unchanged. Cooke had acquired this tall, well-margined copy—for $90—in the 1876 New York auction of William Menzies's celebrated collection of early printing, European Americana, and early American imprints; indeed, Cooke bought heavily at that sale.

Smith compiled his *Generall Historie* during 1623 and 1624 as the fate of the Virginia colony, buffeted by mismanagement, Indian attacks, and disease, hung in the balance. Much

of the narrative consists of four of Smith's previously published works on Virginia and New England, some with extensive additions. Hence Smith deliberately looms large in the *Generall Historie* as pivotal agent and outsized personality. The engraved folding map of "Ould Virginia," for instance, is surrounded by vignettes adapted from John White's watercolors of Virginia Indians, into each of which has been inserted the heroic figure of "C[aptain] Smith."

AAS Wellsprings 13; Cooke Sale III, 2299; STC 22790d.

40. Henry Clinton. *Correspondence between His Excellency General Sir Henry Clinton, K.B. and Lieutenant General Earl Cornwallis.* Probably New York: James Rivington, 1781.

PURCHASED WITH FUNDS BEQUEATHED BY JOSEPH J. COOKE, 1883.

At the third and final Joseph J. Cooke sale

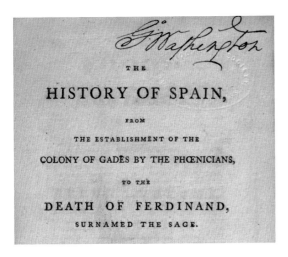 

CAT. 41. Charles John Ann Hereford, *The History of Spain* (details), 1793.

on December 3, 1883, AAS was fortunate to secure for $7.00 one of the few known copies of this pamphlet. Sir Henry Clinton was no stranger to New York, having lived there as a child while his father served as governor of the province. Clinton returned to New York in 1776 as part of the British force which wrested the city from American control, and from 1778 to 1782 he made his headquarters there as commander-in-chief of British forces in North America.

Following General Cornwallis's humiliating and decisive surrender at Yorktown on October 19, 1781, Clinton and Cornwallis mutually launched a furious, prolonged effort to place the blame squarely on the other's shoulders. Knowing that Cornwallis would have several months in London to personally shape public opinion before his own arrival home, Clinton gathered all relevant documents from his headquarters and had them printed in pamphlet form for distribution to government ministers and influential figures back in England. Although the pamphlet bears no imprint, the typography identifies it as very likely the work of James Rivington, Loyalist printer in New York.

Cooke Sale II, 537; Shipton & Mooney 43954.

41. Charles John Ann Hereford.
The History of Spain ... Dublin: J. Exshaw, L. White, and Wm. Jones, 1793.

PURCHASED WITH FUNDS BEQUEATHED BY JOSEPH J. COOKE, 1883.

The Joseph J. Cooke collection was strong in Washingtoniana, and AAS bought extensively from that portion of the Cooke sale. The prize—though at $7.50, by no means the most expensive Washington item purchased by AAS at the sale—was this finely bound two-volume set from George Washington's library. Although lacking Washington's engraved armorial bookplate—not uncommon for books from his personal collection—each volume was boldly signed by Washington on the title page. The inventory of Washington's Mount Vernon library, posthumously prepared in 1800, lists 893 volumes; this set, valued at $3.00, sat in "Case No. 1," apparently on the same shelf with Adam Smith's *Wealth of Nations* and Shakespeare's *Works.*

Per the circular engraved bookseller's label on each pastedown, Washington purchased this set in Philadelphia from Thomas Stephens— who was active as a bookseller, publisher, and editor from 1793-1797 —sometime during his second term as President of the United States. Presumably this copy was also bound in Philadelphia, in tasteful tree calf with modest decoration in gilt and blind. No marginalia are present, but a few folded page corners may evidence Washington's reading. These volumes remain the only ones from Washington's library known to have entered the AAS collection.

Cooke Sale II, 1116.

Old SANTECLAUS with much delight

His reindeer drives this frosty night,

O'er chimney tops, and tracks of snow,

To bring his yearly gifts to you.

Three Prominent Worcester Members and Collectors

Since its founding in 1812, the American Antiquarian Society has been distinctive for being simultaneously a national and a local institution. Although its membership has always been drawn from a broad geographic base, for much of its history the Society has relied heavily upon those members residing in or near Worcester, Massachusetts, for its leadership and financial support. The Worcester of 1812 was a small town with a population of some 2,500, but one whose residents included several well-to-do and nationally prominent figures who willingly embraced Isaiah Thomas's vision as their own. The opening of the Blackstone Canal connecting Worcester with Providence, Rhode Island, and the Atlantic Ocean in 1828 quickly transformed Worcester from an agricultural community into an industrial power-house. As did many other local institutions, the Soci-ety benefited greatly from Worcester's extraordinary growth during the nineteenth century, sharing with its institutional peers a large nucleus of wealthy, civic-minded individuals. Following the Civil War, collec-tions built by three Worcester residents in particular helped to shape the Society and its library: Stephen Salisbury III, Nathaniel Paine, and George Frisbie Hoar.

FIG. 10. Stephen Salisbury III.

Stephen Salisbury III (1835-1905) was the scion of Worcester's wealthiest and most prominent family. In 1767, eight years before Isaiah Thomas brought his press to Worcester, Stephen Salisbury I moved from Boston to establish a branch of the family mer-cantile business. It prospered, and his son, Stephen Salisbury II (1798-1884), vastly expanded the family fortune through canny investments in real estate and Worcester's burgeoning industrial and financial sectors. Stephen II became one of Worcester's most generous benefactors and civic leaders, and served for three decades as AAS president (1854-1884).

Stephen III was elected a member of AAS in 1863. He pursued an abiding interest in Pre-Columbian America, contributing many papers on the topic to the AAS *Proceed-ings*, funding archaeological digs, acquiring museum artifacts for AAS, and increasing its holdings of works printed in, and about, Central and South America. In 1887 he be-came the Society's president, remaining in that office until his death. Salisbury's many bequests included $200,000 and a tract of land for AAS—up to that time its largest sin-gle gift—which enabled the construction of the present Antiquarian Hall, opened in 1910. Also received were the family's business and personal papers, and library, which over time have proven to be of considerable research value.

A contemporary of Stephen Salisbury III, Nathaniel Paine (1832-1917) was born

FIG. 11

FIG. 12

into an old and distinguished Worcester family of more modest means. Industrious and fortunate in his friends and mentors—among them the Unitarian minister and prolific author Edward Everett Hale (who succeeded Salisbury as the Society's president in 1906)—Paine found work at a local bank as an office boy, rising through the ranks until he became its president. Not content simply to monitor Worcester's financial pulse, Paine was a tireless and generous participant in its many social and cultural organizations. To none was he more devoted than AAS, the local institution which most fully embodied his greatest passions: collecting and local history. Elected to membership in 1860, Paine participated in the Society's affairs for fifty-six years, including forty-four years as treasurer. To its *Proceedings,* Paine contributed many papers on local history and genealogy, as well as useful checklists of the early currency, art works, seventeenth-century imprints, pre-1801 broadsides, and manuscripts held by AAS. One manuscript in particular captivated Paine for its literary merits and insights into Worcester history: the engaging diary of Christopher Columbus Baldwin (Cat. 25), which Paine edited for publication in 1901.

A lifelong collector of stamps, coins, medals, photographs, prints, printed ephemera, and manuscripts in addition to books, Paine found the creation of extra-illustrated volumes and scrapbooks to be ideal ways of driving his collecting and of organizing his holdings. Today the dozens of compiled volumes that Paine bequeathed to the Society are unusually rich resources for a wide range of research topics. If not the most valuable, among the most useful are the extra-illustrated volumes documenting Worcester history and the Society's first century, to which Paine added his own photographs, research notes, manuscripts, and ephemera. Paine's bequest also included his substantial library and a generous contribution to the AAS endowment.

Born in Concord, Massachusetts, George Frisbie Hoar (1826-1904) established a law practice in Worcester after graduating from Harvard Law School in 1849. Initially, Hoar recalled, "my dream and highest ambition were to spend my life as what is called an office lawyer, making deeds, and giving advice ... perhaps to earn twelve or fifteen hundred dollars a year, which would enable me to have a room of my own in some quiet house and to collect rare books which could be had without much cost." But in 1852 Hoar began a meteoric rise in state and national politics, becoming a Republican stalwart and renowned orator, Worcester's chief advocate in Washington, and a distinguished member of the U.S. Senate. Rare books and manuscripts were always in his thoughts, however, and Hoar frequently employed his political clout to bibliophilic ends. When bookseller Henry Stevens offered Benjamin Franklin's papers to the United States government in 1882, Hoar made certain that they were purchased for the nation. Perhaps no single achievement pleased him more, however, than his successful negotiations with the Bishop of London for the return to Massachusetts

Fig. 13

in 1897 of the manuscript of William Bradford's "Of Plimoth Plantation," now in the Massachusetts State Library. When back home in Worcester, Hoar participated actively in its political and cultural life. Elected to AAS membership in 1853, Hoar eventually joined his close friend Nathaniel Paine as an officer in the Society, serving as president (1884-1887) between the terms of Stephen Salisbury II and III, and seeking to place AAS acquisitions on a more predictable footing through establishment of a purchase endowment.

Throughout his life Hoar returned for recreation to interests first developed during his Harvard years: classical Greek and book collecting. Visitors to Hoar's home "were as apt as not to find him standing at his desk and advancing [his unpublished translation of Thucydides] by a few lines, or revising it." Then their eyes would turn to Hoar's vast library, which was particularly strong in rare works on American history. Many indeed "could be had without much cost" from booksellers and at auction, though Hoar was among those who paid high prices at the Brinley sales for specific items they could not live without. Following his death in 1904, Hoar's library remained with the family until 1961 when, after a prolonged courtship, AAS was permitted to select what it needed. Just under a thousand books and pamphlets were added to the collections, ranging from seventeenth-century New England imprints to mid-nineteenth-century sermons.

Old Santeclaus with much delight
His reindeer drives this frosty night,
O'er chimney tops, and tracks of snow,
To bring his yearly gifts to you.

CAT. 42. *The Children's Friend*, 1821.

42. *The Children's Friend. Number III. A New-Year's Present, to the Little Ones from Five to Twelve.* New York: William B. Gilley, 1821.

GIFT OF STEPHEN SALISBURY III, 1897.

This cultural landmark is one of the rarest children's books at AAS. In the early United States, New Year's Day was formally celebrated as the major winter holiday, while Christmas was looked down upon by many American Protestants as hopelessly linked to Catholicism and disorderly mob behavior. *The Children's Friend* promotes New Year's Day as a child-centered, family-oriented holiday, but it also features one of the earliest known images of "Sante Claus" driving a gift-laden sleigh pulled by a single reindeer. Just two years later, in the December 23, 1823 issue of the *Troy Sentinel*, the adventures of Santa Claus and his reindeer would be immortalized by Clement Clarke Moore in his poem, *The Night before Christmas.*

William B. Gilley published *The Children's Friend* as a high-end holiday picture book, retailing for the price of 25 cents hand-colored, or 18¾ cents plain. The publisher's advertisement on the back wrapper describes the illustrations as prepared "in a method entirely new"—a reference to the revolutionary process of lithography. The unsigned illustrations were probably lithographed by the firm of William A. Barnet and Isaac Doolittle; their designer may have been Arthur Joseph Stansbury, who collaborated with Barnet and Doolittle on at least one other publication.

This copy was given to Stephen Salisbury III in 1841, when he was six years old, and then carefully preserved in the family library. It is one of over sixty children's books donated by Salisbury to AAS.

Shoemaker 4977.

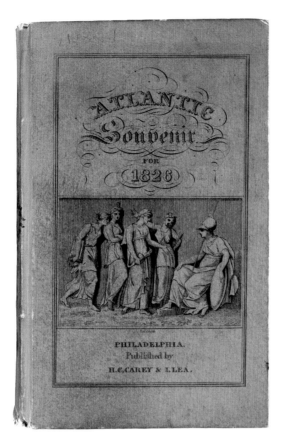

CAT. 43. *The Atlantic Souvenir, 1825.*

43. *The Atlantic Souvenir, A Christmas and New Year's Offering. 1826.* **Philadelphia: H.C. Carey & I. Lea, 1825.**

BEQUEST OF STEPHEN SALISBURY III, 1907.

Stephen Salisbury III's bequest of a portion of his family library remains prized today. The volumes are notable not only for revealing how a well-to-do Worcester family stocked its library during the nineteenth century, but also for their overall fine condition. This significant annual, or gift book, for example, is in almost as-new condition.

Quick to note the success of London publisher Rudolph Ackermann's innovative literary annual, *The Forget Me Not* (itself based on continental European annuals), Philadelphia publishers Carey & Lea signed on as Ackermann's American agents in 1824. But Carey & Lea soon decided that publishing their own annual was the better business option. Two thousand copies of *The Atlantic Souvenir* for 1826, considered the first American literary annual, were published in December 1825, just in time for the holiday market. This anthology of short fiction and verse by popular authors, illustrated with steel-engraved plates, was an instant success. Part of its appeal for purchasers such as the Salisburys was the attractive illustrated binding of green paper over boards, edges gilt, with green silk pull tab at the top edge, housed within a decorative slipcase. The binding alone cost thirty-five cents to manufacture, or fully one quarter of the volume's production cost. Lavishly decorated and bound gift books remained a staple of American publishing up to the Civil War.

Shoemaker 19471.

44-46. Nathaniel Paine. *Isaiah Thomas House.* 1887; *The Worcester Camera Club at Merriam's Corner, Concord Mass.* 1892; and *White Birch Tree (The Wizard), Intervale, N.H.* 1892.

GIFT OF THE NATHANIEL PAINE ESTATE, 1920.

The invention of the albumen photographic process in 1850, and the development of portable cameras in the 1880s, made photography more widely accessible to non-professionals and transformed the way amateur historians recorded the world. Camera clubs sprouted up across the country, gathering together like-minded enthusiasts to share photographic techniques and tips. Because most cameras then worked best out of doors in bright sunlight, recreational photographers often employed them to record vanishing historic buildings and landscapes.

These three images were taken by AAS member Nathaniel Paine, an active participant in the Worcester Camera Club, which started meeting informally in 1885. One image depicts club members on an 1892 outing to Concord, Massachusetts. Paine turned his camera on many significant properties, using the albumen process and also experimenting with cyanotype, in order to capture images he felt had historical importance. The image of Isaiah Thomas's Main Street home in Worcester, Massachusetts, was used by Paine to extra-illustrate a copy of his privately printed *Notes, Historical and Chronological on the Town of Worcester, Massachusetts* (1876). Another image depicts the Wizard Birch in Cathedral Woods near Intervale, New Hampshire. This tree stood in a grove where, in the early 1870s, Henry Ward Beecher preached to the throngs of tourists who flocked to the White Mountains in summer. Today Paine's photographs are important (and often unique) visual records of vanished historical places: the Thomas house, for instance, was torn down early in the twentieth century, and the Wizard Birch no longer stands.

47. *Charleston Mercury Extra … The Union is Dissolved! December 20, 1860.* Charleston, South Carolina: Mercury Office, 1860.

GIFT OF NATHANIEL PAINE

The divisive political events of the 1850s had pitted North against South on numerous issues, including the expansion of slavery into the western territories, tariffs on goods such as cotton, and broader concepts of states' rights vs. federal law. Political compromises made throughout the decade in an attempt to keep the nation together effectively collapsed with the election of Abraham Lincoln in November 1860. South Carolina, heir to the legacy of states' rights lion John C. Calhoun, was the first to address the possibility of leaving the Union. On November 10, 1860, four days after the presidential election, South Carolina brought the issue to a head by calling a secession convention for the following month.

Considered by virtue of timing to be the first Confederate imprint, this broadside announced to the public the convention's declaration, on December 20, 1860, that South Carolina would secede from the United States. This sheet was removed from a wall in Charleston by the Boston-born author Caroline Howard Gilman (1794-1888), who had moved permanently to Charleston following her marriage to the Rev. Samuel Gilman. Gilman mailed the broadside to her daughter Eliza in Salem, Massachusetts. Eliza in turn presented the document to AAS member Nathaniel Paine who, heeding the Society's call to preserve all printed material relating to the unsettling national events, passed the broadside along to AAS.

48. Nathaniel Paine, compiler, *Freaks of Nature Illustrated.* 1891.

GIFT OF THE NATHANIEL PAINE ESTATE, 1920.

Nathaniel Paine's interests were broad, and he compiled extra-illustrated volumes on a wide variety of subjects. Many concerned

CHARLESTON

MERCURY

EXTRA:

Passed unanimously at 1.15 o'clock, P. M., December 20th, 1860.

AN ORDINANCE

To dissolve the Union between the State of South Carolina and other States united with her under the compact entitled " The Constitution of the United States of America."

We, the People of the State of South Carolina, in Convention assembled, do declare and ordain, and it is hereby declared and ordained,

That the Ordinance adopted by us in Convention, on the twenty-third day of May, in the year of our Lord one thousand seven hundred and eighty-eight, whereby the Constitution of the United States of America was ratified, and also, all Acts and parts of Acts of the General Assembly of this State, ratifying amendments of the said Constitution, are hereby repealed; and that the union now subsisting between South Carolina and other States, under the name of "The United States of America," is hereby dissolved.

THE

UNION

IS

DISSOLVED!

CAT. 47. *Charlestown Mercury Extra*, 1860.

CAT. 48. *Freaks of Nature Illustrated,* 1891.

Worcester and various aspects of American history—particularly the American Revolution—as well as coins and currency, theater, and circuses. In so doing, Paine succeeded in preserving much ephemeral, but highly important, primary source material that AAS researchers draw upon heavily today.

This is not properly an extra-illustrated book, but rather a scrapbook containing a compilation of material. The principal text is an article, titled "Freaks of Nature," clipped from the November 8, 1890 issue of *The Illustrated American.* Paine supplemented the article with photographs of people exhibited as freaks, plus pamphlets distributed at exhibitions, newspaper clippings, and advertisements for circuses and other shows he attended. The volume includes images of Moung Phoset and his mother Mahphoon, both of whom suffered from hereditary hypertrichosis. They were first brought from their home in Burma to London; in 1887, they journeyed to the United States, where they were exhibited by P. T. Barnum.

Photographs of tattooed people, snake charmers, and Circassian beauties are also to be found in Paine's volume.

49. *The Charter of the City of Saint John, in the Province of New-Brunswick.* St. John: Lewis and Ryan, 1785.

GIFT OF THE NATHANIEL PAINE ESTATE, 1920.

Nathaniel Paine's many gifts to AAS included not only photographs, extra-illustrated volumes, and manuscripts, but also important Americana. American Loyalists saw the handwriting on the wall long before the Treaty of Paris was signed on September 3, 1783, formally ending the American Revolution. By that date, nearly 30,000 Loyalists had embarked from New York, Boston, and other

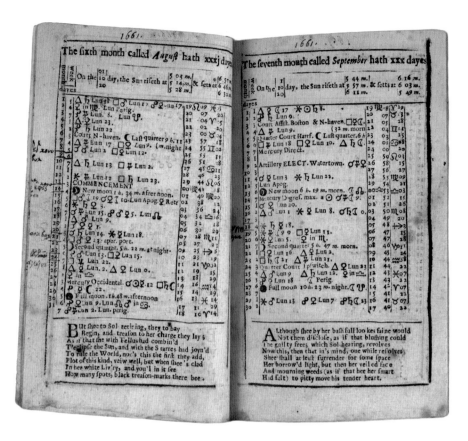

CAT. 50. Samuel Cheever, *An Almanac for the Year of Our Lord 1661.*

ports, most settling in Nova Scotia and the newly established province of New Brunswick. Their removal was overseen by Sir Guy Carleton, who had been appointed in 1782 as Commander-in-Chief of British forces in North America and then as Governor of Britain's Canadian provinces. In 1785 Carleton granted to the Loyalist boom town of Saint John its own royal charter, establishing it, by several decades, as Canada's first incorporated city. Based on the colonial charter of the city of New York, the Saint John charter included specific provisions restricting the rights of the many African-American Loyalists ("people of colour") who had settled there. This very rare early Canadian imprint forms part of AAS's strong, but relatively little-known, collection of pre-1877 Canadiana.

Tremaine 467.

50. Samuel Cheever. *An Almanac for the Year of Our Lord 1661 ...* Cambridge, Massachusetts:

Samuel Green and Marmaduke Johnson, 1661.

GIFT OF THE ESTATE OF GEORGE F. HOAR, 1961.

Among the nearly one thousand items acquired by AAS from the George F. Hoar library was this imprint, one of two recorded copies of Samuel Cheever's 1661 almanac. Early Massachusetts almanacs often were compiled by young Harvard College graduates. The 1660 and 1661 almanacs printed at the Cambridge press of Samuel Green and Marmaduke Johnson, for instance, were the work of Cheever, who was part of the Harvard class of 1659. As was typical of these almanacs, the monthly calendars list the various court and election days, as well as the date of Harvard's commencement. Notably, Cheever filled two densely printed pages with an essay, "A brief Discourse of the Rise and Progress of Astronomy," which concludes: "Whereupon in this last age,

Galilaeus ... and sundry other Mathematicians, have learnedly confuted the Ptolemaick & Tychonick Systeme, and demonstrated the Copernican Hypothesis to be most consentaneous to truth ... although there are ... those who will still be pleased to censure and cavil at [it] ... *Experientia Scientiam, Scientia Veritatem, sed Veritas Odium Peperit* [Experiment has given birth to knowledge, knowledge to truth, but truth to enmity]." Historians have cited Cheever's essay as important evidence for the teaching of new astronomical theories at Harvard and their early dissemination throughout New England.

Drake 2837; Evans 66.

51. Leonard Hoar. *The Sting of Death and Death Unstung, Delivered in Two Sermons ...* Boston: John Foster, 1680.

GIFT OF THE ESTATE OF GEORGE F. HOAR, 1961.

George F. Hoar was already an accomplished book collector by the time of the first Brinley sale in 1879, where he secured, for $45, this especially meaningful prize: a very rare copy of the second and final publication of his eminent ancestor, Leonard Hoar (1630-1675). Born in England, Leonard Hoar emigrated to Massachusetts as a child and graduated from Harvard College in 1650. Hoar then returned to England for twenty years until called to the pulpit of Boston's Old South Church in 1672. Before his installation, however, Hoar was elected the third president of Harvard—the first alumnus to fill that office. His brief tenure was marred by bitter factionalism believed to have been instigated by disappointed rivals such as Urian Oakes (Cat. 84). Despite having earned the respect of many, Hoar was forced out in 1675 and died shortly thereafter. Five years later, this posthumous publication of two sermons Hoar preached in England in 1653 was financed by his nephew Josiah Flint, who indirectly rebuked Hoar's unnamed enemies in the preface.

Brinley Sale I, 777; Evans 286.

52. Jonas Clark. *The Fate of Blood-Thirsty Oppressors, and God's Tender Care of His Distressed People. A Sermon, Preached at Lexington, April 19, 1776 ...* Boston: Powars and Willis, 1776.

GIFT OF THE ESTATE OF GEORGE F. HOAR, 1961.

The George F. Hoar library was particularly rich in works concerning the American Revolution, of which Jonas Clark's sermon is one of the rarest and most significant. Called to the pulpit in Lexington, Massachusetts, in 1755 at the age of 25, Clark remained in that post until his death fifty years later. His few published sermons include the 1768 *Importance of Military Skill, Measures for Defence and a Martial Spirit, in a Time of Peace*, no doubt heard and read by some future Minutemen. An ardent supporter of the Patriot cause, Clark was hosting its leaders, Samuel Adams and John Hancock, in his Lexington home when Paul Revere leapt from his weary mount and pounded on the door shortly after midnight on April 19, 1775. In the ensuing hours, Clark would witness the muster and battle on Lexington Green, and officiate at the burial of the dead.

One year later, Clark delivered this impassioned sermon, which helped to establish the symbolic importance of Lexington and Concord even before independence was declared. From that day, he stated, "we may venture to predict, will be dated, in future history, THE LIBERTY or SLAVERY of the AMERICAN WORLD," depending on whether "God shall see fit to smile, or frown upon the interesting cause, in which we are engaged." Of special significance is Clark's appended "Narrative," in which he offers his own eyewitness account of the battle.

Evans 14679.

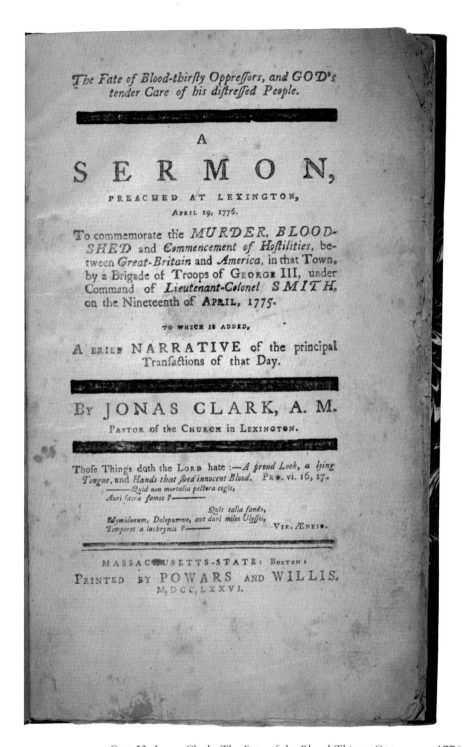

The Fate of Blood-thirsty Oppressors, and GOD's tender Care of his distressed People.

A

SERMON,

PREACHED AT LEXINGTON,

APRIL 19, 1776.

To commemorate the *MURDER, BLOOD-SHED* and *Commencement of Hostilities*, between *Great-Britain* and *America*, in that Town, by a Brigade of Troops of GEORGE III, under Command of *Lieutenant-Colonel SMITH*, on the Nineteenth of APRIL, 1775.

TO WHICH IS ADDED,

A BRIEF NARRATIVE of the principal Transactions of that Day.

BY JONAS CLARK, A. M.

PASTOR of the CHURCH in LEXINGTON.

Those Things doth the LORD hate :—*A proud Look, a lying Tongue,* and *Hands that shed innocent Blood.* PRO. vi. 16, 17.
————*Quid non mortalia pectora cogis, Auri sacra fames ?*————

Quis talia fando,
Myrmidonum, Dolopumve, aut duri miles Ulyssei,
Temperet a lachrymis ?———— VIR. ÆNEID.

MASSACHUSETTS-STATE: BOSTON:
PRINTED BY POWARS AND WILLIS.
M, DCC, LXXVI.

CAT. 52. Jonas Clark, *The Fate of the Blood-Thirsty Oppressors*, 1776.

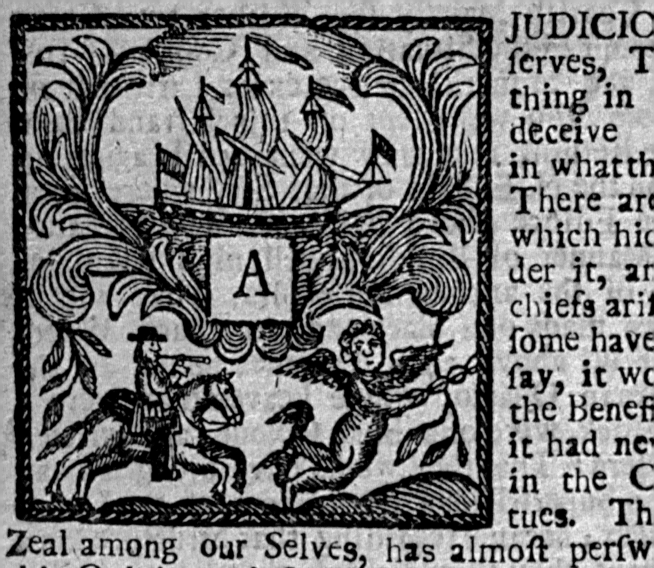

JUDICIO
ferves, T
thing in
deceive
in what th
There are
which hic
der it, ar
chiefs ariſ
ſome have
ſay, it wo
the Benef
it had ne
in the C
tues. Th
Zeal among our Selves, has almoſt perſw
this Opinion. A furious pretended Zeal, w
Matters of Opinion, has been improv'd ag
a Deſign to deſtroy my Reputation and
thoſe who are Strangers to my Perſon: A
ſign might be the better carried on, ſome P
ſo undutiful to the Reverend Dr. Increaſe
ſwade him to prefix his Name to an Adv
laſt Weeks News-Letter and Gazette, whe
Appellation I meet with, is that of a w
Libeller. This Charge I now lye under fro
miſter in the Country, and in order to clea
fr ª give an Account of the firſt Cauſe
etween us

Collecting in the Twentieth Century

As the American Antiquarian Society approached its centennial in 1912, it became increasingly apparent to the Society's officers that it was time to shift direction. The death of AAS president Stephen Salisbury III in 1905 had opened the door to new leadership. Of equal importance, Salisbury's substantial bequest provided the means for the Society to construct an entirely new building—the present Antiquarian Hall—with library stack space to accommodate substantial collection growth. Most of the miscellaneous artifacts in the Society's cabinet had already been transferred to more appropriate institutions, such as the Smithsonian Institution and the Peabody Museum at Harvard, allowing AAS to invest its scarce resources in building its research library holdings. No longer would an *omnium gatherum* approach to collection development be acceptable. Rather, in keeping with Isaiah Thomas's original vision for AAS, and in acknowledgment of its existing collecting strengths, the Society would henceforth focus its energies on early American imprints and the primary and secondary sources necessary for the study of early American history. With the retirement of librarian Edmund Mills Barton in 1908, the search began for a successor, which ended with the spectacularly successful appointment of Clarence S. Brigham to the post.

The story which follows is perhaps best understood in the context of Brigham's outsized personality and consummate skills as a bookman and bibliographer. A graduate of Brown University, Brigham (1877-1963) arrived at AAS after several years as librarian of the Rhode Island Historical Society. Hampered as were his predecessors by inadequate resources, Brigham followed Christopher Columbus Baldwin's example by making the most of little. As AAS Director Clifford K. Shipton recalled, Brigham "would take a field in which [Isaiah] Thomas had left the bare cornerstones, and would buy the largest collection to become available, usually at a time when interest in that field was low. Then he could set out to fill the gaps."

Brigham was also adept at cultivating collectors, bibliographers, and booksellers. Unfailingly generous with his time and formidable bibliographical knowledge, Brigham (assisted by his dedicated staff) worked hard to apprise collectors and bibliographers of the relevant resources to be found at the Society. These professional contacts were reinforced through Brigham's relentless networking, in social circles, Boston's Club of Odd Volumes, the Grolier Club, or various bibliographical and historical societies, and especially at AAS and his Worcester home. Many of Brigham's bibliophilic friends, grateful for his help, appreciative of AAS's zeal for its mission, and made fully aware of how their collections could enhance the Society's holdings, generously favored AAS with donations great and small. The results were nothing short of astonishing: beginning with a library of approximately 100,000 volumes in 1908, Brigham had enlarged the collections to some 600,000 volumes by 1939, securing its status as the preeminent holding of pre-1821 American imprints. (Subsequently that number was reduced as the Society pared post-1876 and foreign works with no connection to America from its collections. Today the total stands at 750,000 volumes.) Particular attention was also paid to AAS's unrivaled early American newspaper collection, which Brigham trebled in size. The example set by Baldwin and Brigham was carefully heeded by Brigham's successors, R.W.G. Vail, Clifford K. Shipton and Marcus A. McCorison, all of whom added meaningfully to the library's holdings.

Charles Henry Taylor, Collector Extraordinaire

Charles Henry Taylor (1867-1941), the publisher of the *Boston Globe,* became a member of the American Antiquarian Society in 1912, the institution's centennial year. Taylor was then forty-five years old—a relative youngster among the membership—and he had been collecting printed Americana in earnest for more than a decade. Taylor's interests were wide-ranging, and he bought primarily from a network of dealers in Boston, Providence, and New York. During his three decades of membership, Taylor proved to be one of the Society's greatest benefactors, donating thousands of books, manuscripts, newspapers, and prints to the collection, as well as generously funding several major acquisitions.

The son of General Charles H. Taylor (1846-1921), who had joined the *Globe* a year after its founding in 1872 and made it a commercial success, the young Taylor grew up around reporters, politicians, and sportsmen of the age. Constantly underfoot at the *Globe,* he learned all aspects of the newspaper business, from running presses to managing the front office. Even though Taylor was surrounded by modern presses and equipment, he was fascinated by earlier printing technologies, collecting eighteenth-century newspapers printed from hand-set type, seeking out impressions of early American lithographs, and acquiring first editions of the nation's great writers.

Taylor's initial gifts to AAS were, appropriately, American newspapers. Immediately after his election to membership, Taylor began to correspond frequently with librarian Clarence S. Brigham, who had just begun working on his bibliography of pre-1821 American newspapers while concurrently acquiring as many as he could for AAS. As the relationship between Taylor and the Society intensified, his collecting interests shifted increasingly from newspapers and the history of American journalism to American lithography. Taylor had begun collecting lithographs in 1904, and he was intrigued by all aspects of the process, from printing to coloring to publishing and distribution. Indeed, Taylor had grown up with lithography, which became far more widespread following the Civil War. *The Globe's* subscription slips, for example, were lithographed in colors, many school books of the era were illustrated lithographically, and his father often offered chromolithographs to subscribers as subscription premiums. But at the very time that Taylor became interested in lithography, it was largely being replaced by photomechanical processes. Thankfully, Taylor realized the historical value of lithography just as it was disappearing and resolved to preserve its history as best he could. He sought out and interviewed retired lithographers, compiled notes on the business relationships between firms in Boston, and purchased hundreds of lithographed books, prints, and ephemera. In a 1923 letter to Brigham, for instance, Taylor noted that he had spoken with John White Allen Scott (1815-1907), who had worked as an apprentice in the late 1820s for the Pendleton firm in Boston, and had also interviewed Nathaniel Currier's son, who provided details on Currier's early partnership with Adam Stodart.

As he tried to make sense of the mass of primary source material accumulating in his

FIG.14

home, office and even in his summer residence on Buzzard's Bay, Taylor soon found himself nearly as much a historian as a collector. At Brigham's insistence, he reluctantly delivered a paper on American lithography to the AAS membership in 1922. "So long as I keep my data to myself," Taylor fretted, "everybody sits up and says 'He is the authority on Early American lithography.' If I deliver the address and it gets into print, somebody is sure to find me out and I will lose the only standing I have in collectors' circles." Two years later, he purchased a large portion of the archive of the Massachusetts chromolithography firm L. Prang & Co., presenting the Society with several dozen salesmen's sample books full of chromolithographed greeting cards, proof sheets, and progressive proofs. Taylor also began to give segments of his vast print collection to AAS. The prints poured in—city views, marine scenes, political cartoons, portraits, and sporting prints all made their way from Boston to Worcester, where they were carefully sorted and recorded. The extent of his gift was tremendous. In 1928 alone, Taylor sent to the Society 383 volumes and 155 pamphlets illustrated with lithographs; 1,010 separately published prints; and 940 pieces of lithographed sheet music. Considered together, Taylor's gifts span the entire field of American lithography, in all its permutations, from the 1820s through 1900. Thoughtfully, Taylor also donated funds so that AAS could promptly catalogue the material. In October 1929, Brigham was able to report that AAS had established in its reading room the nation's first card catalog for a lithograph collection, eventually comprising 4,000 records and providing access by publisher, artist, and title.

Taylor's quarterly gifts of lithographs and lithographically illustrated imprints—supplemented by maps, pamphlets, sheet music, newspapers, photographs, and manuscripts—continued until his death, prompting this memorial tribute from Brigham: "Not since Isaiah Thomas has any one donor given the Library so great a mass of historical material." That "mass of historical material" included important additions to all of the Society's primary collecting areas—this catholicity was perhaps the hallmark of Taylor's generosity. Newspapers from his collection regularly arrived in Worcester, as well as gifts of children's books (eventually totaling over 350) and periodicals, particularly illustrated volumes. Taylor was particularly concerned about recording illustrators in each of the periodicals he donated. In 1923, for example, he sent to the Society several copies of the December 1825 issue of the *Boston Monthly Magazine,* explaining that all should be kept because each was illustrated with a different lithograph. Writing to Brigham in 1927, Taylor reviewed the cataloguing process for his donated prints, specifying, "In addition to making the cards and sheets I think it would do very well to keep a chart of lithographers and dates so that you can check back and see if any of the dates are correct .... Do this in every case. We want to record every bit of information no matter how slight."

Taylor was quick to appreciate the importance of archival material in documenting the book trades. Over the course of his relationship with AAS, he donated many significant manuscript collections, such as the Lee & Shepard papers and the Daniel C. Heath correspondence, which document book publishing, as well as artists' papers, including those of Henry Inman, Bass Otis (who made the first lithograph in America), and David Claypoole Johnston, which illuminate the process of making and distributing art in nineteenth-century America. Taylor also donated authors' papers, such as a cache of Lydia Maria Child's correspondence and manuscripts of

FIG. 15. Charles H. Taylor.

stories by John Sherburne Sleeper. Books were not omitted from Taylor's beneficence. Along with his important gift of Herman Melville first editions, Taylor donated cookbooks, eighteenth-century tracts, bookseller's catalogs, and, of course, lithographically illustrated books.

In 1938, Taylor sent to Brigham his working file on the Newburyport inventor and engraver Jacob Perkins, including original engraved currency, photographic files, and research notes. One of the last gifts to arrive at the Society during Taylor's lifetime, it exemplifies his in-depth, almost journalistic, focus on a topic. Following Taylor's death, his generous bequests to AAS, Harvard University, and the Peabody Museum, which followed his long-standing relationship as a prominent donor to each institution, were described in detail by the Boston newspapers, with the Society receiving first choice of the remaining prints, books, and manuscripts. Brigham accepted almost everything that was not a duplicate, including a large number of Currier & Ives lithographs which Taylor had threatened to "dump" on the Society back in 1928. In the October 1941 AAS *Proceedings*, Brigham fondly remembered his old friend, remarking that for "thirty years, books, pamphlets, newspapers, prints and manuscripts flowed to Worcester in a steady stream." Taylor "collected chiefly to aid libraries and scholarship in general; and the more quickly he could send his gatherings to some permanent depository, the happier he was." Based on the sheer volume and significance of his gifts to AAS, Charles Henry Taylor must indeed have been a happy man.

CAT. 53. Bass Otis. Account Book, 1815-1854.

53. Bass Otis. Account Book, 1815-1854.

GIFT OF CHARLES HENRY TAYLOR, 1931.

Bass Otis (1784-1861) was born in East Bridgewater, Massachusetts, and during a long career spent primarily in Philadelphia and Boston, he specialized in painting portraits. He also made limited attempts in other media, including engraving, mezzotint, and aquatint. Around 1911 Charles Henry Taylor asked Anthony J. Philpott, an editor at the *Boston Globe*, to interview Otis's nephew William Vinton, Jr., who still lived in East Bridgewater. In 1928 Taylor donated Philpott's notes to AAS along with over a dozen other items by or about Otis that he had accumulated, including a self-portrait (Cat. 54).

Three years later Taylor augmented his gift by donating this account book kept by Bass Otis. It lists more than three hundred portraits that Otis painted between 1819 and 1826; in addition, there are records of a smaller number of later portraits, copies of paintings, and prints executed by Otis. The volume also contains a few sketches, such as a study for a portrait of the children of the Philadelphia Quaker merchant and philanthropist Caleb Cresson and his wife Sarah Emlen Cresson.

54. Bass Otis. *Self-Portrait.* Oil on tin, 1860.

GIFT OF CHARLES HENRY TAYLOR, 1928.

Bass Otis painted several self-portraits, leaving a remarkably complete record of his changing physical appearance. The earliest is dated 1812, when Otis was launching his artistic career; two images from the 1830s show Otis in his prime; and this self-portrait, at age 76, is Otis's last known work. It was commissioned by Ferdinand Julius Dreer, a Philadelphia jeweler and arts patron. Charles Henry Taylor purchased the painting at the 1913 auction of Dreer's collection.

Early in his career, Otis experimented with the new artistic medium of lithography. The July 1819 issue of the *Analectic Magazine* featured an article on this novel printing process. It included a lithographed scene by Otis depicting a mill at water's edge—an image which has been called the first lithograph published in America. Because of his abiding interest in the history of lithography, Charles Henry Taylor had long been a student of Otis's career. Indeed, Taylor's article, "Some Notes on Early American Lithography," published in the AAS *Proceedings* in 1922, begins with a biographical account of Otis and his work.

AAS Chief Joys 212; Hewes 91; Weis 91.

CAT. 56. M.E.D. Brown, *Wm P. Dewees, M.D.*, 1834.

55. Nicolas-Eustache Maurin, after Gilbert Stuart. *George Washington, First President of the United States.* Boston: Pendleton, 1825-1828.

GIFT OF CHARLES HENRY TAYLOR

In the 1820s, capitalizing on French advances in lithographic printing, a few American entrepreneurs arranged to have prints produced in France for the American market. Perhaps the best-known examples are the "American Kings," a set of lithographed portraits of the first five American presidents. The brainchild of John Doggett, owner of a Boston looking-glass and carpet warehouse, the prints were lithographic reproductions of portraits painted by Gilbert Stuart. Doggett had exhibited the original paintings in Boston in 1822, but it was not until 1825 that arrangements were made to reproduce them as prints. Lacking a practicable American alternative, Doggett commissioned Boston lithographer John Pendleton to take the

paintings to Paris, where the compositions were drawn on stone by the French artist Nicolas-Eustache Maurin. Pendleton then brought the paintings, the prepared lithographic stones, a French lithographic press, and three trained pressmen back to Boston, where the impressions were printed and sold.

Intrigued by this early instance of transatlantic lithographic printing, Charles Henry Taylor collected multiple examples of the five Maurin prints, including one complete set which he acquired directly from a former printer in the Pendleton firm.

56. M.E.D. Brown, after John Neagle. *Wm. P. Dewees, M.D.* Philadelphia: N. Currier for M.E.D. Brown, 1834.

GIFT OF CHARLES HENRY TAYLOR

William Potts Dewees (1768-1841) was a prominent Philadelphia physician and professor of medicine. Best known for his frequently reprinted textbook, *A Compendious System of Midwifery*, Dewees standardized obstetric practices in the United States and also wrote widely on pediatric medicine. While still an adjunct professor, he commissioned a portrait from Philadelphia artist John Neagle, which shows Dewees standing at a desk, with writing implements displayed nearby and several paintings hanging on the wall. In 1833 and 1834 several lithographers produced images based on Neagle's painting, perhaps to meet a demand for reproductions following Dewees's appointment as chair of obstetrics at the University of Pennsylvania.

This image epitomizes Charles Henry Taylor's deep interest in early American lithography. Created by an American just five years after Maurin's print of George Washington (Cat. 55), the Dewees portrait illustrates how quickly American printmakers mastered the new technology. Although M.E.D. Brown was trained as an engraver, his understanding of the lithographic medium comes across beautifully in the print's atmospheric quality as he captured multiple grades of tone and shadow. As an added bonus (and a fact that would not have escaped Taylor), the print was pulled by a young Nathaniel Currier who, at age twenty, had just completed his Boston apprenticeship and taken his first job, working in Philadelphia as one of Brown's pressmen.

57. *Henry M. Johnson Iron, Steel & Metals. 36 India Street, Boston, Mass.* Boston: Ch. H. Crosby, 1870-1872.

GIFT OF CHARLES HENRY TAYLOR

Charles Henry Taylor was interested in any print, book, or piece of ephemera printed lithographically, not just the prints by such well-known firms as Currier & Ives and Pendleton, and he bought voraciously. This color lithograph, printed with multiple stones, reflects his wide-ranging interests. Charles H. Crosby printed children's books, ephemera, portraits, and advertising prints starting in the late 1850s. He experimented with color printing in the early 1870s, using multiple stones to

print four- and five-color prints. This image of Henry M. Johnson's iron and steel warehouse is typical of Crosby's work.

58. Louis Prang & Co. *Cloisonné Vase.* New York: D. Appleton & Co., 1896-1897.

GIFT OF CHARLES HENRY TAYLOR, 1924-1925.

This outstanding chromolithograph was produced more than seventy years after Maurin's portrait of George Washington (Cat. 55). It employs a complex multi-stone process that lithographers could not even have imagined in 1825. The plate was prepared for the multi-volume work, *Oriental Ceramic Art*, published by D. Appleton from 1897-1899. When volume one was released, Appleton's promotional literature touted the work as "one of the most costly books ever printed," with $500,000 invested in the seventeen-year project. This impression of a tall Asian vase decorated with floral patterns and landscape scenes is an office copy retained in the Louis Prang & Co. archive. Prang & Co. spent eight years producing the work's 116 chromolithographed plates, many of the images requiring fifty different stones to reproduce satisfactorily the glossy ceramic surfaces. Prang considered the set the "chief monument of his life."

Between 1924 and 1931, Charles Henry Taylor donated to AAS sixty bound volumes of salesmen's sample books, proof books, and proof sheets from Prang & Co. The company's archive was dispersed in the 1920s through a network of book dealers in Boston and Springfield, Massachusetts, and Taylor, along with the Boston Public Library, bought avidly.

59. *F. Mayer & Co. Specimen Book. 1863.* New York, 1863.

GIFT OF CHARLES HENRY TAYLOR, 1932.

This sample book contains examples of lithographed and chromolithographed job work printed by Ferdinand Mayer & Co., which was based in New York from 1858

CAT. 58. Louis Prang & Co., *Cloissonné Vase*, 1896-1897.

through the 1870s. Included are nearly 400 examples of labels, blank checks, receipts, share certificates, billheads and trade cards, many decorated with allegorical figures, dogs, street scenes or patriotic subjects. Pasted inside the front cover is a May 1864 solicitation letter, addressed to a stationer in Bangor, Maine, outlining terms and explaining how to read the accompanying price list. The sample trade cards show the firm's impressive reach: F. Mayer & Co. had many clients in New York, of course, but it also did work for businesses in other U.S. cities and in Latin America.

In the 1920s Charles Henry Taylor had purchased a large archive of salesman's sample books from Louis Prang & Co. (Cat. 58), and he continued to pursue materials related to the business side of lithographic production. Taylor acquired this volume for $15 from a dealer in the early 1930s, some four decades after F. Mayer & Co. declared bankruptcy and sold off its presses and stock. Such sample books, which document the day-to-day work done on the presses as well as the marketing techniques employed, are indispensable resources for the study of lithographic printing in the United States.

60. Moritz Furst, designer. American Institute Premium Medal. Struck by William and John Mott, Philadelphia, 1831.

GIFT OF CHARLES HENRY TAYLOR

This bronze medal, awarded in October 1831 to John Pendleton for excellence in lithography, is a rare survivor. Pendleton (1798-1866) had left Boston in 1828 to set up a printing shop in New York, independent from his brother William. It is unknown what specimen of lithography Pendleton submitted to the American Institute for its consideration. One clue may be that the Institute listed Pendleton as operating at 9 Wall St., the address given for his shop in city directories for 1832 and 1833. Several prints by Pendleton bearing the Wall St. address could be contenders for the medal winner, including a portrait of George Washington after Rembrandt Peale, a genre scene of a woman reclining and looking at a miniature, and a view of Niagara Falls.

The medal was one of many premium awards that Charles H. Taylor collected and donated to AAS, although this is the only example awarded for lithography. Taylor was also an avid stamp collector and numismatist, purchasing from a variety of dealers across New England.

61. David Claypoole Johnston. *Taproom.* Watercolor on paper, ca. 1858.

PURCHASED WITH FUNDS DONATED BY
CHARLES HENRY TAYLOR, 1933-1934.

David Claypoole Johnston (1799-1865) was a Boston artist and satirist who produced hundreds of cartoons, book and almanac illustrations, and prints. Johnston had an astonishing eye for detail and this skill, along with his ability to successfully capture an individual's strengths and foibles with a sweep of brush, burin, or lithographic pen, earned for him the name "The American Cruikshank." This watercolor of a tavern interior shows a young girl with a tambourine approaching a well-dressed man reading a newspaper. Another man holding a trumpet is about to drop a coin into the tambourine. The scene is full of details typical of Johnston's work, from the carefully rendered row of bottles behind the counter to the stylish yellow gloves worn by the newspaper reader.

This is one of a set of urban images featuring children made by Johnston in the 1850s. In August 1933, Charles H. Taylor purchased several Johnston lithographs through a Boston dealer and gave them to AAS. That donation prompted Clarence S. Brigham to hunt for more Johnston material, and by October he had made contact with the family. Purchase negotiations proceeded through the autumn, with Brigham making regular trips to Dorchester to help sort the hundreds of prints and thousands of drawings preserved in the Johnston home. Taylor was eager for any details on the collection, which AAS librarian R.W.G. Vail called a "particularly rich haul." In November, Brigham sent Taylor a detailed list of the desired Johnston items, and in December a price was agreed upon, with Taylor funding the entire purchase.

62. David Claypoole Johnston. Assorted ephemera and lens in a case, ca. 1815-1850.

PURCHASED WITH FUNDS DONATED BY
CHARLES HENRY TAYLOR, 1933-1934.

While negotiating to purchase the D.C. Johnston archive, Clarence S. Brigham made several lists of desiderata. One list included the artist's magnifying lens (or loupe), and an assortment of printed job work, including business cards, small pull-tab political cartoons, letterheads, and two impressions of Johnston's first attempt at engraving during his apprenticeship. It is to the credit of both Brigham and Charles Henry Taylor that this ephemeral material, stored in an attic trunk with the artist's papers, as well as sets of proofs for prints and various copperplates and woodblocks, was preserved. The family, in fact, had only hoped to find a purchaser for the lithographs and watercolors, never expecting that AAS would also be interested in the more mundane portions.

CAT. 61. David Claypoole Johnston, *Taproom*, ca. 1858.

THE
New-England Courant.

[Nº 27

From MONDAY January 29. to MONDAY February 5. 1722.

Aliud est maledicere, aliud accusare. Cic.

JUDICIOUS Author obferves, That there is nothing in which Men more deceive themfelves than in what the World call Zeal. There are fo many Paffions which hide themfelves under it, and fo many Mifchiefs arifing from it, that fome have gone fo far as to fay, it would have been for the Benefit of Mankind, if it had never been reckoned in the Catalogue of Virtues. The fatal Effects of Zeal among our Selves, has almoft perfwaded me to be of this Opinion. A furious pretended Zeal, which only regards Matters of Opinion, has been improv'd againft my felf with a Defign to deftroy my Reputation and intereft amongft thofe who are Strangers to my Perfon; And that this Defign might be the better carried on, fome Perfons have been fo undutiful to the Reverend Dr. *Increafe Mather*, as to perfwade him to prefix his Name to an Advertifement in the laft Weeks *News-Letter* and *Gazette*, wherein the mildeft Appellation I meet with, is that of a wicked and curfed Libeller. This Charge I now lye under from the oldeft Minifter in the Country, and in order to clear my felf I shall firft give an Account of the firft Caufe of the Difference between us.

The Week before the *Courant* of *Jan.* 1. came out, a Grandfon of Dr. *Increafe Mather* brought me the following Account of the Succefs of Inoculation in *London*,

A Paffage in the London Mercury, Sept. 16.

'Great Numbers of Perfons in the City and the Suburbs 'are under the Inoculation of the Small Pox. Among the 'reft, the eldeft Son of a noble Duke in Hanover Square, 'had the Small Pox inoculated upon him.

This he faid his Grandfather defir'd me to infert in my next, and affirm'd that he had tranfcrib'd it himfelf, and that it was Word for Word with the Account in the London Mercury. About Noon on the Day that the *Courant* came out, I faw the Four firft Pages of the London Mercury of Sept. 16. and found nothing in them, but that *fhe eldeft Son of a noble Duke in Hanover Square*, had the *Small Pox inoculated upon him INCOGNITO.* Here our young Spark was detected in a downright Falfhood, and loft his Credit with *Courant*; and I had great Reafon too to believe that the firft Part of the above Paragraph was not in the other Half-Sheet of the *Mercury*, becaufe both Paffages related to Inoculation, and might (no doubt) have been as well inferted together. The next Week I inferted a Letter in the *Courant*, which afferted, that the former Part of the Paffage, *viz. Great Numbers of Perfons in the City and the Suburbs are under the Inoculation of the Small Pox*, was not to be found in the London Mercury of that Date, but at the fame time inform'd us, that *there were fome Accounts like it in a Weekly Mercury, which wanted Confirmation, and with the Addition of the Word Incognito.* So that tho' the Author of this Letter cou'd not find the former Part of the above Paffage in the London Mercury, yet his main Defign was to fhow, that thofe who fent the faid Paffage to me, defign'd to impofe on the Publick by leaving out the material Word *Incognito*; and the Truth of this can be prov'd by many who have feen but the firft Four Pages of the faid *Mercury*. However, I am now inform'd by Gentlemen whom I dare believe, that the former Part of the faid Paffage is to be found in the laft Half-Sheet of the *London Mercury* Sept. 16. fo that I have been impos'd on by both Sides, and fhall take Care for the future, not to infert any thing in the *Courant* upon the Word of another.

I come now to confider the Doctor's Advertifement; and fhall firft obferve, that thofe who firft took the Advantage of my Credulity to deceive the World, (by leaving out the Word *Incognito*,) are thofe who now call me a curfed Libeller.

The Doctor firft endeavours to clear himfelf of the Imputation of being one among the Supporters of the *Courant*, but at the fame time acknowledges, that he had paid me for Two or Three of them. He might as well have faid he had paid me for many more, as to have put me to the Trouble of

proving it. Whether he remembers it or no, his Grandfon *Eiles*, by his Order, defir'd me to fet him down as a Cuftomer fome Time ago; but upon the Appearance of a Letter in the *Courant*, wherein a certain Clergyman was touch'd upon, he dropt it as a Subfcriber, but fent his Grandfon almoft every Week for a confiderable Time to buy them; by which Method he paid more for the Paper and was more a Supporter of it, than if his Name had been continu'd in the Lift. At length, being weary with fending, he became a Subfcriber again, and exprefs'd no Diflike of the Paper till after Mr. *Mufgrave* had publifh'd his Grandfon's Letter in the *Gazette* of *Jan.* 15. So that he both had and paid me for one Paper after that which he fo much diflikes. The Truth of this I am ready to declare upon Oath, againft the Teftimony of all the Men in the Country. And that he has been a Subfcriber, and confequently a Supporter of the Paper, the following Letter under his own Hand, will fufficiently prove.

Mr Franklin,

' I Had Thoughts of taking your *Courant* (upon Tryal) for ' a Quarter of a Year; but I fhall not now. In one of ' your Courants you have faid that *if the Minifters of God ' are for a Thing, it is a Sign it is from the Devil*, and have ' dealt very falfly about the *London Mercury*. For thefe and ' other Reafons, I fhall NO MORE be concerned with you.
Your well wifhing, but grieved Friend,
I. Mather.

In the next Place he fays, *In one of his vile Courants, he infinuates, that if the Minifters of God do approve of a Thing, its a fign it is of the Devil, which is a horrid Thing to be related.*

The Words in the *Courant* are in a Dialogue (by an unknown Hand) between a Clergyman and Layman, and are exactly as follows,

Cl. But I find, all the Rakes in Town are againft Inoculation, and that induces me to believe it is a right Way.

Laym. Moft of the Minifters are for it, and that induces me to think it is from the D——l; for he often makes ufe of good Men as Inftruments to obtrude his Delufions on the World.

The Doctor muft know, that Satan once ftood up againft Ifrael, and provoked D A V I D to number the People. *Joab*, his wicked General, was not fo eafily provok'd to this Evil: The King's Word was abominable to him. This is Doctrine which I have often heard from the Pulpit, and if I am condemn'd for publifhing it, I may venture to fay (in the Words of the Doctor's Grandfon, that I have Company of *which I need not be afhamed*.

Again, *And altho' in one of the* Courants *it is declared, that the* London Mercury *Sept. 16. 1721. affirms, That Great Numbers of Perfons in the City and Suburbs are under the Inoculation of the Small Pox; in his next Courant he afferts, That it was fome bufy Inoculator, that impofed on the Publick in faying fo.*

I defire him to confider, that what I declared in one Courant was at his Defire, and what I afferted in the next was at the Inftance of another; fo that I am but a Publifher of what one declares and another afferts.

Then, (after telling us that he has read thofe Words *in* the London Mercury,) he fays, *And he doth frequently abufe the Minifters of Religion, and many other worthy Perfons, in a Manner which is intollerable.*

One of thefe worthy Perfons he hints at, has been fince pretended by the Grand Jury for cohabiting with a Woman as his Wife, who was never known to be fo; and another has not yet been able to clear himfelf of the Charge againft him.

Again, *I can well remember, when the Civil Government could have taken an effectual Courfe to fupprefs fuch a curfed Libel.*

Here the Doctor calls the Courant a *curfed Libel, and yet* tells us the Government *cannot* fupprefs it; by which he owns there is nothing in the Paper againft Law, and plainly proves what he fays to be a Curfe caufelefs, which fhall not come.

Again he fays, *I cannot but pity poor Franklin, who tho' but a young Man, it may be fpeedily he muft appear before the Judgment feat of GOD, &c.*

I fhall make no other Anfwer to this, than, That there is no Man living which doeth good and finneth not, and that I expect and Hope to appear before God with fafety in the Righteoufnefs of Chrift.

I*n*

CAT. 63. *The New-England Courant*, February 5, 1722.

Taylor recognized the rarity of such an archive, and shortly after its acquisition in 1934 he urged Brigham to give a talk on Johnston that would inform listeners about "who he was, and what he was, and about the collection and what a great thing it is for the American Antiquarian Society to have it as a memorial. This may plant the idea of something similar in the minds of other people and that won't hurt the Society at all." With Taylor's financial backing, AAS continued to purchase Johnston material from the descendents through 1939.

63. *The New-England Courant.* Boston, February 5, 1722.

GIFT OF CHARLES HENRY TAYLOR

As a member of the family which controlled the *Boston Globe,* and as the newspaper's treasurer from 1893 to 1937, Charles Henry Taylor avidly collected publications on the history of American printing and journalism. He generously donated to AAS anything it lacked. Among his gifts were runs of many important American newspapers, including this issue—the second earliest at AAS—of *The New-England Courant.*

Only the third newspaper to be printed in Boston, *The New-England Courant* was published by James Franklin from 1721 to 1726. During the *Courant's* first two years, its popularity was bolstered by the publication of fourteen letters from one "Silence Dogood," the nom de plume of James's younger brother and apprentice, Benjamin Franklin. But the *Courant* had a contentious history, as James was often at odds with the provincial government, the powerful Mather family, and other influential Bostonians. In 1723 James was imprisoned by the Massachusetts General Court and ordered to suspend the *Courant,* a ban which James circumvented by issuing the paper under his brother's name. Even after Benjamin ran away to Philadelphia in October of that year, the *Courant* continued to appear under his imprint until it ceased publication.

The front page of this issue contains an extensive article on the smallpox inoculation controversy then raging in Boston. While Cotton Mather and other clergy supported inoculation, many Bostonians disagreed. James Franklin opposed the practice in this and many subsequent articles.

64. *Stephen H. Branch's Alligator.* New York, September 11, 1858.

GIFT OF CHARLES HENRY TAYLOR

This is one of the most unusual newspapers donated to AAS by Charles Henry Taylor. Stephen H. Branch (b. 1813) was well known as a firebrand and eccentric in New York City's antebellum newspaper world. Branch and Horace Greeley became acquainted in the early 1830s when both, aspiring to journalistic greatness, roomed at a New York boarding house for devotees of Sylvester Graham's vegetarian diet. Branch received his nickname, "Alligator Branch," from his *New York Herald* reporting during 1849 when, while crossing the Isthmus of Panama en route to gold-crazed California, Branch described alligators that ran up and down trees like squirrels—one of many fabrications in his dispatches. Nine years later Branch launched the *Alligator,* famous for its extremely outspoken attacks on the corruption he perceived among New York's political elite. AAS possesses a complete run of this muckraking weekly paper, which lasted just twenty-nine issues, some of them written and edited by Branch from a jail cell on Blackwell's Island following a conviction for libel. Branch subsequently edited other periodicals, including *Anaconda, Daily Hand, Grave Digger,* and *Weekly Star.*

This issue contains several articles about the just-completed transatlantic cable, including one complaining that the city would likely spend $150,000 on a celebration while the proprietors of the Atlantic Telegraph Company, which had laid the cable, would not be willing to give even $500 for the relief of the poor. The cable failed after just three weeks.

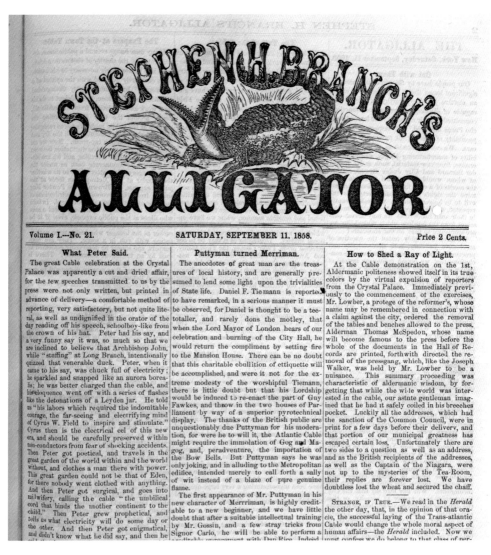

CAT. 64. *Stephen H. Branch's Allligator*, September 11, 1858 (detail).

65. Frances Sargent Locke Osgood. *The Cries of New-York.* New York: John Doggett, Jr., 1846.

GIFT OF CHARLES HENRY TAYLOR, 1921.

Picture books depicting street vendors and their cries were printed in England as early as the late seventeenth century. A century later, American printers began to issue books of London cries for American children. By 1822, prolific children's book publisher Samuel Wood & Sons was issuing pocket-sized chapbook editions of New York cries. This mid-nineteenth century example is in folio picture book format, with wood-engraved illustrations by Nicolino Calyo (1799-1884). The brief cries serve as the basis for descriptive verse by Frances Osgood (1811-1850), a poet and friend of Edgar Allan Poe. The volume includes a description of the newsboy, an urban occupation that was largely born and romanticized in the nineteenth century. The factual description below the rumpled (but not destitute) newsboy reads like a city guide book, which is not surprising, given that the publisher, John Doggett, Jr., also issued New York city directories.

BAL 15301.

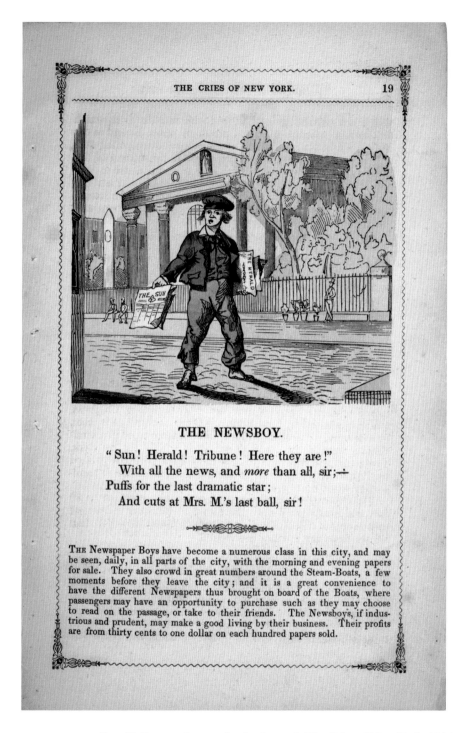

THE CRIES OF NEW YORK. 19

THE NEWSBOY.

"Sun! Herald! Tribune! Here they are!"
    With all the news, and *more* than all, sir;—
Puffs for the last dramatic star;
    And cuts at Mrs. M.'s last ball, sir!

THE Newspaper Boys have become a numerous class in this city, and may be seen, daily, in all parts of the city, with the morning and evening papers for sale. They also crowd in great numbers around the Steam-Boats, a few moments before they leave the city; and it is a great convenience to have the different Newspapers thus brought on board of the Boats, where passengers may have an opportunity to purchase such as they may choose to read on the passage, or take to their friends. The Newsboys, if industrious and prudent, may make a good living by their business. Their profits are from thirty cents to one dollar on each hundred papers sold.

CAT. 65. Frances Sargent Locke Osgood, *The Cries of New-York*, 1846.

A
POEM
On the late distrefs of the
TOWN OF
BOSTON

Remarks of the fudden Flight ef the MINISTERIAL Troops, after plundering and Destroying
[...]bitants they left the town in the greatest confufion imaginable, not allowing themfelves time to
[...]Warlike Stores, In fhort, they fled like Murderers pursued by the Hand of JUSTICE.

✻✻

[...]out AMERICANS with Joy,
[...]d's praife your tongues employ,
[...]foes defigns deftroy,
[...]r Liberties annoy.

[...]and foldiers brave,
[...]hard, your land doth fave,
[...]feeking to inflave,
[...]wn into their grave.

[...]cry once was high,
[...]ht peace and liberty;
[...]d the earth did fly,
[...]r greatnefs did envy.

[...]til greater glory fee:
[...]fons of rebels be,
[...]let her Sons been free,
[...]wn'd the bramble-tree.

[...]e fo in pride did rife,
[...]e and pitying eyes,
[...]hear the oppreffed cry,
[...]umble fuits defpife.

[...]limitted, I fay
[...]whole Realm bear fway:
[...]er they fhall obey,
[...]whole North-America.

[...]ent efpoufe my caufe,
[...]merit and applaufe;
[...]s enforce my laws,
[...]help there's few withdraws:

Before hoftilities commence't,
They have the Town for their defence,
Their Cannon mounted to difpence,
Deftruction to AMERICANS.

When they this Town had fortified,
With ftrong defence on every fide:
There's now no Bridle to their pride,
They think none can their force abide.

They then begin their murderous theme,
Well pleas'd with their curs't plot they feem,
Their victory now a pleafing cream,
Till juftice ov'rthrows their fcheme.

AMERICANS this murder fee,
And could no longer filent be,
But with one mind and heart agree,
To fet unhappy BOSTON free,

In Seventy-Five this war began,
With fighting while the year was run,
With Cannon, bayonet and Gun,
While blood on either fide did run.

Our Colonies unite as one,
Commanded by brave WASHINGTON,
Who to our help together run,
Whofe branded fwords and armour fhone.

Brave WASHINGTON is valiant found,
His Men our tyrant foes furround,
Their cruel Plot he doth confound,
And is at laft with victory crown'd.

By flaughter in A[...]
Doth not blood's gilt [...]
Then bid farewel to [...]
Unlefs blood clences, [...]

Bloods gilt doth c[...]
Nought elfe can waff[...]
If than thy murderer[...]
You draw your fword [...]

You that in Bofto[...]
And have been fcatte[...]
How doth your hear[...]
Your City of thofe m[...]

Give glory to the [...]
Who did defeat thin[...]
That fo few of thy [...]
Or went into captivit[...]

Some that were ne[...]
That joined with th[...]
Through fear and fl[...]
And thofe that ftay'd, [...]

Should you again [...]
And God fhould you [...]
Avoid all luxerous ex[...]
Left God bring [...]

AMERICANS confide[...]
What fate on Britifh [...]
And pattern not by [...]
Left you in vain for [...]

American Literature and Poetry

In 1923, fifteen years after his appointment as AAS librarian, Clarence S. Brigham contemplated a new collecting initiative: nineteenth-century American literature. By virtue of its comprehensive early American imprint collecting, the Society had already amassed one of the finest holdings of pre-1821 American literature. But one would search in vain at AAS for many of the classic works of post-1820 American fiction and poetry. Here was precisely the kind of collecting opportunity that most appealed to Brigham: although many collectors and institutions were building author collections, few were seeking at that time to develop a comprehensive library of American authors; the potential universe of collectible books was large; there were many collectors and booksellers to whom Brigham could turn for assistance; and while the classic rarities were already priced well beyond the Society's modest budget, many of the more obscure items were affordable.

Brigham's interest in nineteenth-century American literature had been piqued the previous year, when the Society was given a collection of 151 association copies formed by Alice Morse Earle (1851-1911). A best-selling author of books popularizing early American social history, a number of which were researched at AAS, Earle had been the recipient of many gift copies inscribed to her by literary friends such as Sarah Orne Jewett, Edith Wharton, William Dean Howells, and Thomas Bailey Aldrich. Some volumes had been enhanced through the in-

Fig. 16

sertion of original correspondence between Earle and the books' authors. Although somewhat out of AAS's traditional collecting scope, Brigham accepted the Earle collection in part because he expected it would attract similar gifts and thus open up a new area of collecting.

Brigham did not have to wait long. The effusive description of the Earle books that he published in the AAS *Proceedings,* and no doubt some personal lobbying, quickly prompted a splendid donation of some six hundred volumes from the library of the Rev. Herbert E. Lombard (1863-1940). Included were many presentation copies of works by leading nineteenth-century American authors. In October 1923 Brigham happily reported to the Society's membership that Lombard's gift "makes an excellent start for a collection of American first editions."

Ever since his election to membership in 1913, Lombard had been one of AAS's most devoted benefactors. Born just south of Worcester, Massachusetts, in the town of Sutton, Lombard was never wealthy. He first supported himself as a schoolteacher and bookkeeper before turning to the ministry. After being called in 1902 to the pulpit of Byfield Congregational Church in Newbury, Massachusetts, Lombard finally found the time and means to pursue his passions for local history and book collecting. Lombard's first interest was American bookplates, to which he soon added presentation copies of American writers and works by Essex County, Massachusetts, authors, including a comprehensive collection of the works of John Greenleaf Whittier.

In 1911 Lombard accepted a position in Worcester, wandered into AAS, and asked Brigham to assign him a useful bibliographical project. "I told him we needed a bibliography of early Newburyport printing," Brigham reminisced, "but that the most arduous part of the undertaking was to examine the long files of Newburyport newspapers for advertisements of imprints." Lombard was game, set to work immediately, and remained an enthusiastic and devoted supporter of AAS until his death. In 1914 came Lombard's first major gift—his collection of some 2,500 American bookplates—after which Brigham considered him the Society's *de facto* curator of bookplates. Lombard worked tirelessly to secure donations and negotiate purchases of bookplate literature and collections, and by 1940 the Society's collection of over 50,000 American bookplates was reputed to be the country's finest. Likewise, Lombard immediately endorsed Brigham's desire to build comprehensive holdings of nineteenth-century American literature. His 1923 gift of books was followed in 1925 by another substantial donation, and Lombard canvassed his wide circle of friends for suitable additions.

In P. K. Foley's 1897 bibliography, *American Authors, 1795-1895: A Bibliography of First and Notable Editions*, Brigham found an authoritative guide to what AAS's nascent American literature collection should contain. Born in Ireland, Foley (1856-1937) opened an antiquarian bookshop in Boston in 1896 and, thanks to his bibliography and uncanny ability to find copies of the books listed therein, was instrumental in developing American literature into a prominent collecting specialty. *American Authors* identified first and notable editions by 311 writers, and Brigham resolved to collect all of the 4,995 titles listed. In 1926 he engaged AAS staff in expanding Foley's guide to include works published by its listed authors from 1895 to 1926, raising the bar by another 2,700 editions. But Brigham thrived on such challenges, and in this particular endeavor he succeeded brilliantly, later writing that "within a dozen years we acquired over 6,000 volumes, or about ninety per cent of all the titles represented in Foley."

While Brigham filled the collection's interstices, he found many donors willing to supply the all-important "high spots." The collector Charles Henry Taylor (Cats. 53-65, 74-75), for instance, had long been a favored client of Foley's, as a consequence of which Taylor's multifaceted interests included American literature. In 1926 AAS was the recipient of Taylor's superb Herman Melville collection; soon thereafter Taylor also donated the nucleus of AAS's James Fenimore Cooper collection.

For early American poetry, Brigham turned to Matt Bushnell Jones (1871-1940), elected to AAS membership in 1924, and already a member of the Grolier Club. Born in Waitsfield, Vermont, Jones received degrees from Dartmouth College and Harvard Law School. In 1904 he joined the New England Telephone and Telegraph Company in Boston, rising to the offices of president and later chairman of the board. Time could always be found, however, for book collecting. Armed with ample resources, Jones soon built an extensive collection of early American printing, with an emphasis on Vermont imprints and early American verse. "It was not enough," Brigham wrote, "for [Jones] to own a book; he must know everything about it and its background."

It was equally important for Jones that his books be available to scholars, hence he regularly donated portions of his collection to various institutions, or simply served as middleman and financier between bookseller and library. AAS, for example, received many of Jones's best pieces of early Americana, including the Vermont imprints it lacked. And from the mid-1920s, Jones "became practically [the Society's] agent, searching the bookstores of New England and New York, checklists of our holdings in his hand, buying to fill our gaps with as much eagerness as any collector buying for his own collection." Jones's enthusiasm was particularly apparent in the hunt for early American poetry, especially ephemeral broadside verse and newspaper carriers' addresses.

FIG. 17

For nineteenth-century American fiction, it was another member of AAS and the Grolier Club who provided the Society with many key pieces. Frank Brewer Bemis (1861-1935) was a native Bostonian who made his fortune in banking and investments. He carefully built an outstanding collection of English and American literature, seeking fine copies in original bindings whenever possible, important association copies, and choice manuscripts. The Keats, Shelley, and Wordsworth portions of Bemis's

FIG. 18

library were particularly fine, as were its holdings of the titans of nineteenth-century American literature. Disinclined to speak about his library, Bemis was well known in the trade but not among collectors until late in life.

Clarence S. Brigham was determined to acquire for AAS what it needed from the Bemis collection, and after two decades of patient waiting, he mostly succeeded. Bemis was elected to membership in 1925, the same year he turned his library over to trustees for eventual sale, the proceeds going to charity. When Bemis died in 1935, Brigham had extracted from him the promise of a substantial bequest—following the precedent set by Brinley and Cooke—to purchase selected items for AAS through the Bemis library trustees. In 1938 Brigham secured appointment as one of the library's two trustees, and later its sole trustee, in which role he oversaw the library's liquidation. Much of it was entrusted to Philadelphia book dealer and collector A. S. W. Rosenbach for sale, but Brigham wrapped up his duties by purchasing for AAS the final 195 volumes—all choice first or significant editions of American literary works—in 1946.

Brigham's timing was excellent: when first Lyle H. Wright and then Jacob Blanck began work on their standard bibliographies, *American Fiction 1775-1900* and *Bibliography of American Literature*, respectively, the AAS collection of American literature was one of the finest available. Wright and Blanck consulted the collection extensively, as can be seen by the number of AAS copies cited in each work. AAS has made continued development of its American literature holdings a high priority. Special emphasis has been placed on areas in which Brigham's collecting was less exhaustive, including popular literature, minor poetry, American editions of foreign authors, and later editions illustrative of the wide range of nineteenth-century American publishing practices.

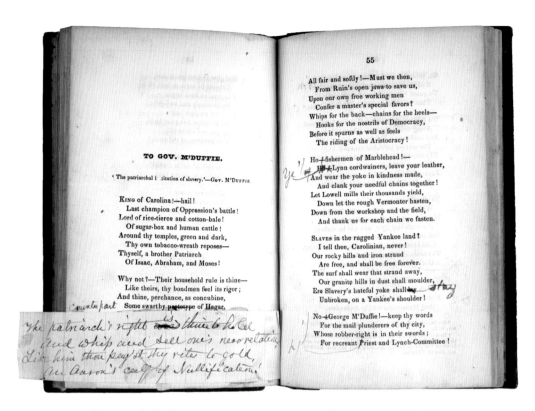

CAT. 67. John Greenleaf Whittier, *Poems Written During the Progress of the Abolition Question,* 1837.

66. William Lloyd Garrison. *Selections from the Writings and Speeches of William Lloyd Garrison.* Boston: R. F. Wallcut, 1852.

GIFT OF HERBERT E. LOMBARD, 1923.

Of the many presentation copies of the works of American authors donated to AAS in 1923 by Herbert E. Lombard, this is one of the most evocative. On December 27, 1851, William Lloyd Garrison inscribed to John Greenleaf Whittier this copy of his selected works, "From his old, attached and admiring friend."

Garrison exerted a profound influence on the young Whittier and can truly be said to have made his career. In 1826, as the twenty-year-old editor of the Newburyport, Massachusetts, *Free Press*, Garrison published the eighteen-year-old Whittier's first poems. Soon the two friends were rooming together in Boston, where Garrison found Whittier his first editorial position. In 1833 Whittier finally committed himself wholeheartedly to the abolition-ist movement, helping to found the American Anti-Slavery Society and devoting his political, journalistic, and poetic talents to the cause. However, the two friends became estranged in 1839 amid the bitter infighting occasioned by Garrison's nonresistance views. Whittier finally broke his silence in 1850, impressed by Garrison's adroit maneuvering and principled stands in the turmoil leading up to the Compromise of 1850 and enactment of the Fugitive Slave Law. This presentation copy of Garrison's book, which reprints Whittier's poem "To William Lloyd Garrison," is an eloquent witness to their reconciliation.

67. John Greenleaf Whittier. *Poems Written During the Progress of the Abolition Question in the United States, between the Years 1830 and 1838.* Boston: Isaac Knapp, 1837.

GIFT OF HERBERT E. LOMBARD, 1923.

Herbert E. Lombard's important 1923 gift to the AAS American literature collection included not only several hundred presentation copies, but also significant holdings of John Greenleaf Whittier first editions, many of them inscribed by the author.

The 1837 *Poems* collected for the first time Whittier's verses written on behalf of the abolitionist cause. Whittier had little editorial control over the volume, but he made amends the following year by carefully editing a revised and expanded edition. This copy of the 1837 *Poems* (the second issue with pages 97-103 added) belonged to Whittier and bears his characteristic purple ink manuscript corrections to several poems. The most heavily revised is "To Gov. M'Duffie," a powerful attack on the South Carolina governor and Nullifier. The date of Whittier's revisions is unclear: some appear in the 1838 revised text, though most do not. Possibly they are much later; but because this was one of the poems Whittier suppressed on artistic grounds from his collected works, these revisions apparently never saw print. "To Gov. M'Duffie" first appeared in Whittier's own *Essex Gazette* (Haverhill, Massachusetts) on July 16, 1836. Interestingly, Whittier has dated this poem "1834" in manuscript, apparently confusing it with another poem with the same title that he did compose that year.

American Imprints 48510; BAL 21705.

68. Michael Wigglesworth. *The Day of Doom, or, a Poetical Description of the Great and Last Judgment.* Cambridge, Massachusetts: Samuel Green, 1666.

GIFT OF MATT B. JONES, 1929.

Perhaps Matt B. Jones's most significant gift to the AAS collection of early American poetry was this substantial fragment of the first American bestseller, and the earliest printed American verse now at AAS. Born in Yorkshire, Michael Wigglesworth (1631-1705) emigrated with his family to New England in 1638. At Harvard he prepared for the ministry before being called, in 1654, to the pulpit at Malden, Massachusetts. Wigglesworth remained in Malden as the town's minister and physician, in between bouts of ill health, for fifty-one years.

In 1662 Wigglesworth published *The Day of Doom*, an ambitious 224-stanza poem describing the Last Judgment in graphic, Calvinistic terms. One by one, groups of unrepentant sinners appear before an unforgiving God, only to be rebuked and cast into eternal hellfire. An immediate success, the first edition of 1,800 copies sold out quickly. A second edition, for which Wigglesworth added marginal notes, was published in 1666. This exemplar is the most complete of the three known fragmentary copies. Wigglesworth later published several other poetical works, though *The Day of Doom*, which was repeatedly reprinted on both sides of the Atlantic into the early nineteenth century, proved the most popular.

Evans 112; Stoddard 7.

69. Job Weeden. *Job Weeden, Salem News-Boy, Begs Leave to Present the Following Lines …* Salem, Massachusetts: Samuel Hall, 1771.

GIFT OF MATT B. JONES, 1930S.

Presumably printed late in 1771 by Samuel Hall, printer of the *Essex Gazette*, for distribution on or about New Year's Day 1772, this small newspaper carrier's address was authored by fifteen-year-old Job Weeden. In entertaining verse, Weeden pleads unabashedly for financial support from his patrons, to whom he faithfully brings the paper even though he is "drenched with Rain or smother'd in Snow." It is one of two known carriers' addresses written by Weeden—a 1768 printing contains similar begging language—who likely was apprenticed to Hall and delivered papers in Salem for his master. Later Weeden opened his own printing shop in Boston and, with a partner, published *The Gentleman and Lady's Town and Country Magazine* (1784-1785), the first American periodical to give special attention to women through fiction and advice.

Matt B. Jones collected this carrier's address as an example of printed verse; he acquired it together with two volumes of poetic

CAT. 70. Elisha Rich, *A Poem on the Late Distress of the Town of Boston*, 1776.

elegies and an 1804 patriotic ode, all of which once belonged to early AAS member Timothy Alden (1771-1839) of Portsmouth, New Hampshire. It is one of over six hundred pre-1820 carriers' addresses housed at AAS. The collection includes the earliest known example, printed in 1734 in Philadelphia for the *American Weekly Mercury*.

Evans 42389; McDonald 133.

70. Elisha Rich. *A Poem on the Late Distress of the Town of Boston ...* Chelmsford, Massachusetts: Nathaniel Coverly, 1776.

GIFT OF MATT B. JONES, 1930S.

The British evacuation of Boston on March 17, 1776, is celebrated in this poem, which also refers to the Stamp Act and the Battle of Bunker Hill. The relief cut of a large cannon and a lighthouse also appeared on Elisha Rich's *Poetical Remarks upon the Fight at the* *Boston Light-House*, a broadside published by Coverly in 1775. This is one of three Rich broadside poems given to AAS by Matt B. Jones.

Jones spent the summers of 1932 and 1933 hunting for pre-1800 American poetry from his vacation home in Cape Elizabeth, Maine, writing daily to AAS with lists of potential acquisitions to be checked against AAS holdings. He sent books, pamphlets, "juveniles," and poetic broadsides by the dozen, telling Clarence S. Brigham to "junk" whatever was not wanted by AAS. Delighted, Brigham kept most of Jones's finds, while actively encouraging him to visit certain shops, auction houses, and collectors known to possess eighteenth-century American imprints. Eventually, Brigham sent Jones an annotated copy of Oscar Wegelin's 1930 bibliography, *Early American Poetry*, with desiderata marked. Jones would occasionally hit a dry spell—"I seem to be temporarily stumped on poetry," he reported in August 1932—and buy newspapers and sheet music instead. By the time of his death in 1940,

I

S PEAK, O Man less recent! Fragmentary fossil,
Primal pioneer of Pliocene formation,
Hid in lowest drifts below the earliest stratum
Of volcanic tufa!

— Older than the beasts, the oldest Palæotherium;
Older than the trees, the oldest Cryptogamia;

CAT. 72. Bret Harte, *The Pliocene Skull*, ca. 1871.

Jones had donated to AAS dozens of broadside ballads recorded by Wegelin, and no fewer than forty-seven unknown to Evans.

AAS Wellsprings 156; Evans 15061; Wegelin 326.

71. Nathaniel Hawthorne.
Fanshawe, a Tale. Boston: Marsh & Capen, 1828.

BEQUEST OF FRANK BREWER BEMIS, 1946.

Among the first editions received from the Frank Brewer Bemis library was this exceptional association copy, in original quarter cloth and tan boards with printed spine label, of Nathaniel Hawthorne's rare first published book, *Fanshawe*. This short Gothic romance owed much to the twenty-four-year-old author's fondness for the novels of Sir Walter Scott, and its setting at "Harley College" closely resembles Bowdoin College, from which Hawthorne graduated in 1825. Fanshawe, the young, retiring, sickly, and morbidly studious hero, was based in part on Cotton Mather's younger brother Nathanael, whose gravestone in a Salem, Massachusetts, cemetery Hawthorne surely would have seen. Financed with Hawthorne's personal $100 subvention, *Fanshawe* received only a tepid critical response, and the 1,000 copies sold poorly. Hawthorne soon disavowed the book and henceforth strove to conceal his authorship. In a fortuitous plot twist worthy of the novel, most of the copies were destroyed in a warehouse fire. This copy bears the ownership signature of noted scholar, critic, and book collector Charles Eliot Norton, member of Boston's famed Saturday Club and a pallbearer at Hawthorne's funeral.

BAL 7570; Shoemaker 33508.

72. Bret Harte. *The Pliocene Skull*.
Washington, D.C.: Peters & Rehn, ca. 1871.

BEQUEST OF FRANK BREWER BEMIS, 1946.

CAT. 74. *The Martial Wreath ...*, 1852-1860. William Cook Collection.

Frank Brewer Bemis owned a significant collection of Bret Harte editions, and his bequest enabled AAS to augment substantially its own holdings. Harte's famous satirical poem, "To the Pliocene Skull," first appeared in the July 28, 1866 issue of the San Francisco newspaper, *The Californian*. It was occasioned by the famous Calaveras Skull, "discovered" deep within a Calaveras County, California mine on February 25, 1866. Though widely understood at the time to be a practical joke, the California State Geologist, Josiah Whitney, considered the skull useful confirmation of his pet theories and proclaimed it, at a July 16, 1866 meeting of the California Academy of Sciences, the earliest human New World fossil, dating from the Pliocene age. No subsequent amount of scientific inquiry, including twentieth-century radiocarbon dating of the skull to ca. 1,000 A.D., has managed to undo the damage unleashed by Whitney's claim.

Harte's poem was reprinted widely, most notably in this edition published just as Harte, having reached the apogee of his fame, fatefully left California behind. It photolithographically reproduces a manuscript version penned, and humorously illustrated, by Edward Martin Schaeffer, M.D. (1843-1917), an employee of the Army Medical Museum. Schaeffer went on to pursue a successful medical career in Washington and Baltimore, but he is not known to have illustrated other books.

BAL 7424.

73. Ralph Waldo Emerson. *Letter from the Rev. R.W. Emerson, to the Second Church and Society.* Boston: I.R. Butts, 1832.

BEQUEST OF FRANK BREWER BEMIS, 1946.

The Frank Brewer Bemis bequest enabled AAS to acquire a number of "first books" of prominent American authors. Among them was Ralph Waldo Emerson's very rare first separate publication, the eight-page *Letter ... to the Second Church and Society.* Following graduation from Harvard, Emerson entered the ministry and, in his late twenties, was called to a Boston pulpit comparable in prestige and compensation to that once held by his father. But his wife's death in 1831 helped to provoke a profound spiritual crisis, leading to Emerson's resignation in October 1832. Emerson had no definite future plan until he embarked on a nine-month tour of Europe, during which he initiated his long friendship with Thomas Carlyle and further refined his emerging Transcendentalist philosophy. On December 22, 1832, just prior to his departure, Emerson penned this valedictory letter to his former congregation. Believing that "Freedom is the essence of Christianity," Emerson explained that, for him, the "grace of God" meant "the liberty to seek and the liberty to utter it." That empowering liberty would prove transformative.

American Imprints 12288; BAL 5175.

74. William Cook. Five poetry booklets and broadsides written, illustrated, and printed by William Cook. Salem, Massachusetts, 1852-1876.

GIFT OF CHARLES HENRY TAYLOR, 1915-1932.

Among Charles Henry Taylor's manifold collecting interests were examples of works written and printed by William Cook between 1852 and 1876. A life-long resident of Salem, Massachusetts, "Billy" Cook (1807-1876) displayed much academic promise until physical and mental illness narrowed his prospects. Cook nevertheless ran a successful private school—where he taught mathematics, bookkeeping, Latin, and Greek—and although never ordained to the ministry, he preached and conducted religious services in his home.

Unable to afford a printer for his verse, Cook instead acquired some battered type from a local newspaper office and fixed up a cast-off press resembling, according to one witness, "an old-fashioned high-back hand-organ," with which he could print a page or two at one pull. Over the next twenty-five years, Cook laboriously produced over forty poetry pamphlets

and broadsides, of which Taylor succeeded in acquiring a nearly complete set for AAS. These were sold on the street or to the visitors frequenting Cook's public "Art Gallery" of original oil paintings. Most were profusely illustrated with Cook's own woodcut vignettes and full-page plates, which he often heightened with graphite or colored pencil. Cook usually stitched his pamphlets into illustrated paper covers, sometimes collecting several in simple printed cloth bindings. Given that Cook was his own printer, publisher, and binder, his imprints exist in innumerable variants. For all of Cook's eccentricity, he was a much-loved Salem fixture, and his works are notable examples of American folk art.

75. Herman Melville. *John Marr and Other Sailors, with Some Sea-Pieces.* New York: The De Vinne Press, 1888.

GIFT OF CHARLES HENRY TAYLOR, 1926.

In his collecting, Charles Henry Taylor—and by proxy AAS—benefited substantially from his strong friendship with Boston bookseller P. K. Foley, whose *American Authors, 1795-1895* clearly delineated a new and exciting collecting field. Taylor was an enthusiastic convert, and in 1926 he presented to AAS a virtually complete collection of Herman Melville first editions.

Included in Taylor's gift were copies of two Melville "black tulips": *John Marr* (1888) and *Timoleon* (1891), each privately printed in only 25 copies. In 1885 an inheritance enabled Melville not only to retire from his position as a New York customs inspector, but to resume a literary career that had been in abeyance since the failure of *Clarel* in 1876. *John Marr*, a collection of sea poems and dramatic monologues, was composed at the same time that Melville was reworking a similar dramatic monologue into the novella *Billy Budd*. Melville slowly doled out copies to favored friends and family. This copy bears Melville's manuscript corrections as well as a presentation inscription to the New York literary critic and anthologist Edmund Clarence Stedman.

AAS Chief Joys 174; BAL 13676.

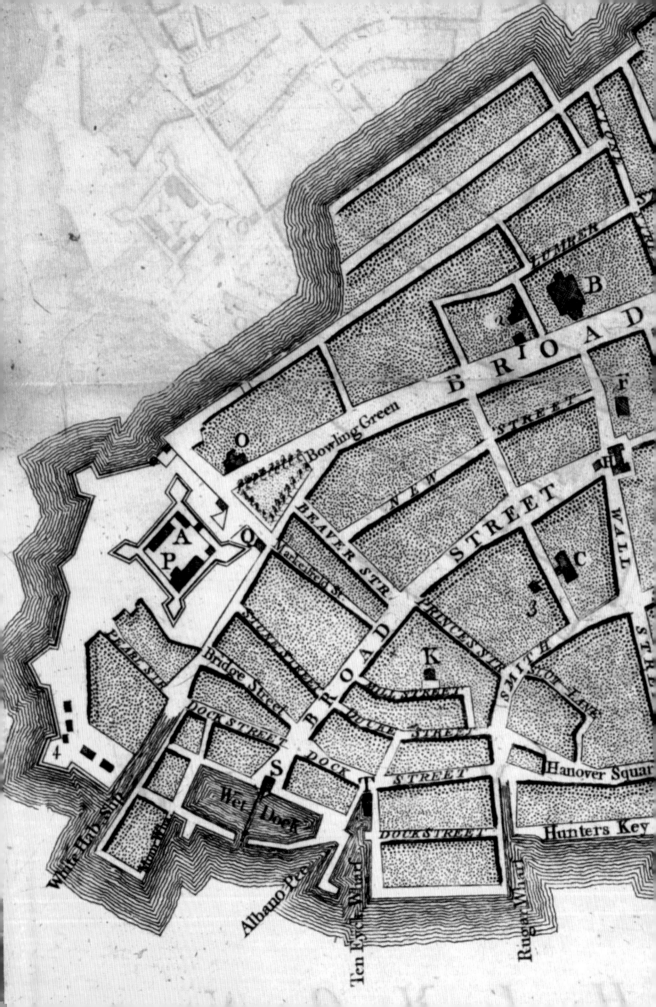

Early Americana

The American Antiquarian Society began to collect Americana at a time—the early nineteenth century—when few others cared to do so. By its centennial year in 1912, the situation had changed utterly: books and manuscripts concerning the European discovery and settlement of the New World had emerged as a leading interest among collectors. Individuals and institutions alike vied against one other in the auction rooms and importuned booksellers for the choice rarities. Although the Society had already succeeded in building, primarily through gift, a formidable collection of early American imprints and Americana generally, improving its quality in the face of stiff competition was a daunting challenge for a modestly funded institution.

But librarian Clarence S. Brigham was not worried, for he knew that time was on the Society's side. In his April 1918 report to the Council, he noted: "If the smaller institutions are ruled out from competing for the wealth of good things offered, the private collector of means and intelligence accumulates and preserves, and in time passes on his holdings for dispersion, or as a memorial of his life interest by a deposit in a public institution." These private collectors would be elected to AAS membership and cultivated. Should personal and institutional goals coincide, collectors would be encouraged to place their treasures at the Society for the perpetual benefit of scholarship. Boston was well stocked with outstanding private libraries rich in early Americana, and Brigham naturally focused his attentions there. Of the many seeds Brigham planted among Boston's book collectors, four in particular eventually yielded unusually significant harvests for AAS: substantial donations of stellar Americana from the libraries of Frederick L. Gay, John W. Farwell, James F. Hunnewell, and his son James M. Hunnewell.

The first collection, comprising nearly 400 choice works from the library of Frederick Lewis Gay, arrived in 1918. Gay (1856-1916) was born into a prominent Boston family which traced its roots back to the Great Migration of 1630. Neglecting to complete his Harvard studies, and uncertain of a profession—indeed, not needing one to make ends meet—Gay found his calling in his family's history. In becoming the consummate antiquarian and genealogist, Gay was active in many of Boston's numerous historical and genealogical societies. Because his researches depended on access to primary sources, Gay began to form a personal library while still in college. Its nucleus was 3,000 volumes Gay inherited at the age of nineteen, which he soon reshaped into

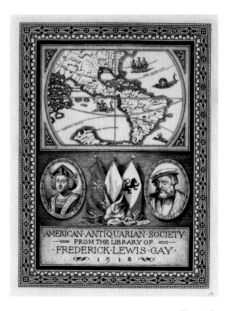

Fig. 19

a comprehensive research library on New England history. To the printed works he added many volumes of transcripts made from relevant documents in British and American archives. And when his researches led him to the English Civil War, Gay began assembling an outstanding collection of seventeenth-century English political tracts.

Elected to AAS membership in 1906, Gay presented as a centennial gift in 1912 one of his most prized manuscripts: a bound volume containing the original minutes for May 1622-June 1623 of the Council for New England, the corporation chartered in 1620 by King James I to settle and govern New England. When Gay died in 1916, he left no written instructions for his library's disposition other than that it was not to be sold, but his heirs understood and acted upon his wishes. The English political tracts went to Harvard, the transcripts and first editions of works by seventeenth-century New England ministers went to the Massachusetts Historical Society, and AAS received a highly important group of early American imprints and European Americana covering all of England's New World settlements, with a concentration on New England.

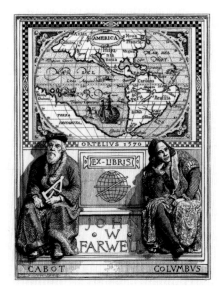

FIG. 20

Gay's contemporary John Whittemore Farwell (1843-1929) did not begin collecting in earnest until around 1900, but his library was deemed by Clarence S. Brigham, on the occasion of its arrival at AAS in 1942-1943, "the most important single gift of rare books that has come to this Library since the days of Isaiah Thomas." Born in Boston, Farwell took over and substantially enhanced the family's business, managing specialized factories that bleached the cotton cloth produced in New England's textile mills so that it could more effectively receive printed patterns. In building his library, Farwell chose to collect the best early Americana he could find, with an emphasis on colonial New England. His interests eventually became known to AAS, which elected Farwell to membership in 1915. Henceforth he was a frequent and generous donor, mainly in response to Brigham's repeated appeals for funds. But following Farwell's death in 1929, his library remained with the family.

Though Brigham was aware of the quality of Farwell's holdings, he admitted that "so quietly and unobtrusively did he gather his books that few of us, even those who were familiar with his library, realized its scope." Hence when Farwell's heirs communicated their decision in 1942 to place its contents at AAS, Brigham surveyed the unexpected windfall with astonishment. In a report of the Council, he outlined the collection's numerous strong points. Farwell possessed fine copies of many classics of sixteenth- and seventeenth-century European Americana, in particular the English works esteemed by collectors but long outside the Society's financial reach. Notable as well were the early American imprints, especially those printed at Cambridge and Boston during the seventeenth century. Farwell also formed an especially fine collection documenting relations between colonists and Native Americans, rich in rare accounts of early military conflicts and Indian captivity narratives. Later in life Farwell developed an interest in the early cartography of North America and Boston in particular, building an impressive holding of atlases and sheet maps superior to that already at AAS.

Another very important source of early Americana for the Society was the Hunnewell family of Charlestown, Massachusetts. When James Hunnewell (1794-1869) went to sea in 1815, he sailed for the Hawaiian Islands, which he explored at length during a several-month layover. His familiarity with native customs proved valuable four years later when, as a crew member on a ship carrying the first American missionaries, he secured permission for them to remain in Hawaii. Hunnewell's Hawaiian trading business prospered, and in 1830 he returned to Charlestown to manage the firm, deputizing others to captain his ships and oversee his Hawaiian interests. His son James Frothingham Hunnewell (1832-1910) joined the family business in 1850, helping to manage its extensive Pacific mercantile interests during the great age of American clipper ships. In 1866 James F. Hunnewell retired from business a very wealthy man and found that there were more rewarding activities to pursue, namely foreign travel and book collecting. By the time of his death, Hunnewell had crossed the Atlantic forty-eight times, though curiously he never journeyed to Hawaii to see the vast changes he and his father had been instrumental in effecting. Book collecting was an activity Hunnewell pursued with unrelenting zeal. As a boy he saved money to buy books, and in 1852 he bought a finely bound set of Sir Walter Scott's works, which he read avidly. Meanwhile Hunnewell's father joined in his son's interest by building a fine collection of Hawaiian imprints—then relatively easy to obtain—and works about Hawaii. During the Civil War years Hunnewell exercised his bibliomania by acquiring as many of the large-format, limited edition works then issuing from American presses as he could afford, many being reprints of rare works on American history. Retirement, extended access to Europe's bookshops, and a resolve to focus on rarities helped Hunnewell advance to the highest rank of American book collectors. By 1900 Hunnewell arguably owned the finest private collection of rare books in the Boston area.

Hunnewell's collecting is well documented through the library catalogs he privately printed on his own press, and the interleaved copies (now at AAS) that he meticulously updated in manuscript (Cat. 83). The range of his interests was remarkable. After his retirement he formed collections of illustrated art museum catalogs and guides, works on antiquities, and on architecture. By 1870, intrigued by the incunabula available from European booksellers, Hunnewell began building an extraordinary collection of fifteenth-century printing—now at Harvard—featuring pre-1476 imprints from as many different presses as possible. Other collections included the works of the English bibliographer Thomas Frognall Dibdin, fine bindings with significant provenance, and tens of thousands of loose maps, prints, and photographs. As for Americana, Hunnewell formed outstanding holdings of Charlestown, Massachusetts, imprints, works by eighteenth-century Boston ministers, and the best extant collection of New England election

FIG. 21

sermons. Motivated by his preparations for two papers delivered at AAS on "Illustrated Americana" in 1889 and 1890, Hunnewell set about forming a collection of the finest illustrated and color plate works relating to American history, though Audubon's double elephant folio he considered too "costly and bulky."

James F. Hunnewell was elected to AAS membership in 1869, and he remained an active and generous member to the end. His library was inherited by his only son, James Melville Hunnewell (1879-1954), a devoted book collector in his own right, who was elected a member in 1927. Realizing that portions of the family library would find an ideal home at the Society, Hunnewell made a series of gifts. The first and most substantial gift, consisting of the illustrated Americana and New England election sermons, was made in 1935. Two years later Hunnewell helped fund the Society's purchase of material gathered by the early Hawaiian missionary Hiram Bingham. This acquisition was augmented in later years by many of Hunnewell's own Hawaiian books. In 1941 came the family's Christopher Columbus collection, as well as a fine group of 270 clipper ship cards. Although James F. Hunnewell's original collection of Charlestown imprints had gone to the Massachusetts State Library, his son formed a second collection which he eventually donated to AAS. The tradition of Hunnewell family membership in, and extraordinary generosity to, AAS continues with the present generation: in 2008 James F. Hunnewell, Jr., Ogden McC. Hunnewell, and Robert C. Hunnewell donated a choice group of early Hawaiian imprints to the Society.

CAT. 76. Edmond Halley, *A New Plan of the Harbour of Boston in New England*, 1702.

76. Edmond Halley. *A New Plan of the Harbour of Boston in New England ...* Watercolor and ink on paper, 1702.

GIFT OF THE ESTATE OF
JOHN W. FARWELL, 1942-1943.

In 1698, Edmond Halley (1656-1742) left his position working under Isaac Newton at the Royal Mint in order to undertake an Atlantic voyage with the purpose of charting the ocean's magnetic fields. Halley had already gained fame for his star maps of the Southern hemisphere and his charts of the Earth's winds. This elegant manuscript map of Boston Harbor, prepared by Halley in 1702 after his return to England, was probably used to create the engraved version which appeared in Book Four of *The English Pilot* (1707). The manuscript map shows more

territory to the north than does the printed chart, and it varies in some details. In 1705 Halley returned to his study of the stars, calculating the orbit of the comet which today bears his name.

Once in the possession of Admiral Lord Richard Howe (1726-1799), commander of the British Navy during the American Revolution, this chart came to AAS as part of John W. Farwell's bequest, which more than doubled the Society's cartographic holdings. Farwell built a major collection of early maps of the English colonies and particularly of New England, while concurrently pursuing interests in early printed books and broadsides. He was very generous with his cartographic collection, allowing access to his Boston home to researchers exploring such topics as piracy, urban development, and mapmaking.

AAS Chief Joys 18.

77. Council for Virginia. *A Declaration of the State of the Colony and Affaires in Virginia. With the Names of the Aduenturors, and Summes Aduentured in that Action.* London: Thomas Snodham, 1620.

GIFT OF THE ESTATE OF
JOHN W. FARWELL, 1942-1943.

John W. Farwell's interest in early Americana was all-encompassing, and from his library AAS obtained many important works concerning the English settlements south of New England. Among these was this optimistic description of the Virginia Colony at a critical juncture in its history. Issued by the Council for Virginia (the governing body of the Virginia Company), the *Declaration* summarizes Virginia's rapid growth in the year since Sir Edwin Sandys had taken control of the Company. Included is a list of the ships sent to Virginia during 1619-1620, along with statistics on the 1,261 passengers they ferried: 650 "Persons for publique use" and 611 "sent for priuate Plantations." Following is an enumeration of the various "Commodities"—iron, hemp, timber, silk, salt, etc.—which the Company hoped would supplant tobacco as the colony's chief exports. Also included are the Virginia Company's revised bylaws, a list of the many stockholders and the amounts invested—the Company of Stationers, for example, ventured £125—and a rosy preview of plans for the coming year. Within two years, however, an Indian uprising in Virginia and bitter factionalism within the Company would nearly doom the colony.

STC 24841.6.

78. Library Company of Philadelphia. *A Catalogue of Books Belonging to the Library Company of Philadelphia.* Philadelphia: Benjamin Franklin, 1741.

GIFT OF THE ESTATE OF
JOHN W. FARWELL, 1942-1943.

One of John W. Farwell's treasures was this copy of the second earliest American library catalog, preceded only by the 1723 catalog of the Harvard College Library, a copy of which is also at AAS. Founded in 1731 by Benjamin Franklin and his friends as a subscription library, the Library Company of Philadelphia proved very successful, soon becoming Philadelphia's de facto public collection. Much of the Library Company's success derived from its ability to carefully select what it acquired, rather than having to rely on donations of less desirable, out-of-date titles. Hence history, literature, and science but not theology predominated among the 375 works acquired during the Library Company's first decade, only a handful of which were in languages other than English. The unsigned "A short Account of the Library" on the catalog's final page was written by Benjamin Franklin, who also printed the catalog.

This copy—one of four to have survived of the 200 printed—had a distinguished provenance prior to Farwell's acquisition. Per the front flyleaf inscription, it was "Bought of William Pickering London, June 1845, in a paper cover, and bound for me by Hayday"—"me" being the formidable Cambridge, Massachusetts, book collector George Livermore (1809-1865). On January 17, 1859, Livermore presented it to noted educator, statesman, Gettysburg orator, accomplished bibliophile and former AAS president Edward Everett.

Evans 4787; Miller 246; Winans 15.

79. John Norton. *The Redeemed Captive. Being a Narrative of the Taking and Carrying into Captivity the Reverend Mr. John Norton ...* Boston: Samuel Kneeland and Timothy Green, 1748.

GIFT OF THE ESTATE OF
JOHN W. FARWELL, 1942-1943.

The Farwell library was especially strong in works on early New England, and on the conflicts among English, French, and Indians as they contested for control of a continent. One highlight, and one of the earliest of the many Indian captivity narratives now at AAS, is John

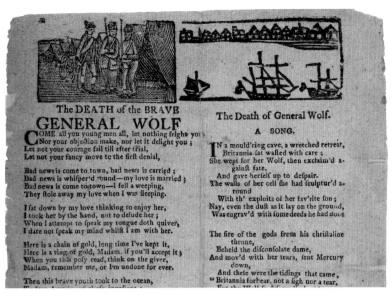

CAT. 80. *The Death of the Brave General Wolf*, between 1775 and 1797 (detail).

Norton's very rare *The Redeemed Captive*. It should not be confused with John Williams's better-known and similarly titled account of the 1704 raid on Deerfield, Massachusetts, though Norton's narrative does cover similar ground.

Following the outbreak of hostilities between England and France in 1744, Massachusetts sought to defend its western frontier by erecting a series of forts. The key outpost was Fort Massachusetts, established near present-day Williamstown. In August 1746, the small garrison of twenty-two soldiers and their families found themselves surrounded by over 900 French and Indians, and it quickly surrendered. The captives, including chaplain John Norton (1715-1778), were marched northward, first to Crown Point on Lake Champlain and then into Canada. In a spare but gripping style, Norton recounts the cruelties and hardships endured by the captives until the survivors were returned to Boston a year later.

Evans 6211.

80. *The Death of the Brave General Wolf*. Massachusetts: Ezekiel Russell, between 1775 and 1797.

GIFT OF THE ESTATE OF
JOHN W. FARWELL, 1942-1943.

The two ballads on this broadside com-memorate one of the most celebrated events of the Seven Years' War: the death in 1759 of General James Wolfe, leader of the combined Colonial and British forces at the Battle of Quebec. Both glorify Wolfe, underscoring his determination not to die on the battlefield until assured that his forces were victorious. The ballad printed on the left side probably originated in England, where the death of Wolfe was romanticized as legend. That on the sheet's right side was written by Thomas Paine, before he emigrated from England to Philadelphia in 1774; its first American appearance was in the March 1775 issue of the *Pennsylvania Magazine*, which Paine edited for publisher Robert Aitken. More abstract than the ballad it is paired with, Paine's song casts a weeping Britannia as its central figure, placing her in a gloomy cave surrounded by depictions of Wolfe's heroic actions and stating, "Nay, even the dust as it lay on the ground was engraved with some deeds he had done."

This is the only known copy of this particular broadside printing. Broadside ballads celebrating Wolfe's heroism were printed and distributed widely in America up until the War of 1812. Several early nineteenth-century printings, for example, can be found among the collection of ballads that Isaiah Thomas donated to AAS in 1814 (Cat. 12).

Wegelin 539.

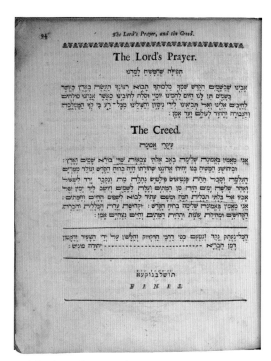

CAT. 81. Judah Monis, *Dickdook Leshon Gnebreet*, 1735.

81. Judah Monis. *Dickdook Leshon Gnebreet. A Grammar of the Hebrew Tongue ...* Boston: Jonas Green ... Sold by the Author at his House in Cambridge, 1735.

BEQUEST OF FREDERICK LEWIS GAY, 1918.

The Frederick Lewis Gay bequest to AAS included among its treasures this copy of the first Hebrew textbook to be written and published in the American colonies. Its author was Judah Monis (1683-1764). Born in Italy and educated there and in Amsterdam, Monis emigrated to New York by 1716, where he was a merchant and rebbe to the Jewish community. In 1722, aided by his public conversion to Christianity, Monis was appointed to the newly established part-time post of instructor in Hebrew at Harvard College, where he would remain until 1760. When not teaching, Monis ran a general store and became a popular figure in what is now Harvard Square.

Hebrew had long been a requirement for Harvard undergraduates, and at first they used manuscript copies of Monis's self-composed Hebrew grammar as their text. After a dozen years of effort, Monis persuaded college officials to fund 1,000 copies of his textbook. The job was executed by Boston printer Jonas Green using Hebrew types—the first complete font made available to an American press—donated to Harvard by English benefactor Thomas Hollis. All incoming students were required to purchase the text, and many of the extant copies display marks of student ownership. This copy belonged to Oliver Peabody, Harvard class of 1745, who later served briefly as Harvard's librarian.

Evans 3931.

82. *Interesting Tracts, Relating to the Island of Jamaica, Consisting of Curious State-papers, Councils of War, Letters ... Down to the Year 1702.* St. Jago de la Vega: Lewis, Lunan, and Jones, 1800.

BEQUEST OF FREDERICK LEWIS GAY, 1918.

Complementing its holdings of early Americana, AAS also has a remarkable collection of British Caribbean imprints: books, pamphlets, almanacs, and newspapers. Given the vagaries of time and climate, many of the

Caribbean imprints at AAS are now of exceptional rarity.

Among them is *Interesting Tracts*, a 300-page quarto work printed in Jamaica, acquired in 1918 as part of the Frederick Lewis Gay bequest. It publishes, mostly for the first time, important documents (originally recorded in manuscript) concerning the seventeenth-century British conquest and rule of Jamaica. The text is based on transcriptions made by Edward Long (1743-1813) from original manuscripts in various British archives. Long served as lieutenant governor of Jamaica before returning to his native England in 1769 to research and write his three-volume *History of Jamaica* (1774). Long's original transcriptions made their way back to Jamaica, where in 1800 they were printed in the colonial capital, St. Jago de la Vega (present-day Spanish Town).

83. James Frothingham Hunnewell. *A Catalogue of Books Belonging to James F. Hunnewell, of Charlestown, Mass.* Cambridge, Massachusetts: The Riverside Press, April 1873.

GIFT OF JAMES MELVILLE HUNNEWELL, 1946.

James F. Hunnewell documented his collecting activities in numerous privately issued publications—Hunnewell's personal copies of these are now at AAS, courtesy of his son James M. Hunnewell.

Hunnewell's first library catalog, privately printed in 1873 in fifty copies, ran to 114 pages. This is his working copy, interleaved and methodically updated to 1891, when a revised catalog was issued. Titles inadvertently omitted from the 1873 catalog were added in red, with several thousand additions neatly noted, first in black ink, then in blue. On March 23, 1888, Hunnewell tallied 5,400 volumes in all, of which the "Library Room" proper held only 3,178. In a handwritten "Prefatory Note," Hunnewell listed his varied collecting interests. These ranged from incunabula to Charlestown, Massachusetts, imprints, to American large paper editions, to Massachusetts election sermons, and illustrated books generally, supplemented by woodcuts, photographs, and 66,140 engravings. Overleaf, Hunnewell added his newest collecting interest, "Illustrated Americana."

84. Urian Oakes. *New-England Pleaded with, and Pressed to Consider the Things which Concern Her Peace ...* Cambridge, Massachusetts: Samuel Green, 1673.

GIFT OF JAMES MELVILLE HUNNEWELL, 1935.

James F. Hunnewell avidly sought Massachusetts election sermons, forming a collection of 165 titles which his son, James M. Hunnewell, donated to AAS in 1935. Thanks to this gift, AAS now possesses the best extant holding of New England election sermons.

Today election sermons are perhaps best known through the Rev. Arthur Dimmesdale's climactic confessional in Nathaniel Hawthorne's *The Scarlet Letter*. But given their symbolic importance, election sermons are important primary documents for colonial American history. They were preached annually in Massachusetts (from 1634 to 1883), Connecticut, New Hampshire, and Vermont on the civil holiday when freemen gathered to elect their legislators. Following their installation, legislators would join the magistrates and freemen to hear a sermon, preached by a prominent minister.

New-England Pleaded with is the earliest election sermon in the Hunnewell gift, and the seventh earliest to be printed. The honor of delivering it was accorded to Urian Oakes, a 1649 graduate of Harvard College who, in 1671, was called back from England to assume the pulpit in Cambridge; from 1675 to 1681 he also served as Harvard's president, succeeding Leonard Hoar (Cat. 51). Oakes's address to the holders of Massachusetts's political and religious authority included a special and eloquent plea for toleration. This is the George Brinley copy, purchased by Hunnewell at the first Brinley sale in 1879.

Brinley Sale I, 834; Evans 180.

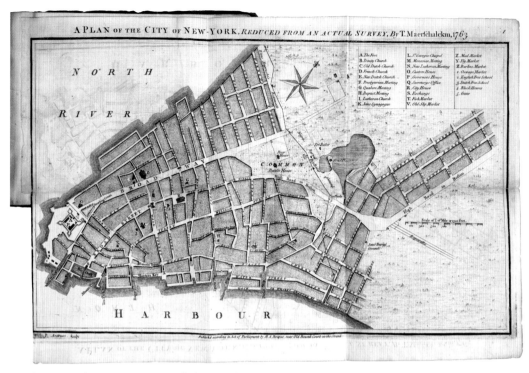

CAT. 85. John Rocque, *A Set of Plans and Forts in America*, 1765.

85. John Rocque. *A Set of Plans and Forts in America. Reduced from Actual Surveys.* London: Mary Ann Rocque, 1765.

GIFT OF JAMES MELVILLE HUNNEWELL, 1935.

In 1935 AAS received from James M. Hunnewell the several hundred volumes of illustrated Americana collected by his father, James F. Hunnewell. One of the gift volumes was this set of thirty engraved plans of French and English forts in the area bounded by New York, Pittsburgh, Niagara, and Louisbourg, as they appeared during the French and Indian War. The plans were executed under the direction of John (or Jean) Rocque, a Huguenot surveyor and mapmaker best known for two multi-sheet maps of London issued in the 1740s. First published in 1763 by Rocque's widow, *A Set of Plans* was reissued (changing only the title-page date) in 1765; today both issues are very rare. The plans are a modest 6 x 7.5 inches in size, save for the first, which is a fine fold-out plan of lower Manhattan, engraved by Peter Andrews after the famous map prepared by city surveyor Peter Maerschalck and published in New York in 1755. This copy

once belonged to William Makepeace Thackeray, whose blind-stamped monogram is faintly visible in the lower right margin; James F. Hunnewell purchased it from London bookseller Henry Sotheran in 1879.

86. *Sandwich Island Gazette and Journal of Commerce.* Honolulu, July 30, 1836.

GIFT OF JAMES MELVILLE HUNNEWELL, 1942.

James M. Hunnewell's many gifts to AAS included much rare Hawaiiana, as for example a virtually complete run of the *Sandwich Island Gazette,* the first English-language newspaper published in Hawaii. Unusually, it was established in opposition to the Hawaiian government and the powerful interests of American Protestant missionaries. Per its prospectus, the *Sandwich Island Gazette* would be "devoted to the interests of Commerce, Navigation, and Agriculture, in the Pacific, and for the diffusion of information upon such topics as may be worthy of notice." Unstated, however, were its affiliation with the local Catholic mission and potential to undermine Hawaii's established institutions. The Catholic Church had so far maintained only a tenuous foothold in Hawaii,

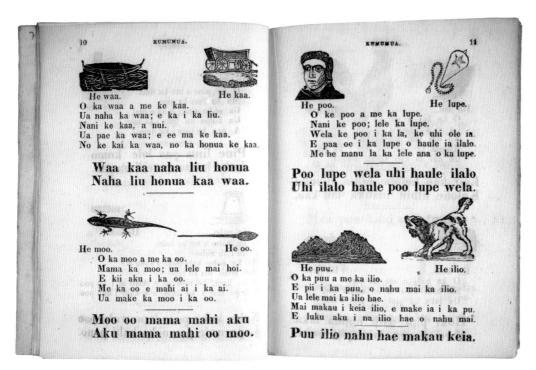

CAT. 87. John Smith Emerson, *O ke kumumua na na kamalii,* 1837.

its priests having been expelled in 1831.

Twenty-four year-old Bostonian Stephen D. Mackintosh established a printing press at the Catholic mission in Honolulu in 1836, producing this first weekly issue on July 30. In it he states: "The appearance of our first number has been delayed by some opposing circumstances beyond our control, but we are now enabled to commence our pleasant task under the kind auspices of His Majesty." The *Sandwich Island Gazette* fulfilled the typical functions of a newspaper while treading carefully through Hawaiian politics—the Catholic religion had been prohibited by law in 1837, and its adherents subjected to persecution. It ceased publication in 1839, shortly after French diplomatic efforts succeeded in lifting the ban on Catholicism.

87. John Smith Emerson. *O ke kumumua na na kamalii: he palapala e ao aku ai i na kamalii ike ole i ka heluhelu palapala.* Second edition. Oahu: Mission Press, 1837.

GIFT OF JAMES MELVILLE HUNNEWELL, 1949.

During the first half of the nineteenth century, the Boston-based American Board of Commissioners for Foreign Missions was busily organizing religious missions worldwide. In 1820 the A.B.C.F.M. established the Sandwich Island Mission Press in order to promote both the Gospel and literacy in Hawaii. Thanks in large part to Hunnewell family gifts, AAS possesses a superb collection of over seventy Mission Press titles, which are frequently used by researchers working on a wide array of topics, including religious history, women's studies, and U.S.-Asia relations.

In English translation, the title of this rare Hawaiian language primer reads: *First Lessons for Children: A Book Teaching the Children Who Do Not Know How to Read Books.* The text, written by American missionary John Smith Emerson (1800-1867), is composed of a set of basic reading exercises. Many of the illustrations are stock cuts imported for the press from the United States, but some, like those of a canoe, a man, and island hills, were printed from woodcuts created locally in Hawaii. The AAS copy is bound in a later wrapper made of printed waste from an unidentified Hawaiian language text, covered with decorative paper featuring an Asian man and what appears to be a caption in Chinese script. This humble primer is a truly transpacific production.

Forbes 1072; Judd 156.

1st Month, JANUARY, hath 31 Days.

D. H. M.			
First Q.	1	5 23	mo.
Full ○	9	4 25	mo.
Last Q.	16	6 43	aft.
New ●	23	0 53	aft.
First Q.	30	6 34	aft.

☊ { 1 ♎ 8; 11 7; 21 7 } deg.

PLANETS places.

D.	☉	♄	♃	♂	♀	☿	☽'s L.
	♑	♈	♎	♍	♏	♒	
1	11	11	29	28	23	0	S. 1
7	18	11	♏ 0	♎ 0	29	5	S. 5
13	24	12	1	3	♐ 6	4	S. 2
19	♒ 0	12	1	3	13	♑ 27	N. 4
25	6	13	1	4	20	22	N. 3

M D	W D	Remarkable days, aspects, weather, &c	☉ rises.	☉ sets.	☽'s Pla.	☽ sets.	☽ south	☽ A
1	A	Circumcis. □ ☉ ♄	7 20	4 40	♈ 16	Morn.	6 25	7
2	2	♀ great. elong.	7 20	4 40	29	sets.	7 10	8
3	3	*Cloudy*	7 20	4 40	♉ 11	1 41	7 55	9
4	4	*with snow*	7 19	4 41	23	2 36	8 42	10
5	5	*or*	7 19	4 41	♊ 5	3 34	9 29	11
6	6	Ephiphany. *cold*	7 18	4 42	17	4 29	10 17	12
7	7	Pleia. s. 8, 16. *rain.*	7 18	4 42	29	5 20	11 3	13
8	A	1st Sund. aft. Epip.	7 17	4 43	♋ 11	6 6	11 49	14
9	2	*Clear and*	7 17	4 43	23	rises.	Morn	15
10	3	*cold.*	7 16	4 44	♌ 5	6 32	0 38	16
11	4	Day's l. 9h. 30m.	7 15	4 45	17	7 28	1 24	17
12	5	*high*	7 15	4 45	29	8 23	2 9	18
13	6	Sirius s. 10, 50.	7 14	4 46	♍ 12	9 25	2 54	19
14	7	*wind,*	7 13	4 47	25	10 26	3 42	20
15	A	2d Sun. aft. Epiph.	7 13	4 47	♎ 9	11 33	4 29	21
16	2	*with*	7 12	4 48	22	Morn.	5 20	22
17	3	*flying*	7 11	4 49	♏ 7	0 38	6 12	23
18	4	☌ ☉ ☿ Oriental.	7 10	4 50	21	1 49	7 8	24
19	5	*Clouds.*	7 10	4 50	♐ 5	2 55	8 7	25
20	6	♃ □ ☉ ☉ enters ♒	7 9	4 51	20	4 4	9 4	26
21	7	Agnes.	7 8	4 52	♑ 5	5 8	10 5	27
22	A	3d Sun. aft. Epiph.	7 7	4 53	19	6 9	11 6	28
23	2	Ar. r. 10, 26. *Snow*	7 6	4 54	♒ 4	sets.	A. 3	●
24	3	*or*	7 5	4 55	18	6 12	0 52	1
25	4	Con. St. Paul. *rain.*	7 4	4 56	♓ 2	7 19	1 46	2
26	5	Day's l. 9h. 54m.	7 3	4 57	16	8 22	2 35	3
27	6		7 2	4 58	29	9 23	3 24	4
28	7	*Clear*	7 1	4 59	♈ 12	10 27	4 10	5
29	A	4th Sun. aft. Epiph.	7 0	5 0	25	11 23	4 56	6
30	2	*and*	6 59	5 1	♉ 7	Morn.	5 44	7
31	3	Day's in. 48m. *cold.*	6 58	5 2	19	0 22	6 32	8

Collecting in Specialized Fields

In realizing Isaiah Thomas's vision of building a comprehensive library of early American imprints, AAS owes its success in part to single-minded persistence. Two hundred years of collecting in a single broad, but ultimately finite, field has inevitably created a collection of formidable scope and strength. But the extraordinary depth and richness to be encountered in so many parts of the AAS collection is due largely to the many specialist collectors who, after painstakingly assembling a library on a single topic, have generously placed it in perpetuity at AAS. All have collected in a manner consistent with the "Code for Collectors" that Edward Larocque Tinker set out for himself in his autobiography: "1. To choose a subject in a little known field, but one that is worthy of study and preservation. ... 2. To amass as complete a collection as possible, and then make a written record of all the new information my enthusiasm and hard work had discovered. ... 3. And lastly, to give or leave my entire collection to some university or other library, so that students of the subject would not be forced to repeat all the work I had done." Of the many collectors who have generously donated their specialist holdings to AAS, four have been selected for closer examination: Samuel Lyman Munson, Edward Larocque Tinker, Frank J. Metcalf, and Thomas O. Mabbott.

Born in western Massachusetts, Samuel Lyman Munson (1844-1930) sought his fortune in nearby Albany, New York. In 1867 he founded the S. L. Munson Co., which would eventually become one of Albany's most important manufacturing companies, employing nearly a thousand workers at its height. Its first product was women's linen collars, though the

FIG. 22

firm eventually added other articles of women's apparel to its line. Munson complemented his business activities with leadership roles in many of Albany's civic organizations. His free time was spent traveling—Munson's journeys included two complete round-the-world trips in addition to many shorter ones—and amassing the nation's largest private collection of almanacs. As a collector Munson started late, not making his first significant almanacs purchase (of early English almanacs) from Boston bookseller George E. Littlefield until around the year 1909. At first Munson collected almanacs from all countries, though American almanacs soon took pride of place. By 1924 his collection numbered over 10,000 items.

When Munson began collecting, Clarence S. Brigham had recently joined the AAS staff, and AAS's own almanac holdings stood at around 4,000 pieces. But Brigham, prompted in part by prominent local AAS member Charles L. Nichols (Cats. 107-110), soon began to acquire almanacs as quickly as he could find them. His reasoning, as explained in his librarian's report of 1910 and restated in 1930, was sound: "[almanacs] furnish, as do few other printed productions, information regarding the establishment and growth of the printing-press in the community in which they were issued, a point that appeals strongly to a library which seeks, as we do, to collect everything that bears upon the history of American printing." Indeed, "no publication, excepting the newspaper, illustrates more clearly and consecutively the history of printing in any town, for nearly every printing firm issued an almanac and the time of its appearance was regular

FIG. 23

and certain." Because both AAS and Munson willingly made their holdings available to the bibliographers then compiling various statewide almanacs checklists, Brigham soon became aware of Munson's collecting. Elected an AAS member in 1918, Munson was quickly appointed to the Council. By 1925, pleased that AAS had succeeded in building the best institutional collection of American almanacs but aware of its deficiencies, Munson offered to give AAS any almanacs it needed from his own collection. AAS selected some 3,800 of Munson's American almanacs.

Like Munson, Edward Larocque Tinker (1881-1968) began collecting late but quickly made up for lost time. Born and educated in New York City, Tinker established a law and real estate practice there after some wanderlust years spent in Texas and Mexico during the Mexican Revolution. In 1916 he married a woman well connected in New Orleans society, and henceforth the Tinkers wintered in their New Orleans home on fashionable St. Charles Street. Fascinated by Louisiana's history and culture, Tinker began collecting works of Lafcadio Hearn while writing his first book, *Lafcadio Hearn's American Days* (1924). Tinker soon donated this collection to Harvard University, for he had already begun the much more challenging task of building a comprehensive library of nineteenth-century Louisiana imprints, especially those documenting the history and culture of its French and Creole populations. He left no stone unturned in the hunt for rare publications, especially newspapers. Tinker reminisced, "I did not confine my search for the old newspapers to New Orleans but went out into the parishes and visited the places where I knew some had been printed. Then I would find the descendants of the original publishers and try to buy any old files they might have. Many had been lost in floods and others burned or eaten by giant cockroaches. However, I managed to get a few that proved to be the only surviving examples. … To me this was as exciting as seeking the treasure of sunken Spanish galleons."

Tinker drew upon his personal library and other sources to write two important books, both published in 1932. The first was his dissertation, *Les Écrits de Langue française en Louisiane au XIXe siècle: Essais biographiques et bibliographiques*, a bio-bibliography of nineteenth-century Louisiana authors who wrote in French, submitted for a doctorate at the Sorbonne. The second, *Bibliography of the French Newspapers and Periodicals of Louisiana,* was published by AAS shortly after Tinker's election to membership. Tinker's first major gift of Louisiana materials was, according to his own description, "part of my collection of French newspaper files, about 200 pounds," sent in 1943. Six years later came the greater portion, the two gifts totaling over 800 volumes plus runs long and short of some 150 newspaper titles. Other periodic gifts followed until Tinker's death. Many researchers have since been pleasantly surprised to find that the Society's Louisiana holdings are nearly on a par with its New England collections.

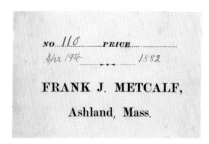

FIG. 24

In 1937 Frank J. Metcalf (1865-1945) was elected to AAS membership on the basis of his reputation as the nation's leading authority on American hymnbooks and hymn writers, and (as Brigham well knew) possessor of an extensive early American hymnbook collection. Born in Ashland, Massachusetts, ten days before Abraham Lincoln's assassination, Metcalf taught school in New England, Texas, and Utah following graduation from Boston University. In 1893 he changed course, accepting a clerkship in the U.S. Army adjutant general's office in Washington. Metcalf was badly injured when the building that housed his office collapsed, killing twenty-two of his colleagues. Following an extended convalescence, Metcalf became an expert in military records and genealogy.

But Metcalf's primary interest was American hymnology and especially its bio-bibliography, to which he fruitfully employed his research skills. His first project was to define the field by compiling a checklist, published in 1917 as *American Psalmody, or, Titles of Books Containing Tunes Printed in America from 1721-1820.* Concurrently Metcalf also collected hymnals as his resources permitted. The bibliography was followed in 1925 by his most important publication, *American Writers and Compilers of Sacred Music,* which provided painstakingly researched biographies of some 150 American hymn composers. Metcalf continued to work on two more ambitious projects: additional biographical sketches (published in part), and a massive bibliography of pre-1881 American hymnbooks, left unfinished at his death. He had laid careful plans, however. To AAS Metcalf bequeathed all of the hymnals it lacked—a total of 2,400 volumes—strengthening an already large collection of early American hymnbooks. He also left his research notes and bibliographical files to the Society.

Thomas Ollive Mabbott (1898-1968) was a frequent donor to the AAS collections even though he was never elected to AAS membership. Like Tinker and Metcalf, Mabbott viewed collecting as an adjunct to his scholarly research. Born and raised in

New York City, he developed at the age of eight a passion for coin collecting that never left him. During the 1920s Mabbott became fascinated with a far different field—fifteenth-century prints and the origins of printing—forming a small but superb collection of rare woodcut and paste prints. These, and other examples in selected American collections, were described in several fascicles Mabbott contributed to Paul Heitz's important series, *Einblattdrucke des fünfzehnten Jahrhunderts*.

Another collecting and scholarly interest was kindled during adolescent visits to the New York townhouse of Mabbott's grandfather. In the library were nineteenth-century periodicals containing original printings of Edgar Allan Poe stories. "It occurred to [Mabbott] that such magazines might be valuable, but when booksellers offered [only] twenty-five and fifty cents apiece for them, he felt it was a buyer's market and began to purchase magazines with Poe texts in them. By the time he was in [high school] he had become attracted to old newspapers," and then to original letters and books by minor American authors. Little wonder, then, that Mabbott trained as a Poe scholar, earning his doctorate at Columbia University in 1923. From his fast-accumulating collection of antebellum periodicals and newspapers, which he read and studied thoroughly, Mabbott gained insights into Poe's literary and journalistic world as well as a wealth of information eventually incorporated into his scholarly monographs on Poe and critical editions of Poe's works. When Mabbott took a position at Hunter College in 1929, domestic space was at a premium, and with New York's library riches close at hand, Mabbott donated his nineteenth-century American newspaper files to AAS. More gifts came later, including issues of flash press, or racy, newspapers from the 1840s. These often salacious papers, targeted to an urban male audience, rarely have survived in collections. Thanks to Mabbott's initial gift, AAS has since built an enviable collection of flash press titles.

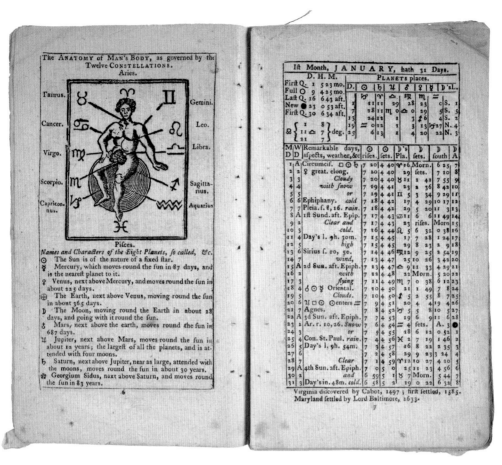

CAT. 89. Benjamin Banneker, *Almanack and Ephemeris*, 1791.

88-89. Benjamin Banneker. Holographic manuscript of his 1792 almanac and ephemeris, with the published edition *Benjamin Banneker's Pennsylvania, Delaware, Maryland and Virginia Almanack and Ephemeris, for the Year of Our Lord, 1792 ... Baltimore: William Goddard and James Angell ..., both 1791.*

Manuscript: GIFT OF WILLIAM GODDARD, 1813; Published almanac: GIFT OF SAMUEL L. MUNSON, 1925.

In 1813 the Baltimore printer William Goddard, who had retired to a farm in his native Rhode Island, donated to AAS one of its most significant manuscripts: the holograph of Benjamin Banneker's first almanac, which God-dard had printed in 1791. Over a century later, Samuel L. Munson's gift of early American almanacs finally enabled AAS to pair the original manuscript with a copy of the rare printed almanac.

Benjamin Banneker (1731-1806), America's first African-American scientist, was born into freedom in rural Maryland and spent most of his life farming tobacco. Largely self-educated, Banneker early on displayed a remarkable talent for mathematics and mechanical apparatus. Beginning in the 1770s, members of the neighboring Ellicott family encouraged Banneker's interest in astronomy, and in 1791 Andrew Ellicott enlisted Banneker's aid in surveying the newly established District of Columbia. By then Banneker had also taught himself to calculate an ephemeris for an almanac. No publisher accepted his calculations for a 1791 almanac, but with the Ellicotts's support, William Goddard agreed to publish Banneker's 1792 effort. Justifiably proud of his work, Ban-

115

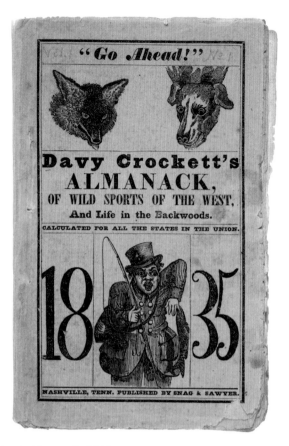

CAT. 90. *Davy Crockett's Almanack*, 1834.

neker sent a copy of this manuscript to Thomas Jefferson, using it as an example of his accomplishment and criticizing Jefferson's views on slavery.

As was typical of the time, Banneker's contribution to the 1792 almanac extended only to the ephemeris and projections of lunar eclipses; the remaining miscellaneous prose content was supplied by others. A comparison of the manuscript with the printed almanac shows that Goddard faithfully followed Banneker's text, editing only for style and space considerations. Prefixed to the text is a long, effusive testimonial from noted Marylander James McHenry. Banneker's almanac was actively promoted by abolitionist societies in Maryland and Pennsylvania, and consequently it sold well; thus encouraged, Banneker continued to prepare almanacs through 1797.

Published almanac: Drake 2226; Evans 23148.

90. *Davy Crockett's Almanack, of Wild Sports of the West, and Life in the Backwoods … 1835.* Nashville: Snag & Sawyer, 1834.
GIFT OF SAMUEL L. MUNSON, 1925.

During the nineteenth century, American almanacs became increasingly topical in content. Many were issued in support of specific causes, such as antislavery or temperance; catered to certain audiences, such as members of religious denominations or fraternal orders; or marketed products, patent medicines in particular. The Samuel L. Munson gift greatly expanded AAS's holdings of topical almanacs.

Among the best known topical almanacs are the "comic" almanacs, filled with jokes, stories, and humorous verse, which first appeared in Boston in 1831 and remained in vogue up to the Civil War. Joining their number in 1835 was *Davy Crockett's Almanack*, published in Nashville. This almanac proved so successful that it continued through 1841 and spawned many longer-lived imitators. The then still-living Crockett almost certainly had nothing to do with this publication, other than to inspire it through the immense contemporary interest in his larger-than-life persona, as popularized through his public appearances, writings, and in the press. Here tall tales of Davy's backwoods exploits are brilliantly melded with the wood engravings typical of comic almanacs. The Nashville series was written and published anonymously—"Snag & Sawyer" is a fictitious imprint—and there is compelling evidence that the later ones (if not all) were illustrated and probably printed in Boston, perhaps by the noted publisher of almanacs and other popular works, Samuel N. Dickinson.

American Imprints 24113; Drake 13405.

91. Caleb Gibbs. Diary, 1778. In *Poor Will's Pocket Almanack, for the Year 1778; Fitted to the Use of Pennsylvania ...* Philadelphia: J. Crukshank, 1777.

GIFT OF SAMUEL L. MUNSON, 1925.

Samuel L. Munson's 1925 gift of 3,782 American almanacs was notable for significantly augmenting AAS's collection of early manuscript diaries. As essential daily references, almanacs were typically printed in much greater quantities than were other products of the American press. Often almanacs were sold interleaved, although purchasers sometimes interleaved their own copies. The blank pages opposite calendar pages invited owners to write brief daily entries. Eighteenth century American diaries were frequently kept in such interleaved almanacs.

This 1778 almanac from the Munson gift contains the brief, but highly important diary of Caleb Gibbs (1748-1818) of Marblehead, Massachusetts. On March 6, 1776, George Washington selected Captain Gibbs to command the newly established Commander-in-Chief's Guard, an elite unit charged with protecting the person, baggage, and papers of Washington and his staff when in camp and

during their travels. Gibbs served with distinction in the post until the disbanding of the Guard in 1783. He began this diary while stationed at Valley Forge, and it records, among other news, the comings and goings of Martha Washington.

Drake 10063; Evans 15238.

92. *Laussat, Préfet colonial, Commissaire du Gouvernement français, ... 30 novembre 1803 ...* New Orleans: Jean Baptiste Le Seur Fontaine, 1803.

GIFT OF EDWARD LAROCQUE TINKER, 1949.

The French colonial prefect, Pierre Clément de Laussat, arrived in New Orleans in late March 1803, only to discover that, thanks to Napoleon's sale of the Louisiana Territory to the United States, he was to oversee not only a transition from Spanish to French rule, but a further transition to U.S. rule. This is one of a series of broadsides by which Laussat arranged an orderly transfer of authority for the courts, the customs office, and the New Orleans municipal government, and made numerous appointments for commissioners, quartermasters, and judges. Printed on the day that France retook possession of Louisiana from Spain, this rare broadside replaces the Spanish courts with a new judicial system, which would remain in place until the United States took formal possession three weeks later, on December 20, 1803.

Edward Larocque Tinker's 1949 gift to AAS included two of Laussat's broadside edicts. Writing to Clarence S. Brigham as the gift was being crated for shipment to Worcester, Tinker modestly stated, "Some of the items are in pretty poor shape: New Orleans is the hardest city in the country on such things. You must remember, too, that this was a strictly working library, so I took things when I could get them, never knowing if later I could get better copies." Fortunately, both Laussat printings were in pristine condition as, indeed, was most of the Tinker gift.

Jumonville 69; Shaw & Shoemaker 4551.

Cat. 93. *Moniteur de la Louisiane*, 1810.

93. *Moniteur de la Louisiane.* New Orleans, February 21, 1810.

Gift of Edward Larocque Tinker, ca. 1950.

The *Moniteur de la Louisiane*, established in 1794 by Louis Duclot, was the first newspaper published in Louisiana. Because so few early issues have survived, its history is difficult to piece together. The earliest known issue—since lost in a fire but preserved in facsimile—was dated August 25, 1794; all other extant issues are from the 1800s. Although founded when Louisiana was under Spanish control, the *Moniteur* was published primarily in French,

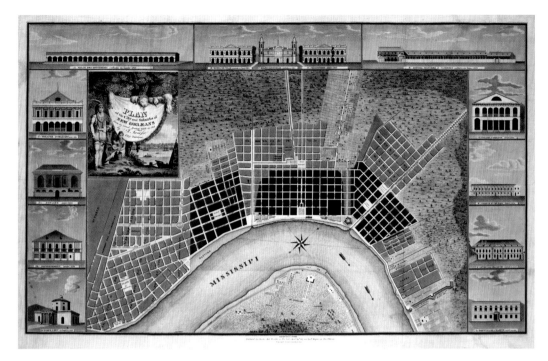

CAT. 94. *Plan of the City and Suburbs of New Orleans*, 1817.

the language of Louisiana's majority population. Over time the newspaper grew in size from octavo to quarto to folio, and it also changed publishers. This 1810 issue lists Jean Baptiste Le Seur Fontaine as publisher, a role he had assumed by 1803 and perhaps as early as 1797. Publication apparently ceased in 1814. When Fontaine died that year, he bequeathed to the city of New Orleans his personal file of the *Moniteur*.

This is one of two issues of the *Moniteur* sent to AAS by Edward Larocque Tinker as part of his very substantial gift of early Louisiana newspapers and periodicals.

94. William Rollinson, after Jacques Tanesse. *Plan of the City and Suburbs of New Orleans from an Actual Survey Made in 1815 ....* New York: Charles del Vecchio; New Orleans: Pierre Maspero, 1817.

GIFT OF EDWARD LAROCQUE TINKER, 1954.

This remarkable engraved plan records the rapid growth of New Orleans, whose population of 7,000 in 1803 had increased to more than 33,000 by 1815. Immigrants from the Americas and the Caribbean flocked to the bustling city seeking opportunity. Mayor Augustin de McCarty attempted to organize the overflowing metropolis, designing new streets, creating a house numbering system, and even writing up garbage removal rules. Drawn up by the city's surveyor in 1815 and published two years later, this map shows the city's seven wards and the breastworks that had proved crucial to Andrew Jackson's victory over the British at the Battle of New Orleans in 1815. Around the perimeter are eleven architectural elevations of important structures, including hospitals, churches, and theaters, and a decorative cartouche of a Native American family flanking a view of the city's bustling port.

This is one of many maps of Louisiana, South America, and the Caribbean given to AAS by Edward Larocque Tinker, who presented it at the Society's 1954 annual meeting. In accepting the map, Librarian Clifford K. Shipton commented on its rarity and acknowledged AAS's heavy reliance on gifts in expanding its cartographic holdings: "We have never been in the position to press the collection of maps as vigorously as the other segments of the field of graphic arts, but over the years we have acquired a surprising number of rare or unique pieces."

95. *Les Cenelles. Choix de Poesies indigenes.* Nouvelle Orléans: H. Lauve et cie., 1845.

GIFT OF EDWARD LAROCQUE TINKER, 1950.

Edward Larocque Tinker wrote widely on his adopted home of New Orleans. Several of Tinker's works reflect his interest in New Orleans' rich nineteenth-century literary culture. Of all the rare Louisiana imprints in Tinker's library, perhaps none was more prized or of greater personal interest than this very rare copy of *Les Cenelles,* the first anthology of African-American verse to be published in the United States.

Antebellum New Orleans was home to a large, prosperous, and well-educated Creole population of free people of color. But being regarded as neither black nor white, Creoles chafed under Louisiana's racial prejudice and legal restrictions. Armand Lanusse (1812-1867), a Creole schoolteacher and author, edited a short-lived literary periodical, *L'Album littéraire* (1843) and compiled *Les Cenelles* to demonstrate that Creoles were fully capable of education and literary attainment. This finely printed and typographically whimsical volume contains eighty-five poems by seventeen Creole authors, including Lanusse and Victor Séjour (1817-1874), who subsequently won fame in France for his popular dramas. The poems, all in French and heavily influenced by French literary culture, reflect the authors' strong European ties; indeed, several of the poets were educated in France, or emigrated there to pursue careers denied them in Louisiana.

Jumonville 1382.

96. Félix de Courmont. *Le Capitaine May et le General de la Vega sur les Bords du Rio Grande, Opera comique en un Acte ...* Nouvelle Orléans: J. L. Sollée, 1847.

GIFT OF EDWARD LAROCQUE TINKER, 1950.

Thanks to the generosity of Edward Larocque Tinker, AAS possesses rich holdings on the diverse cultural life of antebellum Louisiana. The New Orleans stage is well documented through contemporary editions of works originally composed for local performance. One is this very rare one-act opera, *Le Capitaine May,* with a verse libretto by Félix de Courmont and music by Fourmestreaux, about whom virtually nothing is known. *Le Capitaine May* takes as its subject the first acknowledged hero of the Mexican-American War, Captain Charles A. May. On May 9, 1846, May led his squadron at the Battle of Resaca de la Palma (at what is now Brownsville, Texas), silencing the Mexican artillery, capturing Mexican General Rómulo de la Vega, and securing the war's first decisive American victory.

A year later, May's heroic exploits were dramatized for an American audience. Although written in French, the libretto was printed with a serviceable English translation in parallel columns, the printer charmingly inserting question marks in place of many exclamation points ("I am overpowered with fear and alarm?"). The music, unfortunately, is lost. Courmont apparently emigrated to New Orleans sometime after 1835. During the mid-1840s he published this libretto as well as a periodical containing nothing but his own verse; he also edited a short-lived French-language newspaper before disappearing from the historical record.

Jumonville 1540.

97. James Lyon. *Urania, or a Choice Collection of Psalm-Tunes, Anthems, and Hymns ...* Philadelphia: possibly William Bradford, 1761.

BEQUEST OF FRANK J. METCALF, 1945.

Upon his death in 1945, Frank J. Metcalf bequeathed to AAS his collection of nearly 2,500 American hymnals. From these AAS selected what it lacked and, per Metcalf's wishes, sent the remainder to Boston University, where

Metcalf's volumes form the core of its hymnals collection.

One of Metcalf's most prized hymnals, which he wrote about extensively but did not acquire for his collection until 1934, was this rare copy of James Lyons's *Urania*. Lyons (1735-1794) graduated from the College of New Jersey (later Princeton) in 1759, where the commencement ode was set to music of his own composition. Before entering the ministry, Lyons conducted a singing school in Philadelphia and, when enough subscribers had been found, published *Urania*. Lyons selected ninety-six compositions, including psalm tunes and anthems, suitable for an eclectic mix of religious denominations. Most were obtained from English tune books, though Lyons included some original compositions of his own as well as others by American composers Francis Hopkinson, Giovanni Palma, and William Tuckey. Engraved on pp. 190-191 is the first American printing of "God Save the King," here set to new lyrics appropriate for a sacred hymn and identified as "Whitefield's" tune. Later it was repurposed for an American audience as "My Country, 'Tis of Thee."

Britton & Lowens 371-372; Evans 8908.

98. Frank J. Metcalf. *American Psalmody, or, Titles of Books, Containing Tunes Printed in America from 1721-1820*. New York: C. F. Heartman, 1917.

PURCHASED FROM THE HEIRS OF BISHOP ROBERT W. PEACH, 1938.

In the process of building his collection of American hymnals, Frank J. Metcalf became not only the leading authority on American hymn books, but also their foremost bibliographer. His 1917 book *American Psalmody*, with a checklist of nearly 800 pre-1821 printings, secured his reputation.

Metcalf presented this deluxe copy of *American Psalmody*—one of eight on Japan vellum—to his collecting colleague Robert Westly Peach (1863-1936). The presiding bishop of the Reformed Episcopal Church, Peach amassed what was then the largest private collection of American hymnals. In so doing, Peach heavily annotated this copy, noting which of the copies listed therein were his and recording subsequent acquisitions. AAS purchased Peach's 6,000-volume collection in 1938; when merged in 1945 with Metcalf's own holdings, the Society's collection of early American hymnals became the world's best.

99. *The Weekly Rake*. New York, July 9, 1842.

GIFT OF THOMAS O. MABBOTT, 1946.

It was Edgar Allan Poe scholar Thomas O. Mabbott who donated to AAS the nucleus of its collection of racy newspapers. Also known as "sporting newspapers" or the "flash press," such papers catered to an urban male audience eager to read about, and partake in, a city's sporting, theatrical, and sexual pleasures. Frequently edited by young men barely in their twenties, racy newspapers were notorious for their frank coverage—typically couched in terms of high moral dudgeon—of various sexual practices, sexual services and where to find them, scandalous behavior, the criminal underworld, malicious gossip, and extortionate threats of exposure, spiced with appropriate advertising and crude but titillating illustrations. Following a format borrowed from British examples, racy newspapers could be found even in smaller cities from the late 1820s to the Civil War. They reached their peak in New York (1841-1843) before the courts began shutting them down on libel and obscenity charges; later sporting papers such as the *National Police Gazette* were far more subdued. Racy newspapers circulated in the thousands of copies, but today they are of extreme rarity. Recent gifts and purchases have increased AAS's holdings to nearly 200 issues, which are heavily used by researchers.

The Weekly Rake was edited by nineteen-year-old Thaddeus W. Meighan. Shortly after this issue came out, he was charged and found guilty of obscenity along with the editors of New York's competing racy newspapers: the *Flash*, the *Libertine*, and the *Whip*. Meighan moved on to write for the *Whip* until further charges prompted his transition to mainstream journalism.

THOMAS
DEANE

The Book Trades

The history of the American book trades—printing, publishing, distribution, bookselling, papermaking, type founding, bookbinding, illustration—has been a primary collecting interest for the American Antiquarian Society ever since 1812, when Isaiah Thomas donated his initial cache of primary source material. Over the past two centuries the Society has developed holdings in all aspects of the American book trades, some collected up through 1876, others extending beyond that date. A particularly striking aspect of these collections is the role played by booksellers in their formation, first in gathering the material and then in placing it at AAS. Although private collectors have also done much to help the Society build its book trades holdings, booksellers typically have shown special interest and creativity in preserving the primary sources. Nowhere is this more apparent than in the collections of American booksellers' and auction catalogs, and of American bookbindings.

When Clarence S. Brigham became librarian at AAS in 1908, he discovered that it "owned almost no catalogues of book dealers or of book auction sales," a weakness keenly felt by this consummate bookman. By October 1917, Brigham was able to report that the Society now had "practically complete files of the catalogues of American book auction houses, many of them being priced and in the case of important sales with the names of buyers inserted ... about ninety percent of the catalogues of American book dealers and a very large proportion of the English catalogues. The collection contains over fourteen thousand pieces ...." The AAS collection proved invaluable to George L. McKay when compiling his *American Book Auction Catalogues 1713-1934: A Union List*, published in 1937. Ever since, AAS has actively developed the collection through purchase, gift, and by simply saving the catalogs sent its way, so that today the Society's holdings continue to rank among the nation's best.

Two booksellers—Arthur Swann and William J. Campbell—stand out among the many who helped to build the book catalogs collection. Both donated long runs of auction catalogs, annotated in particularly thorough and insightful ways so as to reveal the trade's inner workings. Born in England, Arthur Swann (1875-1959) began his American career at Anderson Galleries before moving to the rival American Art Association. He later worked at the newly established firm of Parke-Bernet in 1937. Swann donated his personal set of over two hundred American Art Association book sale catalogs to AAS, each bearing annotations he made on bids and buyers as the sale took place.

William J. Campbell (1850-1931) was a Philadelphia antiquarian bookseller who early on gained Brigham's confidence. Campbell was adept at offering large groupings of early Pennsylvania books and pamphlets—Brigham liked to buy pre-1821 imprints in bulk for AAS whenever possible—and he also served as the Society's agent at Philadelphia book auctions. Aging and anxious that his collection of some 600 annotated Philadelphia book auction catalogs—including a long run of Stan. V. Henkels catalogs, an essential reference for any Americana specialist—be preserved, Campbell offered them to AAS. He could not afford to give them away during depths of the Depression, but Campbell did offer very generous terms, which the Society accepted. Campbell made something of a specialty out of the auction agent business, providing this service to many prominent collectors and book dealers, and his annotated catalogs bear unusual and important witness to this often overlooked aspect of the antiquarian book trade.

Another aspect of the book trade well represented at AAS is bookbinding. Today the Society possesses what is arguably the finest assemblage of early American bookbindings, a distinction owed primarily to the antiquarian booksellers who gathered many of the volumes and placed them at AAS. Chief among them was Michael Papantonio (1907-1978), who was one of the first to identify early American bindings as a neglected, and potentially important, collecting field. Papantonio apprenticed at the Brick Row Bookshop in New York before establishing his own business. After the end of World War II he partnered with John S. Van E. Kohn to open the Seven Gables Bookshop in New York. For the next thirty years Seven Gables was a mecca for collectors of American and English literature, and a training ground for junior booksellers. AAS bought heavily from the firm, as did many other libraries and collectors.

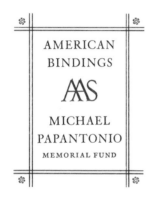

FIG. 25

In the later 1930s, Papantonio began setting aside fine early American bindings as they came his way, but it was not until 1948 that he began to collect seriously and systematically. Papantonio recalled, "There was not a great deal of material on the market, and some I simply could not afford, owing to the importance or value of some of the finer examples. ... However, there was a considerable supply of nicely bound Bibles and the Book of Common Prayer." Book trade colleagues were particularly helpful in steering the odd fine binding his way. Papantonio's collection received its first public viewing in 1962, when the Grolier Club invited him to exhibit twenty-five of the finest examples. Ten years later Papantonio brought several rare book librarians, including AAS's Marcus A. McCorison, to his home for a private viewing. That evening a plan was hatched for a traveling exhibition of sixty examples from the Papantonio collection, ranging in date from ca. 1670 to 1864. The exhibition revealed the fruits of Papantonio's informed and persistent collecting, and the accompanying catalog, *Early American Bookbindings from the Collection of Michael Papantonio*, became an essential reference. Following the exhibition, Papantonio designated AAS as the permanent home for his nearly 1,000-volume collection. It began to arrive in yearly gift installments, the bulk coming in 1978 as Papantonio's bequest.

The Papantonio gift, when added to examples of fine bindings already in the Society's collection, established at AAS one of the world's foremost collections of early American bindings, exceptional for its overall condition and quality. A number of Papantonio's friends generously provided for the collection's growth by establishing an endowed fund dedicated for the purchase of notable early American bindings. In 1989 AAS substantially enriched the collection by purchasing approximately one thousand pre-1877 American bindings gathered by the Brattleboro, Vermont, bookseller Kenneth G. Leach (1926-2007). In 1997 Carol Goodspeed Smith presented to AAS the fine collection of nineteenth-century publishers' bindings formed by her late father, the eminent Boston bookseller George T. Goodspeed (1903-1997).

124

100. American Art Association. *Illustrated Catalogue of New Jersey Memorabilia ... Comprising the Extensive Library of the Late William Nelson ... to be Sold on November 22-23, 1915 ...* New York: American Art Association, 1915.

GIFT OF ARTHUR SWANN, 1933.

It is to Arthur Swann that AAS owes some of the most important book and art auction catalogs in its comprehensive collection. In 1933, Swann donated to AAS his personal, annotated set of American Art Association catalogs; he also arranged the gift of auctioneer Thomas E. Kirby's marked set—substantially complete for 1898-1923—of American Art Association book and art auction catalogs. Together these constitute the auction house's official file copies.

When studied in tandem, the Swann and Kirby sets permit one to recreate each auction in extraordinary detail. For instance, Swann's copy of the 1915 William Nelson sale records, in the left-hand margin, all advance bids submitted to the auction house; as each lot sold, Swann noted in black crayon the winning bid and buyer. Kirby's copy, from which he conducted the sale at the rostrum, contains the City of New York's auction permit for the sale and various annotations: the small penciled figure at left is the auctioneer's confidential pre-sale estimate, the circled number in black crayon is the opening bid (derived from the advance bids), and the large black crayon number is the winning bid; a "d" in the left-hand margin and added name indicate that a duplicate copy was sold to that client. Clarence S. Brigham's three-page list of the bids he placed at the sale on AAS's behalf has also been preserved—AAS secured 15 of 112 lots on which it bid.

McKay 7607.

101. Stan. V. Henkels. *Catalogue no. 1116. Valuable Americana ... of the late Hon. Garret D. W. Vroom ... to be Sold ... Oct. 15 & 16, 1914 ...* Philadelphia: Stan. V. Henkels, 1914.

PARTIAL GIFT OF WILLIAM J. CAMPBELL, 1931.

For nearly twenty-five years, Philadelphia bookseller William J. Campbell engaged in a productive relationship with AAS, offering many items in addition to serving as AAS's agent at Philadelphia auctions. Shortly before his death, Campbell sold his virtually complete, annotated run of Stan. V. Henkels catalogs dating back to 1905 to AAS. In 1942 AAS also acquired eighteen volumes of Henkels's own records of his sales, thus ensuring the preservation of a unique window into this period of American book collecting.

Campbell's annotated catalogs are important for documenting a little-known aspect of the book trade: the role of the auction agent. In this 1914 Henkels sale, for instance, Campbell acted as agent for a dozen collectors, institutions, and dealers, as well as buying on his own account. In the margins Campbell noted in code each client's bids, later adding the buyer's name and hammer price. Inside the back cover Campbell listed his clients—most under code names, with a key—and tallied the lots each won. The western Americana collector Henry Raup Wagner, for instance, was "Arkansas," bookseller P. K. Foley was "Vermont," and AAS was simply "Antiquarian." All told, Campbell bought 95 of the sale's 665 lots for $181.30, earning $12.33 in commissions (five percent to dealers, ten percent to others). Forty-three lots sold to New York bookseller John E. Scopes; famed Americana dealer Lathrop C. Harper attended the sale's first day, but left his second-day bids in Campbell's capable hands. Alas, AAS secured only one lot, for $1.10.

McKay 7443.

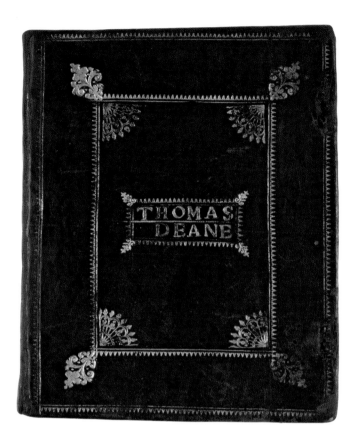

Cat. 102. John Ratcliff, Bookbinding, ca. 1670.

102. John Ratcliff. Bookbinding, Boston, ca. 1670, on: Nathaniel Morton. *New-Englands Memorial or, a Brief Relation of the Most Memorable and Remarkable Passages of the Providence of God ...* Cambridge, Massachusetts: Samuel Green and Marmaduke Johnson for John Usher, 1669.

Purchased from the Papantonio estate as the gift of Frank L. Harrington, 1979.

This volume—the earliest known extra-gilt American binding, bound in Boston shortly after publication—was the keystone of Michael Papantonio's celebrated collection of early American bookbindings. It first came to his attention in a 1950 Hodgson's auction in London, where Papantonio was outbid by H. R. Creswick, Librarian of Cambridge University; fortunately, the volume reappeared in a 1963 Sotheby's auction, where Papantonio finally secured the prize. Although one of a few select bindings omitted from the 1978 Papantonio bequest, AAS was permitted to acquire it.

Morton's famous narrative of the Pilgrims and the Plymouth Colony was the first historical monograph published in British North America. This copy was bound for Thomas Deane (1640?-1686), an English merchant who made his fortune in Boston before returning home in 1678. The stamps and roll tools identify it as the work of John Ratcliff, who arrived from England in the early 1660s to bind copies of the Eliot Indian Bible, and remained in business until 1682. Although earlier gold-tooled American bindings exist, none come close to matching this binding's stamped and roll-tooled cover decoration, its gilt ownership markings, or its twelve gilt false spine bands. Two fore-edge clasps once held the binding closed, though only the catches remain.

Evans 144; Papantonio 1.

CAT. 103. Francis Skinner, Bookbinding, ca. 1750.

103. Francis Skinner. Bookbinding, Newport, Rhode Island, ca. 1750, on: Jeremiah Burroughs. *Two Treatises of Mr. Jeremiah Burroughs. The First of Earthly Mindedness ...* London: Peter Cole, 1649.

BEQUEST OF MICHAEL PAPANTONIO, 1978.

Few volumes in the Michael Papantonio bequest are as unusual as this one, which remains virtually unique among the corpus of early American bindings. Bound in sheepskin, the covers are tooled to a panel design using a single decorative roll, the center completely and curiously filled with a large calligraphic panel stamp reading "Newport" pointing upward on the front cover and downward on the back; the spine and edges apparently were left undecorated.

The distinctive roll tool identifies this binding as the work of Francis Skinner of Newport,

Rhode Island, an attribution confirmed by the ownership inscription, "Fras: Skinners.," on the first text page. Born in Boston, Skinner (1709-1785) sold books there before relocating to Newport in the 1730s, where he worked as a bookbinder for five decades. Modern binding historians Willman and Carol Spawn attributed over one hundred bindings to Skinner, most unimaginatively bound "in the paneled style he had learned as an apprentice ... [which] had become unfashionable by the mid-eighteenth century." In this singular variation, however, Skinner creatively employed a large engraved panel stamp probably intended for leather pocketbooks, or the "Cartouch Boxes" advertised on his binder's ticket—many bookbinders were capable of fashioning a wide range of decorated leather goods. This copy also bears the contemporary signature of James Cahoone, possibly the Newport ship's captain or his son of the same name; whether Skinner bound it for himself, or possibly for Cahoone, is unclear.

Papantonio 6; Wing B6125.

BOOKS

TO BE SOLD BY

ISAIAH THOMAS

AT HIS BOOK-STORE

In *WORCESTER*, MASSACHUSETTS

Consisting of many celebrated Authors in

HISTORY,
VOYAGES,
TRAVELS,
GEOGRAPHY,
ANTIQUITIES,
PHILOSOPHY,
NOVELS,
MISCELLANIES,
DIVINITY,
PHYSICK,
SURGERY,
ANATOMY,

ARTS,
SCIENCES,
HUSBANDRY,
ARCHITECTURE,
NAVIGATION,
MATHEMATICKS,
LAW,
PERIODICAL PUBLI-
CATIONS,
POETRY,
PLAYS,
MUSICK, &c. &c.

Two Worcester Collectors

FIG. 26. Waldo Lincoln.

The American Antiquarian Society has been immensely fortunate in that many of its presidents have also been highly accomplished collectors and generous donors. Even if they may not have collected as assiduously as did the Society's founder and first president, Isaiah Thomas, they have embraced his vision of building at AAS the collection of early American printing, and of making that collection the centerpiece of the Society's many activities. This was particularly the case during Clarence S. Brigham's first two decades as the Society's librarian, when his acquisitions initiatives were staunchly supported by two succesive presidents, Waldo Lincoln and Charles Lemuel Nichols.

Waldo Lincoln (1849-1933) was born into one of the oldest and most prominent families of Worcester, Massachusetts. His great-grandfather, Levi Lincoln, capped a distinguished political career by serving as Attorney General of the United States during Thomas Jefferson's administration. His son, Levi, Jr., served as Massachusetts governor from 1825 to 1834 and later as vice president of AAS. His grandson, Waldo Lincoln, met the civic obligations and high expectations inherited from his forebears. In 1907, shortly after his retirement from active business and nine years after his election to membership, Lincoln assumed the presidency, an office he would hold for the next twenty years. Lincoln hired Clarence S. Brigham as librarian in 1908 and actively supported Brigham's expansion of the Society's collections. Under Lincoln's leadership, AAS moved into its present building in 1910 and celebrated its centennial in 1912. When a new stacks addition proved necessary, Lincoln raised the necessary funds for the 1924 addition.

Lincoln was closely engaged with the Society's activities, visiting the library almost daily when in Worcester. If there was no business to transact, then Lincoln occupied himself organizing collections, preparing a card index to a portion of the collection of maps and bringing some semblance of order to its diverse holdings of printed ephemera. Whether it was Clarence S. Brigham's idea that Lincoln should also collect, we do not know, but collect he did, in a highly focused way. Lincoln's primary interest was American cookbooks, a field which he essentially pioneered

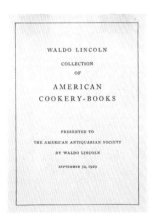

FIG. 27

FIG. 28. Charles L. Nichols.

FIG. 29

and then defined for future collectors. By 1929 Lincoln had built the best extant collection of pre-1900 American cookbooks, numbering some 860 volumes, which he donated to the Society. That same year the Society published Lincoln's *Bibliography of American Cookery Books, 1742-1860* which, in its present third edition, remains the standard guide. Lincoln's second chief collecting interest arose from his winter vacations to the Caribbean. Early West Indies imprints, especially newspapers, were highly desirable adjuncts to the Society's collection of early American imprints, as England's colonies in North America and the West Indies once maintained close ties. The newspapers Lincoln acquired and brought back to AAS, while relatively modest in number, now constitute one of the best such collections in the United States.

Lincoln retired as AAS president in 1927, and his successor was Charles Lemuel Nichols (1851-1929). In many respects Nichols and Lincoln were kindred spirits. Nichols's father was a prominent Worcester physician, and Charles followed suit, supplementing his highly regarded medical practice with leadership roles in many local institutions. And like Lincoln, Nichols found welcome diversion from his professional responsibilities in bibliographical pursuits. Elected a member in 1897, Nichols had already spent many hours in the Society's library, and much of his collecting was influenced by it. His holdings of New England almanacs were noteworthy, but Nichols's chief pride was his superb collection of early Worcester imprints, which he used to write his *Bibliography of Worcester* in 1899. As a Worcester resident and admirer of Isaiah Thomas, Nichols was naturally drawn to Worcester printing, but the hook was the discovery that the collection Thomas had presented to AAS of his own imprints contained significant gaps. These Nichols was mostly able to fill after thirty years of careful collecting. Nichols was particularly successful in acquiring many of the children's books published by Isaiah Thomas Sr. and Jr., imprints which Thomas apparently did not preserve. Because children's literature remained a specialty of nineteenth-century Worcester printers, Nichols soon found himself interested generally in early American juveniles—especially editions of Mother Goose—to AAS's considerable benefit.

CAT. 104. *The Royal Danish American Gazette*, 1776.

104. *The Royal Danish American Gazette.* Christiansted, St. Croix, Vol. VII, No. 911, September 11, 1776.

GIFT OF WALDO LINCOLN, 1926.

The Waldo Lincoln collection of eighteenth- and nineteenth-century West Indian newspapers numbers several thousand issues—many being the only known copies—and is one of the most important to be found anywhere.

The Royal Danish American Gazette was the first newspaper published in what is now the Virgin Islands. It was founded in 1770, when publisher Daniel Thibou relocated from St. Kitts to establish the first press on St. Croix. Portions were printed in Danish for the benefit of St. Croix's sizable Danish population. We know that it had a fairly wide circulation, for a number of its articles were reprinted in contemporary American newspapers. Scholars have recently taken renewed interest in the significance of the West Indies for early American history; but given the tropical climate, relatively few primary sources survive in West Indian libraries.

131

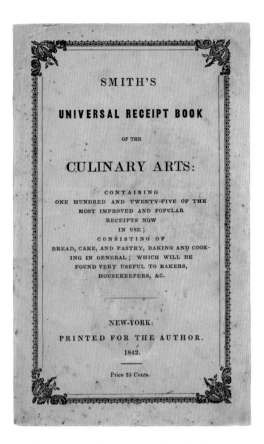

CAT. 105. Sidney Smith. *Smith's Universal Receipt Book of Culinary Arts*, 1842.

105-106. Sidney Smith. *Smith's Universal Receipt Book of Culinary Arts, Containing One Hundred and Twenty-five of the Most Improved and Popular Receipts Now in Use ...* New York, 1842, and Louise-Béate-Augustine Friedel. *The French Cook: A Full and Literal Translation of "La petite Cuisinière habile" ...* New York: Wm. H. Graham, 1846.

GIFT OF WALDO LINCOLN, 1929.

Waldo Lincoln collected American cookbooks with a single purpose in mind: to acquire only those which were not already owned by AAS. In 1929 he merged his holdings with the AAS collection. Lincoln's *Bibliography of American Cookery Books, 1742-1860*, was published by the Society that same year. The Society has since issued two revised editions, both compiled by Eleanor Lowenstein; the most recent (1972) expanded Lincoln's original listing to 835 editions, the vast majority now represented in AAS's pre-1877 American cookbook collection.

Lincoln's central focus was on finding unusual and unrecorded editions. These two examples, both in fine condition, were the only copies known in 1929, and Lincoln's copy of Sidney Smith's cookbook remains so today. Nothing is known of Smith other than his claim in the cookbook's introduction to having "an experience of twelve or fifteen years in the confectionary and culinary departments in the [United States's] most extensive and fastidious epicurean establishments." Friedel's popular *La petite Cuisinière habile* was first published in Paris in 1814; when reprinted in New Orleans in 1840, it became the first French cookbook to be published in the United States. *The French Cook* is an uncredited translation and one of several cookbooks from the 1840s that helped to introduce French cuisine and culinary methods to an American audience.

Lowenstein 289 & 380.

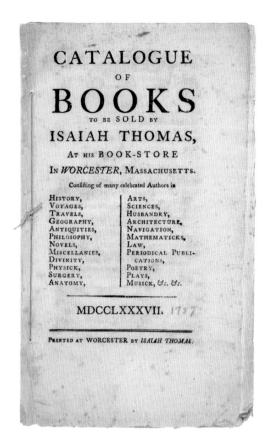

CAT. 107. Isaiah Thomas, *Catalogue of Books to be Sold,* 1787.

107. Isaiah Thomas. *Catalogue of Books to be Sold by Isaiah Thomas, at His Book-Store in Worcester ...* Worcester: Isaiah Thomas, 1787.

BEQUEST OF CHARLES LEMUEL NICHOLS, 1929.

In preparing his definitive bibliography of Worcester printing from 1775 to 1848, Charles L. Nichols discovered that the collection formed by Isaiah Thomas of his own imprints and later donated to AAS was significantly incomplete. Nichols henceforth set himself the task of filling the gaps, and thanks to his efforts, AAS now possesses a virtually complete collection of Thomas imprints.

One of Nichols's best finds was this pristine example—one of three known—of Isaiah Thomas's first published catalog. Following the close of the Revolution, Thomas rapidly developed his Worcester printing and bookselling business, obtaining substantial stocks of new type from England, expanding his retail stock and bindery, and venturing into children's and schoolbook publishing; he also established a local paper mill. This catalog briefly lists some 550 titles arranged under such subjects as "Divinity," "History, Miscellanies, &c.," "Novels, Sentimental Works, &c.," "Tragedies & Comedies," "Physick, Surgery &c.," "Dictionaries," "Classical and School Books," and "A very large Assortment of BOOKS, bound and gilt, with Cuts, suitable for CHILDREN." To these Thomas appended a full range of "Stationary," account books, bookbinding skins and gold leaf, and related supplies. The following year Thomas expanded his business still further, establishing in Boston the first of many partnerships he formed with printers and booksellers throughout New England.

Evans 20745; Winans 121.

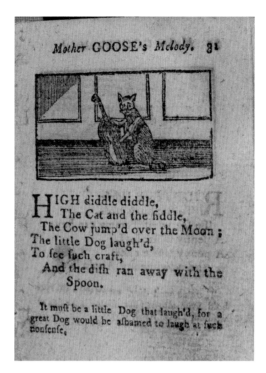

CAT. 109. *Mother Goose's Melody*, 1799.

108. Thomas White. *A Little Book for Little Children. Wherein Are Set Down Several Directions for Little Children. And Several Remarkable Stories Both Ancient and Modern, of Little Children.* Boston: Timothy Green for Nicholas Buttolph, 1702.

GIFT OF CHARLES LEMUEL NICHOLS, 1927.

This edition of Thomas White's *A Little Book for Little Children* is the second earliest American children's book containing religious biographical narratives, the earliest being James Janeway's *A Token for Children,* issued two years earlier (Cat. 36). Despite its innocuous title, *A Little Book for Little Children* is a grisly compilation of biographies of early religious martyrs, drawn partly from John Foxe's *Book of Martyrs.* Like *A Token for Children, A Little Book for Little Children* also contains brief biographies of several pious children who died young. Both were printed by Timothy Green (1679-1757), whose long career in Boston, and

later New London, Connecticut, is documented in the AAS collection by over 325 imprints. Given the somber subject matter and sophisticated text, this book was probably read more by older children and youth, as opposed to "little children." This copy, one of three so far recorded, contains the inscriptions of Elizabeth Jackson (1683-1772) and her brother Joshua Jackson (1696-1745) from Rowley, Massachusetts. *A Little Book for Little Children* is the earliest of the many eighteenth-century titles donated to AAS by Charles L. Nichols.

AAS Chief Joys 176; Evans 1056; Welch 1428.1.

109. *Mother Goose's Melody: or Sonnets for the Cradle ...* Third Worcester ed. Worcester: Isaiah Thomas, Jun., 1799.

GIFT OF CHARLES LEMUEL NICHOLS, 1927, AND CHARLES E. GOODSPEED, N.D.

Charles L. Nichols's interests in Isaiah Thomas imprints and in editions of Mother

Ride a cock horse
To Banbury cross
To see what Tommy can buy;
A penny white loaf,
A penny white cake,
And a two penny apple pie.

Ride away, ride away, Johnny shall ride,
And he shall have pussy-cat tied to one side;
And he shall have little dog tied to the other,
And Johnny shall ride to see his grandmother.

CAT. 110. *Mother Goose's Quarto*, ca. 1824-1827.

Goose is perfectly merged in this, the only known copy of the third Worcester edition. Both Isaiah Thomas and his son were well aware of the continuing market for Mother Goose nursery rhymes, and other publishers imitated their small picture book format well into the nineteenth century. Thomas's editions are noted for their plentiful woodcuts (one appears on nearly every page), uncluttered pages devoted to a single rhyme, and humorous commentaries. For example, the editor (possibly Thomas, Sr.) comments about the laughing dog in "High Diddle Diddle": "It must have been a little dog that laugh'd, for a great dog would be ashamed to laugh at such nonsense."

The unique AAS exemplar is actually a composite copy. In 1927 Charles L. Nichols presented to the Society an incomplete copy which he had purchased at the estate sale of Mother Goose bibliographer Henry Whitmore. This copy was sophisticated with leaves from another imperfect copy that had been donated by Boston bookseller Charles E. Goodspeed.

Evans 35847; Welch 905.3.

110. *Mother Goose's Quarto: or Melodies Complete.* Boston:

Munroe & Francis, ca. 1824-1827.

GIFT OF CHARLES LEMUEL NICHOLS, 1929.

This hand-colored copy is among the earliest (and handsomest) examples of the Munroe & Francis square-format editions of Mother Goose rhymes. Here Isaiah Thomas's picture book format is taken a step further by the insertion of three-quarter-page wood engravings. On the opposite page, the engraving of a man on horseback for "Ride a Cock Horse" dispenses with a border—the seamless transition between illustration and text essentially gives the entire page a more modern feel. The wood engravings were cut by Boston artists Abel Bowen (1790-1850), Nathaniel Dearborn (1786-1852), and Shubael D. Childs (fl. 1823-1835). Bowen in particular enjoyed a prolific career as an engraver, and AAS presently possesses no fewer than 570 imprints containing his wood engravings. Munroe & Francis, and later George W. Cottrell, continued to reprint this square-format edition of Mother Goose up to the Civil War.

1836:

Adapted to the latitude of the

CHOCTAW COUNTRY.

Hvtvk toksvli achukmma, icha in nan vlhpoba yoke.

Nitvk vt pi kvnihia takla 'ko
Nana achukma bieka
Ahnit, achunanchit eho hoyashke,
Chahta okla hvsh puta ma.

Westward Expansion

The American Antiquarian Society's location in Worcester, Massachusetts, and its particular emphasis at the time on pre-1821 American imprints, presented Clarence S. Brigham and his successors with some collecting challenges. Perhaps the most significant was one of balance. As the contents of New England libraries, attics, and barns were transferred to the Society through gift and purchase, the collection necessarily developed a strong New England flavor. But the nineteenth-century history of the United States was in large part the story of westward expansion. As the Society sought to improve its holdings through the year 1876, the collecting of imprints relating to the South, the Midwest, and the West emerged as a priority. Given its relatively modest acquisitions funding, AAS benefited greatly from generous donors to fill the library's various regional gaps. Thanks to Edward Larocque Tinker, for example, AAS now has strong holdings relating to nineteenth-century Louisiana (Cats. 92-96). More recently, through an innovative arrangement with noted Ohio collector and bibliographer Richard P. Morgan, the Society has formed an outstanding collection of pre-1851 Ohio imprints. As for westward expansion generally and the history of the far West, AAS can boast of exceptional holdings, thanks primarily to the generosity of two donors in particular: Donald McKay Frost and Thomas W. Streeter.

In his 1947 report to the membership, librarian Clifford K. Shipton remarked: "Much of next year I shall spend in processing and preparing the inventory of the great collection of Western Americana which [Donald McKay] Frost is giving to the Library. We have not been buying in this field, for it is our policy not to compete on the market in fields in which there is active collecting interest." While AAS did not have the funds to compete with the day's great Western Americana collectors for the rarities, it also did not need to, for it had known for some time that Frost's outstanding collection, already deposited at the Society, would remain there.

Born into a well-to-do Charleston, South Carolina, family, Donald McKay Frost (1877-1958) received his bachelor's and law degrees from Harvard before returning to Charleston to practice law. In 1912, however, ill health forced him to sever his local connections, return to the more salubrious New England climate, and join a Boston law firm. Professional success and an advantageous marriage enabled Frost to retire from active business in 1924, after which time he devoted himself to various social and cultural pursuits. Chief among these was book collecting. This interest apparently first manifested itself at Harvard, where he began to collect contemporary English authors. Shortly after World War I Frost's interests shifted decisively to Western Americana, perhaps because of the vacations he spent in the West. Boston was an ideal place for Frost to form a Western Americana collection, for he could, and did, rely heavily on Goodspeed's Book Shop and the formidable talents of its Americana specialist, Michael Walsh. Frost was in many ways the ideal customer: interested in collecting comprehensively, including later editions and secondary literature; possessed of considerable financial means and unafraid of paying

FIG. 30

high prices; a gentleman with impeccable manners, even upon learning that a choice item had been diverted to a rival collector; and a stickler for condition, willing to keep trading up until the best possible copy had been obtained. Frost was well able to hold his own against stiff competition from other major Western Americana collectors.

Frost once claimed to "enjoy everything about [books] except writing them," and although he left behind little written scholarship, he knew his collection intimately. Perhaps his favorite books were the classics of western exploration, which Frost would study each summer by retracing the explorers' steps out west, on foot and horseback. Although Frost and Clarence Brigham knew each other socially, it was not until 1938 that Frost took a real interest in AAS. Asking Brigham for help in researching a particular western expedition in the newspaper collection, Frost found that Brigham was most willing to assist. Brigham typically worked seven days a week, devoting weekends to personally helping his friends explore the collections and dealing with the booksellers who came with offers or to buy duplicates. Frost became a regular Saturday visitor and a member of the Society in 1939; shortly afterward he joined the Council. By 1936 Frost's library had grown so large that the ping pong room of his home was renovated to hold it. Six years later it seemed advisable to place the by then very valuable 4,000-volume collection—constituting fully sixty-five percent of the titles enumerated in the revised 1937 edition of Henry Raup Wagner's bibliography, *The Plains and the Rockies*—on deposit at AAS. During the later 1940s Frost began to donate it in stages, and on his death in 1958 he endowed a substantial acquisitions fund for its continued growth.

Frost's gifts came just as another collector, Thomas Winthrop Streeter, began to give portions of his own extraordinary library to AAS. The son and grandson of prominent New Hampshire lawyers, Streeter (1883-1965) attended Dartmouth and Harvard Law School before opening his own legal practice in Boston. In 1917 Streeter married, moving to New York City to pursue a broader business career. Streeter now found more time to indulge two personal interests acquired during his college days—American history and book collecting—the latter at first limited mostly to "after dinner" books suitable for showing to guests. Soon Streeter realized that a better course would be to combine the two interests, and he gradually resolved to focus his collecting on, in Lawrence Wroth's words, "'beginnings,' books relating to first explorations of [American] states and areas, first settlements, and cultural foundations in the form of first and significant issues of the press in the individual colonies or states." Westward expansion and Texas loomed particularly large among Streeter's collecting interests. Throughout the 1920s Streeter bought assiduously, forming a rare book collection of impressive scope and richness.

With the Depression, however, came financial reversals, and Streeter was soon forced to sell much of his colonial Americana (though eventually he was able to buy back a portion of it). Even if he could not then afford high spots, Streeter could still collect purposefully, and he wisely chose to acquire works documenting the nineteenth-century American transportation revolution. Early railroad and canal reports could be had cheaply, and before long Streeter had assembled a collection second in importance only to that at the New York Public Library. By 1937 Streeter's finances had improved to the point that he could resume collecting as he had in the 1920s, and the next dozen years would prove to be the key period in his library's formation.

FIG. 31

In 1939 a chief beneficiary was AAS, which Streeter first encountered in 1932 when librarian R.W.G. Vail requested his assistance with the Texas section of Joseph Sabin's *A Dictionary of Books Relating to America*. Much correspondence ensued with Vail, Clarence S. Brigham, and Clifford K. Shipton on a wide range of bibliographical topics. Streeter was promptly elected to AAS membership in 1933, and in 1942 he joined the Council. Also voluminous were the gifts Streeter began to send AAS's way. With his election to vice president in 1949, Streeter generously began to donate the bulk of his magnificent railroad and canal collection, including all of the pre-1841 material plus later imprints concerning southern New England railroads; the remainder was divided among several other institutions. The gifts continued during and after Streeter's term as AAS president (1952-1955), including more railroad material, many works concerning the settlement of Canada's western provinces, and the major part of his collection of separately printed Indian treaties.

During the 1950s and early 1960s Streeter continued to collect with an eye to filling gaps in his superlative Americana holdings, though his attention was increasingly turning to their ultimate disposition. The Texana which had served as the basis for his five-volume *Bibliography of Texas, 1795-1845* (1955-1960) had been sold to Yale in 1956, but Streeter was reluctant to part with the bulk of the library gracing his Morristown, New Jersey home. When death did come in 1965, Streeter's will revealed a carefully thought out plan along the lines of George Brinley's ninety years earlier. Directing that the collection was to be sold at auction, Streeter bequeathed a total of $414,000 to eighteen different institutions which, if they chose, could be spent at the forthcoming sales. Spend they did: the seven Streeter sales conducted by Parke-Bernet Galleries in New York from October 1966 to October 1969 raised $3,104,982 for 4,421 lots, electrifying the book world with its record-setting prices. AAS's generous share amounted to $78,000, which was entirely exhausted in purchasing 126 lots, mostly items concerning westward expansion in the second, third, and fourth sales. Much significant material too modest to sell individually still remained in Morristown, and the Streeter family permitted AAS to purchase on generous terms over 800 additional pieces, including a large collection of mid- and far-western railroad material. Also given to the Society was the massive eighty-seven-volume working catalog of Streeter's great library (Cat. 129).

CAT. 112. Henry James Warre, *Camp in the Mountains, July 24, 1845.*

111-112. Henry James Warre. *Breakfast, July 19, 1845, Our First View of the Rocky Mountains* and *Camp in the Mountains, July 24, 1845.* Both watercolor on paper, 1845.

GIFT OF DONALD MCKAY FROST, 1947.

Perhaps the most stunning of Donald McKay Frost's gifts to AAS was a remarkable set of eighty-six finished watercolors and pencil sketches made by British artist Henry James Warre in 1845 while exploring the Oregon Territory and its contested northern border with the British-held Columbia District. The ongoing border dispute came to a head in the early 1840s, with Britain proposing the Columbia River as the dividing line, and American expansionists calling for the annexation of all territory up to the Alaskan frontier: "54° 40' or Fight!" Worried about war, the British government sent Warre (1819-1898) and a small con-

tingent of British military engineers on a secret, fourteen-month mission to survey the region and sketch its topography should military action be needed. The dispute was peacefully resolved in 1846, when the Oregon Treaty established a compromise border along the 49th parallel.

Warre's sketches show Native American villages, open landscape, snow-covered mountains, and river scenes. They are often annotated with information about mountain passes, river fords, and safe places to camp. On July 19, 1845, the expedition first sighted the Rocky Mountains, and Warre recorded the event at sunrise by sketching a vista of the distant peaks. Many of the finished watercolors were later reproduced as hand-colored lithographs in Warre's *Sketches in North America and the Oregon Territory* (London, 1848), one of the great illustrated books depicting the American West. Donald McKay Frost's donation to AAS included a fine copy of the published book in addition to Warre's watercolors.

113. **American Society for Encouraging the Settlement of the Oregon Territory.** *A General Circular to All Persons of Good Character, Who Wish to Emigrate to the Oregon Territory* **Charlestown, Massachusetts: William W. Wheildon, R.P. & C. Williams, 1831.**

GIFT OF DONALD MCKAY FROST, 1947.

Donald McKay Frost's gifts to AAS included many key works concerning the settlement of Oregon, among them this pamphlet authored by Hall J. Kelley. A graduate of Middlebury College, Kelley (1790-1874) settled in Boston, where he taught school and authored several popular textbooks. By the mid-1820s Kelley's interests had shifted to the Oregon Territory, which he had not seen but was determined to settle and Christianize. In 1829 Kelley founded the American Society for Encouraging the Settlement of the Oregon Territory, redoubling his efforts to seek public and private support for Oregon settlement.

A General Circular marked the apogee of Kelley's campaign. Subtitled "Manual of the Oregon Expedition," it outlined Kelley's plans for recruiting settlers to undertake a transcontinental journey in 1832 and to sell $200,000 worth of stock in the enterprise. In addition to extolling Oregon's climate and resources, delineating the overland route, and sketching plans for settlements and civil government, Kelley offered his readers a rationale for seizing Indian lands. Approximately 500 prospective settlers invested $20 each in the enterprise, for which they received a certificate entitling them to Oregon land after occupying and improving it for two years. Together with *A General Circular,* Frost gave AAS an unused booklet of twenty-five land certificates, that could be purchased from the agents whose names are listed facing the pamphlet's title page. Kelley was forced to abandon the expedition, though some of his recruits did make the Oregon trek.

American Imprints 5722; Wagner-Camp 44a.

114. **James Harvey Barnum.** *The Traveller's Guide, or, the Life of James H. Barnum.* **Great Barrington, Massachusetts: James H. Barnum, 1847.**

GIFT OF DONALD MCKAY FROST, 1948.

Barnum's *Traveller's Guide* is perhaps the rarest and least known of the many western overland narratives presented to AAS by Donald McKay Frost. Born in Danbury, Connecticut, in 1788, Barnum left home at the age of thirteen, travelling the globe as a "sea-faring man" for thirty-two years and spending most of a dozen more exploring the North American continent. In 1845, now rooted to the soil of Sheffield, Massachusetts, as laborer and sawyer, Barnum sat down to write his autobiography, self-published in nearby Great Barrington two years later in fifty-two densely printed pages. This copy in original printed wrappers may be the finest of the five or six known.

Barnum's adventures included merchant and whaling voyages on most of the seven seas, "one year and eight months" as captive on board a pirate ship prowling the Indian Ocean, distinguished naval service on Lake Erie during the War of 1812 (the longest and most detailed section), and extensive land forays in Africa and South America. Interspersed are accounts of several years spent in northern Ohio, followed by hunting and trapping expeditions in the west and down to New Orleans before Barnum again went to sea. Although Barnum claims to have "travelled from Boston to Oregon, by land," the section on his trans-Mississippi adventures is suspiciously short and vague.

Wagner-Camp 126.

115. **Zenas Leonard.** *Narrative of the Adventures of Zenas Leonard ... Who Spent Five Years in Trapping for Furs, Trading with the Indians ...*

Clearfield, Pennsylvania: D.W. Moore, 1839.

GIFT OF DONALD MCKAY FROST, 1948.

From Donald McKay Frost AAS received fine copies of many great rarities of Western Americana, including Zenas Leonard's *Narrative*. Born and raised in Clearfield, Pennsylvania, Leonard left the family farm in 1830 at age twenty, soon securing a position as clerk to a trans Mississippi fur trapping and trading expedition. Leonard eked out a trapper's living until, in 1833, he joined the exploring party of Captain Joseph Bonneville. Leonard was among those selected to accompany scout Joseph Walker on an expedition seeking an overland route from the Great Salt Lake to California. After many travails, the group successfully crossed the Sierra Nevada, wending its way through Yosemite—they were perhaps the first white men to see it—before arriving safely in Monterey. Their route became the famous California Trail which was later followed by thousands of westward-bound pioneers. Leonard continued to roam through much of the northwest before returning to Clearfield in 1835.

Leonard's vivid stories of trapping, trading, Indian customs, and western landscapes proved so popular locally that he was compelled to write them down. Initially serialized in the *Clearfield Pioneer & Banner,* Leonard's account attracted so many new subscribers that the newspaper's publisher reissued as it a book. Today it remains a highly important, and very rare, primary document of Western exploration.

AAS Chief Joys 121; American Imprints 56805; Wagner-Camp 75.

116. John Ross Dix. *Amusing and Thrilling Adventures of a California Artist, while Daguerreotyping a Continent ...* Boston: Geo. K. Snow for John Ross Dix, 1854.

GIFT OF DONALD MCKAY FROST, 1947.

Following the 1848 discovery of gold in California, Easterners who resisted the gold bug were nonetheless intensely interested in what was transpiring 3,000 miles to the west. This rare pamphlet documents an enterprising attempt to satisfy that curiosity: the giant "Pantoscope" of John Wesley Jones. An Illinois lawyer, Jones made his way overland to California in 1850, where he conceived an ambitious scheme to prepare a giant panoramic painting of California's gold fields and boom towns—soon expanded to feature the entire western landscape. Jones engaged a team of artists and daguerreotypists, whose sketches and 1,500 photographs (none seem to have survived) would lend the painting an unrivalled verisimilitude. After documenting California, Jones's team braved the elements and Indians on the trek eastward, becoming the first to have "ever Daguerreotyped a herd of Buffalo on their native Plains."

Back in Massachusetts, Jones supervised the painting of his "Pantoscope," a rolling panorama measuring ten feet high and over a thousand feet long. From 1852 to 1854 the panorama toured the northeast before appreciative paying audiences, who watched the canvas unroll while listening to "appropriate music" and Jones's lively narration. This souvenir program contains breathless accounts of the dangers Jones's party faced out west, glowing newspaper testimonials, and poetry evocative of the scenes depicted. Its compiler was "John Ross Dix," the pen name of expatriate English journalist George Spencer Phillips.

Wagner-Camp 240.

117. *Frontier Scout.* Fort Rice, Dakota Territory, June 15, 1865.

GIFT OF DONALD MCKAY FROST, 1947.

Thanks to Donald McKay Frost, AAS owns a complete run of the second newspaper printed in the Dakota Territory, preceded only by a paper of the same title issued at Fort Union the previous summer. Located in south central North Dakota, Fort Rice was a 500-foot square wooden stockade erected in the summer of 1864 to protect vital transportation routes from increasingly frequent Lakota attacks. Initially it was manned by "galvanized Yan-

FRONTIER SCOUT.

Capt. E. G. Adams, Editor. LIBERTY AND UNION. Lieut. C. H. Champney, Publisher.

Vol. 1. FORT RICE, D. T., JUNE 15, 1865. No. 1.

For the Frontier Scout.

ABRAHAM LINCOLN.

BY CAPTAIN E. G. ADAMS.

Chief of our country's glory,
  Thy death her greatest shame,
Forever live in story,
  A proud historic name!

Talk not of ages olden—
  Of deeds in old time done;
But talk in this age, the golden,
  Of the peer of Washington.

He was the last great martyr
  That sealed with blood his trust;
For gold I would not barter
  The least grain of his dust.

In the triumph hour of glory
  Our Country's Father died:
And shameful was the story,
  As of Christ, the Crucified.

When the bays upon his forehead
  Were budding into leaves,—
Slain by a death as horrid
  As torture 'twixt two thieves.

The nation reeled to stagger,
  In a paroxysm of grief;
When the foul assassin's dagger
  Was shaken o'er our Chief.

And the voice of lamentations
  Went out throughout all lands,
Like a Niobe of nations
  Stricken Columbia stands!

From every tower and steeple
  The knell of sorrow rings,
And wails the mighty people
  Like a harp with million strings.

He has vanished from our vision,
  And with Elias talks;
In the fields of Life, elysian,
  With the throng redeemed he walks.

His clay-cold brow is altar
  Where we lay our hands and swear
That we will never falter
  To true allegiance bear.

From the home of thy perfections
  Look down upon our clime,
And behold in our affections
  Thy monument sublime.

PEACE!—The storm has spent itself in fury. The last shaft of lightning killed our Chief Magistrate. The world reeled a moment, and all was over. The clouds broke, and rolled magnificently away, showing the clear celestial blue. 'Twas like the rending of the veil when the great Messiah died. Across the weeping Heavens the bow of everlasting peace spreads itself like the wings of an angel. All hail thou dawn of the Golden Age!

For the Frontier Scout.

"Alone—All Alone."

A few years since, while a student in the venerable old "Harvard," a favorite place of resort for me was the quiet grounds of Mount Auburn,—the city of the dead, at Cambridge, Massachusetts.

One lovely summer evening, feeling more blue than usual, I quietly strolled within this sacred enclosure to seek retirement from the busy scenes of active life, and indulge in a student's dyspeptic reflections.

The cool evening breeze bore on it the fragrance of a thousand flowers,—the little artificial fountains, constantly playing, kept time to the vesper songs of the many feathered minstrels, who find their sweet homes amid the verdant foliage, which over-hangs the last resting place of loved ones.

The sun had just sunk behind the western hills, the moon—fair queen of night—was gilding with her silvery light the tombstones which tell to the passing stranger the brief history of the sleeping one.

Taking my seat by the side of one of these tombstones, and drawing forth my memorandum book, I commenced to note down some of the inscriptions on the surrounding monuments. These furnished food for reflections, and half an hour had passed, when I was startled from my dreamy meditations by the words, "ALONE—ALL ALONE," uttered in a sad but musical tone. I turned towards the spot from whence came the voice, and saw, a short distance from me, at the foot of a monument, a middle aged woman, attired in deep mourning, kneeling over a freshly made grave. She was evidently paying her tokens of love for some near and dear one who had recently been torn from her by the ruthless hand of death. My interest and sympathies were enlisted, and silently I watched the stricken mourner, seeking to read the history of the bereavement by the monument and inscriptions upon it.

It was a plain marble shaft, surmounted by a silver harp, on which were strung five golden cords. Two of these were large—the other three were small. One large cord had been broken, as also had two of the smaller ones. A moment's reflection told me their significance. This silver harp was an emblem of the family circle; the golden cords wore the living members of that once happy home. The severed ones indicated the ravages of death. Two, only, now remained unbroken—a large and small one—parent and child. The family harp, whose cords once vibrated in sweet harmony, had been roughly swept by the icy hand of Death, and at his chill touch, one by one, the strands had broken, till now, all but two had ceased to give forth their melody.

"Alone—all alone," sobbed the woman, and raising her hand to the emblematic harp, she broke the other little cord, and with the act came fresh bursts of grief. "Another cord is sundered," she sobbed, "only one more left. Oh! God, may that soon be broken, that our harp may be strung anew in heaven!"

Silently I stole away, for I felt that such sorrow was too sacred to be interrupted; but the memory of that scene can never be erased from my mind. "Alone—all alone" has a thousand times since in imagination fell upon my ear, and I seem again to see that lone mother kneeling over the new made grave of her darling child, whom she had just laid beside her husband and other two little angels, and listen to her broken-hearted sobs.

"Alone—all alone." Reader, did you ever realize the full meaning of those words? Did you ever feel hovering around you the gloomy clouds of desolation, till over your heart came stealing the chilling realization that the ones you cherished most dearly were gone forever from your fireside, and that you were left "alone—all alone." MEDICUS.

The First U. S. Vols. Receiving the Stars and Stripes.

It was on the 4th, of June 1864 at Norfolk, Va., the Regiment was to receive the Stars and Stripes. Every man had been laboring with great care to put his musket, equipments and clothes in the best condition. Each one prepared himself as for a wedding feast. The Regiment was to be married by the most solemn compact to the United States' service. Genl. Shepley had come with his staff, and addressed them with deep feeling, a hollow square was formed, and Col. Dimon replied in behalf of the Regiment. Nature smiled beautifully on the scene, the air was redolent with perfume, the sky was clear and blue as that of Italy, and the circle of the landscape seemed like a vast amphitheatre for some glorious display of patriotism. When their youthful Colonel turned to his Regiment to confirm his promises of their unswerving allegiance to that flag that fluttered so beautifully in the breeze of summer, every man fell on his knees, as if by instinct, and so was the solemn compact confirmed.

I had seen many beautiful sights, but nothing that could parallel this. The tears gushed from my eyes, and to my mind it was a glorious premonition of the time that has at length arrived. Happy Regiment! choosing the good part, like Mary of old.

CAT. 117. *Frontier Scout*, 1865.

CAT. 119. Broadside advertisement for *The Vigilantes of Montana*, 1866.

kees"—former Confederate prisoners of war who had enlisted in the Union Army rather than wait indefinitely in prison camps for parole or exchange.

In order to ward off the stress of isolated frontier living, the soldiers engaged in various diversions, including theatrical performances and the publication of their own newspaper printed on a portable press. Captain E. G. Adams and Lieutenant C. H. Champney of the First United States Volunteer Infantry Regiment served as editor and publisher respectively. In this inaugural issue, Adams encouraged the troops to contribute poems, stories, and adventures. "When this is done our paper is formed, a living, speaking, embodiment of the society in which we dwell." The last of the fifteen weekly issues appeared on Oct. 12, 1865, shortly before Adams and Champney left the fort. Most issues were printed on sheets of ruled blue ledger paper.

AAS Chief Joys 110.

118-119. Thomas J. Dimsdale. *The Vigilantes of Montana, or Popular Justice in the Rocky Mountains ...* Virginia City, Montana Territory: Montana Post Press, D.W. Tilton & Co., 1866, with advertising broadside: *Now Completed and for Sale! An Impartial and Correct History of The Vigilantes of Montana Territory! ...* D.W. Tilton & Co., 1866.

GIFT OF DONALD MCKAY FROST, 1947.

Among Donald McKay Frost's many gifts to AAS were two of the earliest Montana imprints. One was a copy of Thomas J. Dimsdale's classic, and very rare, account of life and lawlessness in Montana's frontier towns, and of the vigilantes who cleaned them up. After gold was discovered in southwestern Montana Territory in 1862, thousands of prospectors quickly descended on the boom towns of Bannack and Virginia City. Also seizing opportunity was

Henry Plummer who, upon being elected Bannack's sheriff, deputized his criminal cronies as "road agents" with carte blanche to rob and murder as they pleased. In December 1863, a group of Montanans secretly formed a vigilance committee and, within two months, captured and summarily executed Plummer and two dozen of his desperadoes.

Dimsdale's lively and vivid narrative was initially serialized in part in Virginia City's weekly newspaper, the *Montana Post*. Shortly after Dimsdale's untimely death, *Montana Post* publisher D.W. Tilton reissued the work in book form. Facing the title page is a full-page advertisement showcasing Tilton's job printing business. The spectacular, and very rare, broadside which Tilton printed to advertise Dimsdale's book—printed in red and blue employing thirteen different wood and metal typefaces—demonstrates that his shop was indeed capable of "all kinds of fancy and ornamental printing." The quality of Tilton's printing even received a contemporary mention in the *New York Times*: "Some of their job-work in colors would be creditable to any office." Fittingly for a gold rush town, copies of *The Vigilantes of Montana* were priced at $2.25 in "Greenbacks" or discounted to $2.00 if purchased with gold dust.

120. Madison, Indianapolis, and Lafayette Rail-Road Company. *An Act to Incorporate the Madison, Indianapolis and Lafayette Rail-Road Company, Passed ... February 2, 1832.* Madison, Indiana: Arion & Lodge, 1832.

GIFT OF THOMAS W. STREETER, 1950.

An avid collector of rare Americana during the 1920s, Thomas W. Streeter was forced to part with much of his collection following the 1929 stock market crash. He soon rebounded by embarking on a new, relatively untraveled, and inexpensive collecting field: publications documenting the early nineteenth-century canals and railroads whose construction launched a transportation revolution. By 1950, when Streeter resolved to give it away, his collection of pre-1841 canal and railroad material was the best in private hands. The bulk of it was donated to AAS, which Streeter was then serving as a vice president; smaller portions went to Dartmouth College, the University of Virginia, and several other institutions. Once merged with AAS's own mid-nineteenth-century holdings, the combined Streeter-AAS collection became perhaps the best in existence.

Streeter's gift was notable for its comprehensiveness and for its many rarities. This modest pamphlet, for example—one of two recorded copies—is the earliest Indiana imprint devoted to railroads. In 1832, Madison, Indiana, was a bustling Ohio River port and major entry point for settlers moving northward. A group of Madison businessmen secured from the state legislature this charter for Indiana's first railroad, intended to link Madison, Indianapolis, and Lafayette.

American Imprints 13514.

121. Knox & M'Kee. *Transportation to the West. Wheeling, May 20, 1834 ...* Wheeling, West Virginia: Times Press, 1834.

GIFT OF THOMAS W. STREETER, CA. 1955.

In 1955, during his last year as AAS president, Thomas W. Streeter augmented the 1950 gift of his railroad collection with nearly 200 additional imprints relating to American transportation. Among them was this small handbill promoting the use of Wheeling, [West] Virginia as a transportation hub. Wheeling's population then numbered fewer than 8,000 people, but its Ohio River location offered an easy connection between the large urban centers of the east and such western boom towns as Cincinnati and Nashville. Here agents Knox & M'Kee outline in detail the advantages of using their shipping route between Baltimore and Wheeling; the 300 miles could be covered either in ten days by two daily wagon lines affiliated with the Baltimore & Ohio Railroad, or in fourteen to sixteen days by private wagon companies. From Wheeling, goods would be forwarded by steamboat to "the interior" at Cincinnati, Louisville, Nashville, and St. Louis. Details of insurance are given down to the half cent, and it is advised that packages should be "strongly strapped or coopered and legibly marked with the owner's and consignee's name."

122. *Indignation Meeting! Down with All Monopolies! ...* Wooster, Ohio: 1853.

GIFT OF THOMAS W. STREETER, CA. 1955.

This broadside announces a meeting called by a group of outraged wheat farmers and grain wholesalers of Wayne County, Ohio. The board of directors of the Ohio and Pennsylvania Rail-Road Company had given to one of its members, Zadok Street, exclusive use of all rail cars in Wooster, Ohio. Street apparently locked out local growers and moved his own wheat to and through Wooster by rail, causing grain prices to drop and pricing local farmers, now obliged to move their crops by wagon, out of the market. It was resolved at the meeting that the company's action was "unfair and unjust to the citizens of this county, who gave their means to build this road and it justly merits their disapprobation and indignation." The conflict filled the pages of Ohio newspapers through much of the summer, with accusations coming from both sides. After hints of libel were raised and countered with talk of free speech, one farmer wrote to the local paper, "We spoke fearlessly and independently, and have not one word to retract. If they treat us gentlemanly, we will do the same in return—but if they undertake to swindle, we have the privilege and satisfaction to let the public know it." Due to their very ephemeral nature—they were printed on inexpensive paper and were intended to be posted out of doors for public reading—broadsides like this are rare survivors of the historical record.

123. *Holisso hushi holhtena isht anoli. Chahta Almanac for the Year of Our Lord 1836: Adapted to the Latitude of the Choctaw Country.* Union, Oklahoma: Mission Press, John

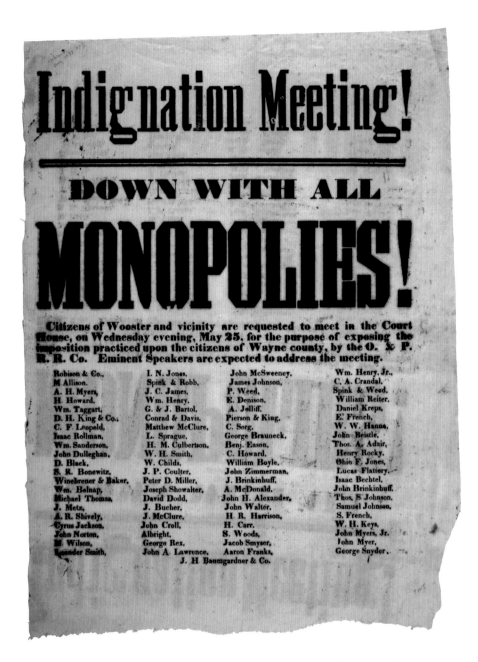

CAT. 122. *Indignation Meeting!* 1853.

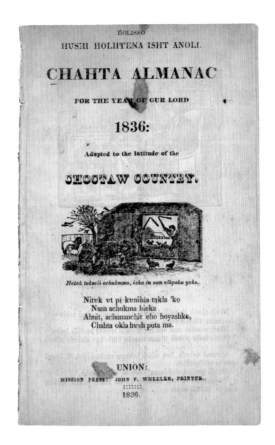

CAT. 123. *Chahta Almanac*, 1836.

Mission Press, John F. Wheeler, 1836.

GIFT OF THOMAS W. STREETER, BEFORE 1960.

During his thirty-two years of AAS membership, Thomas W. Streeter proved to be a constant and generous donor, greatly enriching the collections in numerous ways. To AAS's large collection of early American almanacs, for example, Streeter gave one of the earliest known Oklahoma imprints: this unique copy of the first Oklahoma almanac.

Printing arrived in what is now Oklahoma in late 1835, following the Cherokee removal. In 1828, with the assistance of missionary Samuel Worcester, John F. Wheeler established a press at New Echota, Georgia, where he printed the *Cherokee Phoenix* newspaper and

other imprints set in Sequoyah's Cherokee syllabary, many of which are at AAS. After the press's seizure by Georgia authorities in 1835, Wheeler followed Worcester westward to the new Indian Territory established for members of the displaced Five Civilized Tribes. There Wheeler opened a new press at the Union Mission, where he issued publications in Creek, Cherokee, and Choctaw. Among these was this almanac, which was based on New England models. It was edited and translated by the Rev. Loring S. Williams.

Drake 9406.

124. David Rice. *A Lecture on the Divine Decrees, to Which is Annexed a Few Observations on a Piece Lately Printed in*

Lexington ... Lexington, Kentucky: John Bradford, 1791.

PURCHASED WITH FUNDS BEQUEATHED BY THOMAS W. STREETER, 1967.

At the Thomas W. Streeter auction sales, AAS used Streeter bequest funds to acquire David Rice's *A Lecture on the Divine Decrees*, one of three known copies of the earliest extant book printed in Kentucky. Several earlier imprints were advertised in contemporary newspapers, and the title page of Rice's *Lecture* notes another, but no copies of these have been located.

Printing began in Kentucky nearly four years earlier, when John and Fielding Bradford established a press in Lexington. Setting up shop in a log cabin, with equipment obtained from Philadelphia, the Bradfords began to publish the *Kentucke Gazette* on August 11, 1787 (AAS holds a good run of the paper). Special sorts, relief blocks, and large display types were cut as needed from local dogwood—the unusual rough-edged title-page ornament may well be one of these homespun wood types. This copy was formerly bound in a tract volume with the old (but not original) blue wrappers added after disbinding. Rice (1733-1816) was a prominent Presbyterian minister whose unpopular antislavery views prompted his removal from Virginia to frontier Kentucky.

AAS Chief Joys 69; Shipton & Mooney 46273; Streeter Sale III, 1624.

125. Northwest Territory. *Laws of the Territory of the United States North-West of the Ohio* ... Cincinnati: W. Maxwell, 1796.

PURCHASED WITH FUNDS BEQUEATHED BY THOMAS W. STREETER, 1967.

The most expensive AAS purchase at the Streeter sales, acquired after spirited bidding, was this copy of the first book printed in Ohio, then part of the Northwest Territory. Often referred to as the "Maxwell Code" after its printer, William Maxwell, it was issued in an edition of 1,000 copies. However, of the twenty-odd copies known to survive, only five (including this one) are perfect. Today this copy is an important part of AAS's outstanding collection of pre-1851 Ohio imprints.

Directed by Congress to draft a civil and criminal code for the Northwest Territory, then rapidly gaining new settlers, Governor Arthur St. Clair and the Territory's two judges expedited their work by selecting thirty-seven laws from the Massachusetts, New York, Pennsylvania, and Virginia state codes. William Maxwell was charged with printing these, together with the text of the Northwest Ordinance, in July 1795. Printing this 225-page quarto volume in between his newspaper and jobbing work took Maxwell a good seven months, the typesetting and presswork clearly revealing its frontier origins.

Evans 30916; Streeter Sale III, 1319

126. Florida General Assembly (1817-1818). *Report of the Committee Appointed to Frame the Plan of Provisional Government for the Republic of Floridas* ... Fernandina, Florida: R. Findley, December 9, 1817.

PURCHASED WITH FUNDS BEQUEATHED BY THOMAS W. STREETER, 1967.

At the second Streeter sale, AAS acquired a rare copy of the third earliest Florida imprint. From 1783 to 1784, Loyalist refugees briefly operated a printing press in St. Augustine until Britain ceded Florida to Spain. This 1817 report is the only known specimen of printing made in Florida between 1784 and 1821. The Fernandina press, on Amelia Island, probably existed for less than a month; apparently it also issued a newspaper, *El Telegrafo de las Floridas*, though no copies survive. In 1817 the British adventurer Gregor MacGregor and a band of American filibusters took over Amelia Island, only to lose control to the French adventurer Luis-Michel Aury and his band of Haitian mercenaries. Aury first planted the Mexican flag, then permitted the largely American population to form a "Republic of Floridas"—the *Report* prints the text of its proposed constitution. Prompted by Aury's privateering, smuggling, and open slave trading, as well as the threat of a Mexican foothold in Florida, a naval squadron seized Amelia Island for the United States in late December 1817. Streeter acquired this fine copy from A.S.W. Rosenbach in 1939.

Shaw & Shoemaker 40836; Streeter Sale II, 1198.

127. José Mariano Romero. *Catecismo de Ortologia. Dedicado á los Alumnos de la Escuela normal de Monterrey.* Monterey, California: Agust. V. Zamorano, 1836.

PURCHASED WITH FUNDS BEQUEATHED BY THOMAS W. STREETER, 1968.

This extremely rare Spanish language text, of which only two copies are known, is a landmark in the history of early California printing. The text is a series of questions and answers covering the alphabet, vowels, consonants, diphthongs, basic punctuation, and a brief lesson about numerals. Agustín Juan Vicente Zamorano (1798-1842) was a Mexican government official and the first printer active in colonial California. He was printing letterheads from woodblocks as early as 1826. Zamorano began printing with movable type in 1830, but his commercial printing venture truly started in June, 1834, when a printing press and type arrived on the Boston-based ship *Lagoda*. Zamorano produced at least twenty-one imprints, ten of which were broadsides. The *Catecismo* is just one of four book-length Zamorano imprints; among them is another text prepared for the normal school in Monterey: a book of arithmetic tables titled *Tablas para los Niños que Empiezan a Contar* (1836). Thomas W. Streeter obtained this copy from the great Western Americana collector and bibliographer Henry Raup Wagner.

Streeter Sale IV, 2484; Suzuki & Pulliam 28.

128. *Denver City and Auraria, the Commercial Emporium of the*

Pike's Peak Gold Regions, in 1859. Possibly St. Louis, 1860.

PURCHASED WITH FUNDS BEQUEATHED BY THOMAS W. STREETER, 1968.

Also acquired with the Streeter gift was this key piece—the first Denver directory—for the Society's collection of early American city directories. Denver was founded in 1858, in what was then Kansas Territory, after gold was found nearby. The early boom soon was transformed into a full-fledged stampede, reminiscent of California in 1849, when major gold deposits were discovered in 1859. Within two years the newly created Colorado Territory boasted some 100,000 settlers.

This very rare directory contains a brief history and description of Denver and the adjacent settlements of Auraria and Highland, followed by a "List of Business Men," arranged by occupation, and fifteen pages of advertisements for local businesses. At front is a two-page lithographed plan of the city and a full-page wood-engraved view of Denver (which is more impressionistic than accurate). Both the plan and the view were the work of St. Louis artists; indeed, this directory was most likely printed there. Most of the few known copies end at page 44, but the fine Streeter copy in original wrappers contains an additional thirty-two pages of advertisements and promotional text for St. Louis, St. Joseph, Missouri, and Elwood, Kansas—all stops along the route to Colorado.

AAS Chief Joys 134; Spear p. 118; Streeter Sale IV, 2137; Wagner-Camp 355.

129. Thomas W. Streeter. "Catalogue of the American Library of Thomas W. Streeter." Volume 3 (of 87), ca. 1941-1965.

BEQUEST OF THOMAS W. STREETER, 1970.

Thomas W. Streeter was not simply a collector, but a bibliographer and scholar who was thoroughly familiar with the treasures collected for his library. With the assistance of his

CHICAGO, BURLINGTON AND QUINCY RAILROAD.

THE
Shortest and most Direct Route

From CHICAGO, MILWAUKEE, DETROIT, TOLEDO, CLEVE-
LAND, BUFFALO, and the NORTH, EAST and WEST generally,
to BURLINGTON, PEORIA, GALESBURG, QUINCY; and
from all points in Western and Central ILLINOIS, to IOWA, MIS-
SOURI, KANSAS, and NEBRASKA, and all points in the

PIKE'S PEAK GOLD REGIONS.

Close connection with the HANNIBAL AND ST. JOSEPH RAILROAD,
and GREAT OVERLAND EXPRESS to DENVER CITY, AURARIA,
SALT LAKE CITY, and CALIFORNIA.

CAT. 128. Advertisement in *Denver City and Auraria*, 1860.

private librarians, Streeter recorded his knowledge in an extensive series of loose-leaf volumes, numbering eighty-seven at the time of his death in 1965. Described were 4,848 books, pamphlets, broadsides, newspapers, and maps arranged per a complex geographical, chronological, and subject classification. Not included were the collections Streeter had given or sold before his death, such as the bulk of his railroad and Texas materials, as well as thousands of lesser items. The original catalog was bequeathed to AAS, while a carbon copy—heavily used by Parke-Bernet Galleries staff in preparing the seven-volume Streeter sale auction catalog—is now at the New-York Historical Society.

Shown here is part of Streeter's entry for the 1649 Cambridge Platform, which sold for $80,000—the auction's highest realization—at the second Streeter sale in April 1967. The penciled notes provide details of acquisition, provenance, location of other copies, its shelving location within Streeter's library, and the 1955 appraisal valuation determined by Michael J. Walsh of Goodspeed's Book Shop. On the preceding recto is a full title-page transcription, collation, physical description, and references; following is Streeter's three-page typescript essay on the work's significance. Many of Streeter's essays bear his extensive manuscript revisions—at some point these would be replaced by retyped versions. Also included are clippings from booksellers' catalogs, related correspondence, and other information.

JOHNSON's BOOK STORE

Children's Book Collecting

The AAS children's literature collection is not merely a gathering of attractive milestones. It certainly has them, as evidenced by the books selected for this exhibition. But the children's literature collection, now numbering over 24,000 titles, is more appropriately described as a comprehensive—indeed, the best—collection of books and pamphlets published for children and youth in British North America and the United States from the seventeenth century through 1876. (McLoughlin Bros. picture books, which AAS actively collects through the year 1899, are the one notable exception to this chronological endpoint.) This constantly growing collection is also thoroughly catalogued, enabling researchers to discover relevant titles on the widest possible range of topics, including, for example, diet, disease, religion, gender role, race relations, temperance, debt, child abuse, and play.

Although Isaiah Thomas printed many books for children, by the time of Clarence S. Brigham's arrival in 1908 the only examples to be found at AAS were the handsomely bound volumes of the *Youth's Library* from Thomas's personal collection. Thanks to Brigham's vision and tenacity, the AAS children's literature collection was transformed from an odd assortment of juveniles and school books—many of them donated by their authors and publishers—into a world-class collection of great depth and research value. Aiding Brigham in his quest for children's books were a number of dedicated and astute collectors, including Wilbur Macey Stone, Charles Lemuel Nichols (Cats. 107-110), d'Alté A. Welch, Ruth Adomeit, Elisabeth Ball, and Herbert Hosmer. Brigham was also ably assisted by many booksellers, in particular the bookman Benjamin Tighe.

FIG. 32

Wilbur Macey Stone (1862-1941) was among the earliest American collectors to build a substantial library of eighteenth- and nineteenth-century American and English children's literature. A successful New York patent attorney and mechanical engineer, he was also a scholar and bookplate designer. Stone's relationship with AAS began in 1912, when he inquired whether it held any copies of Isaac Watts's influential children's hymnal, *Divine Songs*. Brigham promptly responded with a list of the fourteen editions printed between 1773 and 1845 then at the Society. In characteristic fashion, Brigham ended his letter with a request: "In case you bring out any printed material upon the subject, I should be happy to be informed of it." Thus began a fruitful collaboration between the two men that lasted until Stone's death. Stone peppered AAS staff with queries about how to date Isaiah Thomas's mostly undated children's chapbooks, which Brigham enlisted the aid of AAS member and resident Thomas expert Charles Lemuel Nichols in answering. Before long, Stone and Brigham were exchanging duplicate children's books and encouraging each other's collecting. Taking added inspiration from the many illustrated materials, including children's books, then being donated by Charles Henry Taylor (Cats. 53-65, 74-75), Brigham began to develop the children's literature collection as a major resource in its own right.

By the time of his election to membership in 1931, Stone was making regular research trips to AAS. He wrote to Brigham after one such visit, "It is always a great pleasure to sit in with you and talk about old juveniles etc. It is also very pleasing to me to see the Antiq. Soc. so very much alive." The fruits of Stone's research included *The Divine and Moral Songs of Isaac Watts* (1918), a comprehensive bibliography of the many English and American editions of Watts's masterwork. Upon his death in 1941, Stone bequeathed his outstanding collection of *Divine Songs* editions to AAS. In contrast to the fourteen editions owned in 1912, a century later the Society can boast of possessing over 200 editions issued between 1730 and 1876, thanks in no small part to Stone's generosity.

FIG. 33

No doubt inspired by Stone, Brigham started to hunt assiduously for Isaiah Thomas chapbooks that could be brought "home" to AAS. Toward that end, he was helped not only by Charles Lemuel Nichols, but especially by Worcester bookseller Benjamin Tighe. Benny Tighe (1895-1975), was born in Woonsocket, Rhode Island. He did not attend college, but educated himself through private reading and first-hand experience rummaging through thrift stores, attics, and barns for books, pamphlets, and ephemera. In June 1919 he placed his first newspaper advertisement seeking old books in the *Worcester Telegram,* and Tighe's initial contact with AAS apparently came at about the same time. In 1927 his long-running advertisement elicited a response that uncovered a Thomas chapbook bonanza. Oscar T. Loring invited Tighe to visit him in Oakham, Massachusetts, to look at some old books. Tighe recalled in his memoir: "When I drove up to his home, he asked if I had come alone. When I assured him that this was the case, he informed me that he had a cudgel that he would not hesitate to use on anyone whom he did not want there … He allowed me in to see a closet shelf upon which were at least fifty Isaiah Thomas juveniles of the 1786-1788 period, all in their original wrappers or covers … Although these rarities did not command much of a price in those days, I realized the great importance of this find." When Tighe asked Loring to name a price, the elderly man countered that he was expecting Brigham to see the books, and in turn asked Tighe for his offer. Apparently Loring, alerted to the books' potential value after reading Tighe's advertisement, had already contacted Brigham, who soon braved Loring's cudgel and secured the chapbook bounty. Gracious in defeat, Tighe continued the hunt, eventually placing several fine caches of eighteenth- and nineteenth-century American juveniles at the Society. These accumulated riches in turn served to attract collectors Elisabeth Ball and Herbert Hosmer to AAS.

One collector who clearly enjoyed the camaraderie of both Brigham and Tighe was James d'Alté Aldridge Welch (1907-1970), the greatest twentieth-century collector of early

American children's books. Welch started collecting in his teens. A librarian at the New York Public Library introduced him to Wilbur Macey Stone, who invited Welch to view his collection. Welch was taken not only by its sheer volume, but also by Stone's care in housing his little books in cardboard boxes with tidy title labels, a practice that Welch would emulate with his own collection. Although he also collected English children's books—that portion of his library is now at UCLA—Welch soon focused his energies on acquiring the more plentiful and affordable early American juveniles.

FIG. 34

In 1939, d'Alté Welch contacted AAS, seeking to purchase duplicates for his collection. Shortly thereafter Welch accepted a position as professor of biology at John Carroll University in Cleveland, where he earned a reputation as an expert on Hawaiian tree snails—hence his bookplate, which depicts a kneeling boy holding a book while observing a snail. Welch soon resolved to compile a comprehensive bibliography of early American children's books, in which endeavor he quickly found an ally in Clarence S. Brigham. The bibliography's gestation—as well as Welch's growing friendship with Brigham and election to AAS membership in 1955—is delineated in their extensive correspondence during the 1940s and '50s. So that he would have ready access to the books to be described in the bibliography, Welch arranged to microfilm the pre-1821 American children's books at AAS and at selected institutional and private libraries. This effort was partially funded by an American Council of Learned Societies grant secured in 1960 with AAS's assistance. Welch's *Bibliography of American Children's Books Printed Prior to 1821* was initially serialized in the AAS *Proceedings* from 1963 to 1967. Tragically, as Welch was revising the bibliography for publication in book form, he was injured in a failed robbery attempt and died several months later, on January 4, 1970. But AAS saw to it that Welch's monumental work, which remains the standard bibliography on the subject, was published in 1972.

Welch was comprehensive in his collecting: he sought with equal fervor both the finely metal-engraved picture book and the moral tract. Fine examples of this catholic approach are reflected in copies of a rare Newport, Rhode Island, edition of the sober tale *The Children in the Wood,* and of *The Courtship, Marriage and Pic-nic Dinner of Cock Robin & Jenny Wren,* which is among the earliest American color-printed picture books. An unfailing friend of AAS, Welch bequeathed his unsurpassed collection of over 800 early American children's books to the Society, where they have since been catalogued, digitized for the Readex *Early American Imprints* series, and used—both in paper and digital form—by researchers worldwide.

Through his enthusiasm for collecting and for AAS, Welch helped to bring another major collector—Ruth Adomeit—into the AAS fold. Adomeit (1910-1996) started collecting children's and miniature books while a student at Wellesley College, when her father, the nationally known artist George G. Adomeit, gave her two miniature books.

FIG. 35

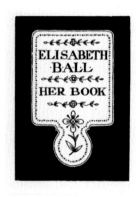

FIG. 36

In 1943 she met d'Alté Welch, a fellow Cleveland resident, and their friendship—in part also a friendly rivalry—mutually kindled their collecting interests. At his urging, Adomeit first visited AAS in 1945 to see the children's book collection. She chose to focus her collecting on miniature "thumb" Bibles, and like Welch, Adomeit compiled the definitive bibliography in her field, *Three Centuries of Thumb Bibles* (1980). Welch's death was a loss keenly felt by Adomeit, and her decision to bequeath over 1,000 children's books (including many children's miniatures) to AAS was undoubtedly based in part on a desire to place her collection with his in perpetuity. Elected to membership in 1983, Adomeit regularly trekked to Worcester, often combining her visits with scouting expeditions in Manhattan book shops, back road estate sales in New England, and everything in between. Upon her death in 1996, Adomeit left funds to establish at AAS a substantial endowment for the purchase of pre-1850 children's books, ensuring that the collection would continue to grow.

Adomeit and Welch counted as a mutual friend the great children's book collector Elisabeth Ball (1897-1982) of Muncie, Indiana. The daughter of book collector George A. Ball, Elisabeth Ball amassed an outstanding collection of English-language juveniles, now dispersed among AAS, the Morgan Library & Museum, the Lilly Library, the Free Library of Philadelphia, and Ball State University. Elected to AAS membership in 1962—the second woman to be so honored—Ball took great interest in developing the AAS collection. A golden opportunity soon came, courtesy of Benjamin Tighe. Welch once wrote of Tighe, "Rare children's books seem to flow to Benjamin Tighe like iron filings to a magnet," and in 1969 Tighe offered the Society what it needed from among more than 600 children's titles. From these AAS director and librarian Marcus A. McCorison selected more than 230 titles that filled gaps and improved defective AAS copies. Welch and book dealer Michael Papantonio appraised the lot at $20,000, a princely sum for AAS at the time. Elisabeth Ball generously funded the purchase but at the time elected to remain anonymous, perhaps due to her close relationships with other institutions. The Helen and Benjamin Tighe Collection of American Children's Books is notable for the rarity, beauty, and significance of its contents; over fifty items are only known copies.

Tighe's finds also helped to attract the attention of picture book collector Herbert Hosmer (1913-1995). An elementary school teacher and puppeteer from Lancaster, Massachusetts, Hosmer first wrote to AAS in 1939, requesting information on portraits painted by his eighteenth-century ancestor, Winthrop Chandler. An artist himself, Hosmer descended from an artistic family that also included the nineteenth-century wood

FIG. 37

engraver, lithographer, and picture book publisher John Greene Chandler (1815-1879). Shortly thereafter, Hosmer paid a research visit to AAS to work on his 1941 facsimile edition of Chandler's *Remarkable Story of Chicken Little*. Always seeking to cultivate potential donors, Clarence S. Brigham notified Hosmer when AAS acquired its first copy of *Chicken Little* (a later edition) from Tighe in 1947. Twenty-seven years later, Tighe found for the Society the extremely rare Roxbury, Massachusetts, first edition of *Chicken Little*, thereby cementing relations between a delighted Hosmer and AAS.

In 1978, Hosmer presented AAS with an important gift: nearly 1,000 McLoughlin Bros. picture books that he had acquired from Ruth Miller, the daughter of McLoughlin vice-president Charles Miller. Many were published during the days of McLoughlin Bros.'s greatest creativity and commercial success, 1870-1900. Also included were 760 pieces of original artwork from the McLoughlin business archives, dating from the firm's establishment in 1858 to its sale to Milton Bradley in 1920. In a departure from AAS's traditional 1876 end date, AAS actively collects McLoughlin Bros. picture books issued through the year 1899 because these serve as a bridge between the roughly produced picture books of the mid-nineteenth century and the polished creations available from publishers today.

The collecting of children's books at AAS is a vital activity with a bright future, thanks to support from the Ruth Adomeit Fund (for pre-1850 imprints) and from the complementary Linda F. & Julian L. Lapides Fund (for post-1850 imprints), established in 1986. Dear friends of Ruth Adomeit and Herbert Hosmer, AAS members Jack and Linda Lapides, former state senator and retired librarian respectively, endowed their fund to ensure that the vision shared by Brigham, Stone, Taylor, Nichols, Welch, Adomeit, Tighe, Ball, and Hosmer continues to be realized.

130. Isaac Watts. *Divine Songs, Attempted in Easy Language, for the Use of Children.* Fourteenth ed. Boston: N. Coverly, 1775.

BEQUEST OF WILBUR MACEY STONE, 1942.

The first edition of *Divine Songs*, written by Isaac Watts (1674-1748), an English dissenting Protestant minister, was published in London in 1715. Fifteen years later the first American edition—of which the only known copy is held at AAS—was published in Boston by Daniel Henchman. *Divine Songs* is a collection of simply worded poems, some of which, such as "I Sing the Almighty Power of God" and "Cradle Hymn," are still mainstays of church hymnals. Watts understood the pull of play for children, and he attempted to gently remind them of their religious duty in "The Child's Complaint": "Why should I love my sport so well? So constant at my play? And lose the thoughts of Heaven & Hell? And then forget to pray?" Many of the poems use allusions to nature and aspects of everyday life to encourage children to contemplate divine immortality. Watts influenced several generations of children's writers, including the English poets Ann and Jane Taylor, whose *Original Poems for Infant Minds* enjoyed great popularity on both sides of the Atlantic throughout the nineteenth century.

This edition has a particularly handsome title page layout. Nathaniel Coverly (1744?-1816) was also a prolific publisher of primers and almanacs. In his bibliography, *The Divine and Moral Songs of Isaac Watts* (1918), Wilbur Macey Stone credited AAS with a dozen early American editions; at present, due in no small part to Stone's generosity, AAS possesses over 200 pre-1877 American editions of this title.

Bristol B4163; Shipton & Mooney 42981; Welch 1408.18.

131. Isaac Watts. *Watts Divine Songs for the Use of Children.* Philadelphia: J. Johnson, 1807.

BEQUEST OF WILBUR MACEY STONE, 1942.

This somewhat rare edition of *Divine Songs* is unusual because of its metal-engraved illustrations. If illustrated at all, most editions of *Divine Songs* contained wood engravings, which were less expensive to produce because the woodblocks could be printed in the same pull with the letterpress text; metal engravings, on the other hand, necessitated sending the sheets a second time through a rolling press. Jacob Johnson was one of the few early nineteenth-century American publishers to systematically issue children's books illustrated with metal engravings. The title plate whimsically features cherubic angels—a distinct departure from the solemn creatures generally gracing juveniles before 1820. Unlike many illustrations depicting children as passively seated in church, the frontispiece shows children engaged in a very public display of piety, kneeling in prayer before the minister in his pulpit. The engravings are by the elusive G. Love, who was active in Philadelphia between 1806 and 1813.

Rosenbach 357; Shaw & Shoemaker 14170.

132. Isaac Watts. *Divine Songs, Attempted in Easy Language, for the Use of Children.* Boston: Samuel T. Armstrong, 1819.

BEQUEST OF WILBUR MACEY STONE, 1942.

Although Watts wrote about the joys of play and the natural world, some of his divine songs were devoted to the serious subjects of conversion and death. In this edition, the macabre imagery of a skeleton representing human mortality punctuates the wood engravings to "The Danger of Delay" and "Solemn Thoughts of God and Death." The first poem is illustrated by a scene of girl and boy joining hands, as if to dance, while a seated musician of color fiddles a tune, all oblivious to the skeleton waving his bony arms through the window. The illustration to "Solemn Thoughts" on the facing page shows Father Time, sickle in hand accompanied by skeletal mortality, armed with his fatal spear.

These detailed wood engravings are the work of the Rev. Jonathan Fisher (1768-1847), the minister of the Blue Hill, Maine, Congregational Church, and all-around Renaissance

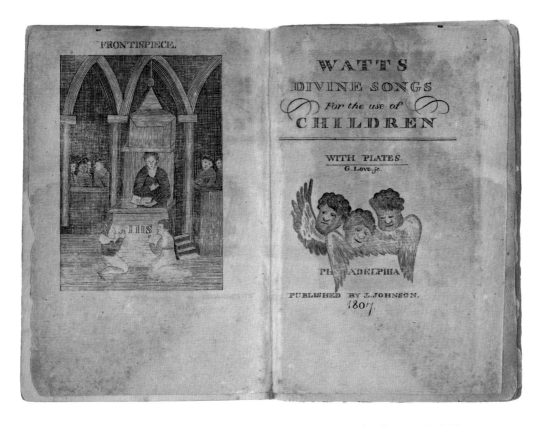

CAT. 131. Isaac Watts, *Watts Divine Songs for the Use of Children*, 1807.

man: he was a painter, poet, inventor, naturalist, teacher, and self-taught engraver. Fisher's work is visually arresting both in composition and execution.

Shaw & Shoemaker 50057; Welch 1408.71.

133. Isaac Watts. *Watts' Divine and Moral Songs. For the Use of Children*. New York: Mahlon Day, 1829.

BEQUEST OF WILBUR MACEY STONE, 1942.

This edition of *Divine Songs* contains wood engravings by Alexander Anderson (1775-1870), a master of his craft who dominated American children's book illustration between 1800 and 1840, when a national market for children's book publishing began to flourish. The example of the prophet Elisha is used to illustrate Watts's hymn "Against Scoffing and Calling Names." The barefoot prophet is taunted by a crowd of children for being bald; in response, God calls upon some she-bears, who tear the children apart. The wood engraving deftly tells the story: the taunting children pay no heed to the heroic prophet in the foreground, or to the bears emerging from the forest. On the opposite page, the wood engraving to "The Sluggard" provides an intimate view of a sleeping man: the clothes hung hastily on a chair and the pair of shoes cast on the floor suggest a disorderly lifestyle. The image of Elisha and the children is based upon an earlier engraving Anderson executed for Philadelphia publisher Benjamin Johnson's 1804 edition of *Divine Songs*. These two illustrations are unsigned, but their powerful composition suggests Anderson as their creator. Publisher Mahlon Day (1790-1854) was a prominent Quaker and prolific publisher who specialized in the children's market. AAS holds over 250 examples of his juvenile imprints.

Pomeroy 1341(a); Shoemaker 41450.

134. *The Book of Nouns, or, Things Which May Be Seen.* Philadelphia: J. Johnson, 1802.

BEQUEST OF D'ALTÉ A. WELCH, 1970.

This, the only known copy of an early American miniature picture book, is unusual for the secular nature of its subject matter. *The Book of Nouns* introduces the reader to everyday words, using pictorial metal engravings. Over one hundred pages long, the book features two leaves of engravings followed by two pages of text, which only partially correspond to each other. In the ongoing list of nouns, the modern reader will find both familiar and unusual professions such as farmer, fowler, fisherman, glover, gardener, hostler, hosier, hatter, and harper. Jacob Johnson (1771?-1819) was, like New York's Samuel Wood, a major publisher of illustrated children's books; in fact, Wood sold Johnson's children's books in his shop.

This copy boasts a distinguished provenance, for it bears the bookplates of both d'Alté A. Welch and his mentor Wilbur Macey Stone. Inspired by Stone's shelves of neatly boxed juveniles, Welch constructed protective covers for his own books. For *The Book of Nouns* he fashioned a protective case out of a particularly charming Christmas card remnant. The typed card bearing a title page transcription and collation shows Welch the bibliographer at work—these cards served as the basis for the entries in his *Bibliography of American Children's Books Printed Prior to 1821.*

Bradbury B33; Shaw & Shoemaker 1924; Welch 112.1.

135. *The Affecting History of the Children in the Wood.* First Newport ed. Newport, Rhode Island: H. & O. Farnsworth, 1799.

GIFT OF THE FAMILY OF D'ALTÉ A. WELCH, CA. 1971.

The Children in the Wood is a somber tale of two orphaned children entrusted to an uncle's care. Resolving to steal his wards' inheritance, the uncle hires two men to kill the children in the wood. After the men argue about whether to commit the murders, one kills the other and abandons the children. The brother and sister wander until they die of starvation and exposure. Justice is eventually served: the escaped murderer confesses his guilt before being executed for another crime, and the uncle languishes in debtor's prison contemplating his evil deeds. The frontispiece to this edition depicts the tale's most popular image: the dead siblings lying on the forest floor as robins gently bury them with leaves.

First printed as a broadside ballad in late sixteenth-century England, *The Children in the Wood* was later widely reprinted in America both in ballad form and as an illustrated prose chapbook. The title had a long life with late nineteenth-century publishers such as McLoughlin Bros., who transformed the tale into a full-color picture book. To the modern eye, *The Children in the Wood* seems like morbid and disturbing fare, but this morality tale struck a profound and lasting chord among readers young and old: the innocent children are ultimately cared for by God "the kind Father," and the evildoers are duly punished with execution, imprisonment, and earthly torment. It is also a landmark in the depiction of early modern childhood: the children are described as inherently innocent, providing a cultural counterweight to the Christian belief—prominently held in Puritan New England—in infant depravity.

The donor d'Alté A. Welch was the single greatest collector of early American children's books. As a teenager, he visited Wilbur Macey Stone (Cats. 130-133), and was immediately inspired to collect children's books. Welch balanced a successful academic career with his bibliographic pursuits. His *Bibliography of American Children's Books Printed prior to 1821,* published by AAS in 1972, remains the standard reference. After Welch's untimely death in 1970, his widow Ann Goddard Welch donated his collection of American juveniles to AAS.

Evans 35086; Welch 173.3.

136. *The Courtship, Marriage, and Pic-nic Dinner of Cock Robin & Jenny Wren, with the Death and Burial of Poor Cock Robin.*

CAT. 137. Card from *The Mother's Remarks*, 1803.

Harrisburg, Pennsylvania: G.S. Peters, 1837.

GIFT OF THE FAMILY OF D'ALTÉ A. WELCH, CA. 1971.

Cock Robin is a beautiful example of a picture book printed and published by Gustav Sigismund Peters (1793-1847), the first color printer in the United States (see also Cat. 140). Peters's picture books, with their signature teal blue, salmon pink, and chartreuse green colors, are highly collectible today. *Cock Robin* was a very popular nursery rhyme in the eighteenth and nineteenth centuries; indeed, the AAS children's literature collection presently holds nearly one hundred editions issued between 1780 and 1900. The wedding's pageantry is conveyed by the goldfinch's efforts in giving fair Jenny away, the jovial wedding feast, and the nightingale's concert. Unfortunately, a different type of pageantry is depicted in the succeeding pages: poor Cock Robin is murdered by a wicked sparrow's arrow, and the funeral is presided over by Parson Rook, Clerk Lark, and wren pallbearers.

137. *The Mother's Remarks on a Set of Cuts for Children. Part I-II.* Philadelphia: T. S. Manning for Jacob Johnson, 1803.

PURCHASE, 1911; PLATES: BEQUEST OF D'ALTÉ A. WELCH, 1970.

This set of two books, fifty-four metal-engraved cards, and a decorative wooden case constitutes one of the earliest known educational games issued by an American publisher. Acquired by AAS decades before the history of the book or childhood studies became accepted academic fields, *The Mother's Remarks* offers important insight into early American pedagogy and visual culture. It came to AAS in parts: the books and case were purchased at auction in 1911, and six decades later the

161

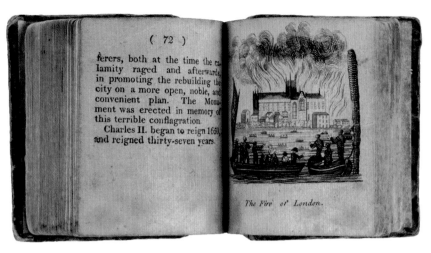

CAT. 138. Alfred Mills, *Pictures of English History*, 1815.

d'Alté Welch bequest supplied the missing cards.

The Mother's Remarks is based upon *Mrs. Lovechild's Book of Two Hundred and Sixteen Cuts*, issued by legendary London children's book publisher Darton and Harvey in 1799. This game was intended for use immediately following school lessons. A pupil would select a card, each bearing six numbered images corresponding to entries in the books. Then the student would spell out the word for each object using the accompanying alphabet letters (here on an uncut sheet). A teacher could also read aloud each object's book entry. The words, images, and descriptions become increasingly complex as the set progresses.

One of the cards features an engraving of Jacob Johnson's bookshop window. Like his Worcester counterpart Isaiah Thomas, Johnson eagerly provided American issues of English children's books to his young customers, reflecting the transatlantic nature of children's print culture in the young Republic. A label on the box is signed by American engraver William Ralph, who probably also executed the cards' 324 images. The case title, *Douceurs*, refers to the sets of twelve pictorial images engraved on each sheet, which were then cut in half to make two six-image cards.

Rosenbach 288; Shaw & Shoemaker 4688; Welch 909.

138. Alfred Mills. *Pictures of English History, in Miniature, from the Reign of Henry VI to the Death of Lord Nelson*. Philadelphia: Johnson and Warner, 1815.

BEQUEST OF D'ALTÉ A. WELCH, 1970.

Illustrated histories for children soon became a staple of children's book publishing in the early American republic. This is the only known copy of the earliest American edition of *Pictures of English History*, which was based upon an 1809 London edition in two volumes. The metal-engraved illustrations are by the book's author, English artist Alfred Mills (1776-1833), who also prepared illustrated miniature histories of ancient Greece and Rome, as well as various illustrated thumb Bibles. Although intended for children, with plentiful illustrations and simply worded text, the book's subject matter was definitely serious and, at times, disturbing. Mills's illustrations include the burning of London in 1666, the execution of Anne Boleyn, and a scene of the two young princes being murdered by Richard III's henchmen. In no small way, this book would have provided ample proof of the moral corruption of an absolute monarchy—a lesson that would help to instill in American children a love for their republican form of government.

Bradbury B121; Welch 849.1.

139. *Bible History.* **New York: S. Wood, 1814.**

GIFT OF RUTH ADOMEIT, 1983.

This is a fine example of an early nineteenth-century "thumb Bible," or a collection of Bible stories issued for children in miniature format, under about two and one half inches tall. Samuel Wood (1760-1844) was one of the major early nineteenth-century American publishers of children's books. The AAS collection includes some three hundred titles issued under Wood's name, including many miniature books, inexpensive chapbooks, and school books.

Ruth Adomeit was the compiler of *Three Centuries of Thumb Bibles* (1980), which remains the standard bibliography. In her acknowledgments, Adomeit glowingly thanked Clarence S. Brigham not only for encouraging her collecting interests, but also for providing ready access to the AAS miniature book collection; she also referred to d'Alté A. Welch as "a good friend whose enthusiasm was so contagious and who taught me so much about book collecting." This copy, which bears the bookplates of both Welch and Adomeit, is a testament to their friendship.

Adomeit A29; Bradbury B95; Rosenbach 484;
Shaw & Shoemaker 30903; Welch 856.5.

140. *A Short History of the Holy Bible.* **Harrisburg, Pennsylvania: G. S. Peters, 1840.**

GIFT OF RUTH E. ADOMEIT, 1995.

Besides publishing picture book editions of nursery rhymes (Cat. 136), Gustav Sigismund Peters also issued illustrated Bible stories for children. This collection of eighteen leaves begins with Cain and Abel and ends with the parable of the Prodigal Son, offering the young reader highlights from both Old and New Testaments. Before releasing this English translation, Peters had published this color picture book in German, under the title, *Kleine biblische Historien, aus dem Alten und Neuen Testament* (Harrisburg, 1838), a copy of which is also held at AAS. This copy, collected by Ruth

Adomeit, reflects her interest in acquiring Peters picture books, to the great benefit of the AAS children's literature collection.

141. *The St. George Juvenile.* **St. George, Utah Territory, December 15, 1868.**

GIFT OF RUTH E. ADOMEIT, CA. 1995.

Ruth Adomeit's interest in juvenile print culture was not only passionate, but wonderfully eclectic, and her collecting followed suit. Her numerous gifts to AAS included thumb Bibles, picture books, and also amateur newspapers. One of the most unusual of the latter is this first number of an amateur newspaper issued in the early days of the Utah Territory. St. George was established in 1861 as a cotton growing mission by Mormon leader Brigham Young, and to this day the area is known as "Utah's Dixie." The newspaper's fifteen-year-old editor and proprietor, Joseph Wetherbee Carpenter (1852-1928), was born in Iowa but moved west to Utah with his Mormon family. The *St. George Juvenile*, like many other amateur papers, is a curious blend of poetry, maxims, and advertisements. The frontier flavor exudes from an ad for locally produced French chalk and Spanish whiting on page 3, which proclaims, "Patronize home industry, and develope [sic] the resources of this state." Carpenter published his newspaper for approximately three years but no complete file is known.

142. J. J. Jackson. *Nonsense for Girls.* **New York: McLoughlin Bros., ca. 1874.**

GIFT OF RUTH E. ADOMEIT, 1995.

Nonsense for Girls, one of over 1,000 children's books donated to AAS by Ruth Adomeit between 1995 and 1996, is an excellent example of McLoughlin Bros.'s leadership in the development of color printing technology in post-Civil War America. *Nonsense for Girls* clearly capitalizes on the success of Edward Lear's *Book of Nonsense.* Its illustrations, by

There was a young person named JULIA, whose tastes were so very peculiar;
That she eat little gnats, and made puddings with rats, which did'nt agree with Miss Julia.

There was a young lady named GRACE, who actually ran in a race;
But she tumbled down flat, and spoiled her best hat, besides getting scratched in the face.

CAT. 142. J. J. Jackson, *Nonsense for Girls*, ca. 1874.

McLoughlin Bros. staff artist Charles J. Howard, feature colorful caricatures of foolish girls, with accompanying limericks. The pictures humorously depict some rather disagreeable girls who indulge in overeating, messiness, cooking with rats, and trying to run a race in girl's clothing.

AAS staff provided full rare book cataloguing for the Ruth Adomeit donation as items were received. When Adomeit saw printouts of the catalog records in 1996, she was pleased that researchers would have ready access to her books not only at AAS, but also from around the world via the Internet.

143. John Greene Chandler.
Remarkable Story of Chicken Little. Roxbury, Massachusetts: J. G. Chandler, 1840.

PURCHASED FROM BENJAMIN TIGHE, 1970.

Chicken Little is a verse adaptation by John Greene Chandler (1815-1879) of the traditional tale, *Chicken Licken*. Chandler simplified the text and added his own lively illustrations. *Chicken Little* is a cautionary tale about the fatal effects of unbridled fear. This extremely rare first edition was printed for sale at a Bunker Hill Monument fundraising fair. In a tongue-in-cheek review dated September 14, 1840, published in the fair's periodical, *The Monument*, Sarah Josepha Hale likens *Chicken Little* to Byron's *Childe Harold*, and writes of poor Chicken's demise, "We could have wished for a different kind of poetical justice, but we forbear to trench on the province of the author." The engravings, which were probably hand-colored in Chandler's shop, have a spontaneous, almost cartoonish quality that would certainly appeal to children. Indeed, Chandler's version of *Chicken Little* was reissued by various American publishers through the 1860s, and it has left a lasting imprint on American popular culture.

Did you ever hear of Chicken Little, how she
disturbed a whole neighborhood by her foolish
alarm?

CAT. 143. John Greene Chandler. *Remarkable Story of Chicken Little*, 1840.

This little treasure—a testimony to Benjamin Tighe's prowess as a book scout—delighted Chandler's descendant, children's book collector, and AAS member Herbert Hosmer. Acquisitions such as this one served as a reminder to Hosmer, underscoring AAS's continued commitment to juvenile literature. It likely helped to encourage his eventual 1978 donation of his archive of McLoughlin Bros. picture books and original art.

144. Hans Christian Andersen.
Good Wishes for the Children. Cambridge, Massachusetts: The Riverside Press, 1873.

PURCHASED FROM BENJAMIN TIGHE, 1967.

Benjamin Tighe's expert eye helped him find many remarkable American children's books for AAS, including this rare edition of Andersen fairy tales, published during the author's lifetime with his full approval. Only recently have the identities of the translator and illustrator—"A.A.B. and S.G.P."—been confirmed. A copy recently acquired by an AAS member is inscribed to George H. Mifflin of the Riverside Press from "Adie A. Bigelow and S.G. Putnam." Artist Sarah Gooll Putnam (1851-1912) pursued a successful career as a portraitist of Boston's elite. Her diary, held at the Massachusetts Historical Society, reveals that Adeline A. Bigelow (b. 1840) initially proposed the idea of an illustrated translation on October 31, 1873, with the book being published less than two months later. Both Putnam and Bigelow were young society ladies who pre-

165

CAT. 144. Hans Christian Andersen, *Good Wishes for the Children*, 1873.

pared this edition as a fundraiser for Boston Children's Hospital. Drawing directly onto lithographic stones delivered by the publisher to her house, Putnam prepared the thirty-six illustrations using young friends and relatives as models. The images were drawn with great delicacy and mastery of composition, as in this example of "The Little Match-Girl," with its white-on-black effect of the barefoot match girl making her way in a lonely cityscape amid falling snow.

Clearly published in a small edition for a wealthy audience, this edition was issued in lithographed paper-covered boards. A review in the January 1, 1874 issue of *Current Literature* remarks, "The delicately-tinted cover will not endure being handled by children who do not wear kid gloves."

145. *People of All Nations: A Useful Toy for Girl or Boy.* Albany: H. C. Southwick, ca. 1812.

GIFT OF ELISABETH BALL, 1969.

Children's books depicting ethnic groups in native costume were highly popular throughout the nineteenth century. *People of All Nations* is a fairly early example in miniature format. The book arranges ethnic groups alphabetically, providing young readers with a secular counterpart to the religiously inspired alphabet in *The New England Primer*, then a universally recognized source of alphabet instruction.

Alphabet books are rich repositories of culturally recognized racial and ethnic stereotypes, and *People of All Nations* provides much fodder: J is for the wandering Jew with sack of

CAT. 145. *People of All Nations*, ca. 1812.

clothes; M is for a Mahometan man smoking his hookah. The book also includes images of well-dressed European residents, tradesmen with their wares, and Native Americans in traditional dress. For this reason, picture books of ethnic groups are indispensable to researchers seeking to understand cultural attitudes toward race and ethnicity.

Helen & Benjamin Tighe Collection of
American Children's Books.
Bradbury B79; Welch 982.3.

146. Charles Perrault. *Contes du Tems passé de Ma Mere l'Oye ... Tales of Passed Times by Mother Goose ...* Septieme ed. New York: J. Rivington, 1795.

GIFT OF ELISABETH BALL, 1969.

Charles Perrault (1628-1703) was a French government official who wrote adaptations of fairy tales in his spare time. His collection *Contes des Fees* was quite popular on both sides of the Atlantic, and his versions of *Little Red Riding Hood*, *Cinderella*, and *Puss in Boots* have become classics of children's literature.

This early American edition, issued by James Rivington with engravings by a twenty-year-old Alexander Anderson, is one of just three known complete copies. The text layout is unusual for a children's book in that the French and English texts are presented on opposite pages, generally facing each other. The volume includes Anderson's whimsical engraving of the wily *Puss in Boots*. The focus of the engraving is on Puss who, having already cajoled a pair of boots out of his impoverished master, brags that he can be of much better service to his master alive than cooked as a meal. Puss's confident stance dominates the image, literally leaving his master in the shadows.

Helen & Benjamin Tighe Collection of
American Children's Books.
Evans 29300; Welch 985.2.

147. *The Entertaining History of Jobson & Nell: Illustrated with Humorous Engravings.* Philadelphia: Wm. Charles, 1814.

GIFT OF ELISABETH BALL, 1969.

Jobson & Nell is a humorous and slightly raucous tale of a cobbler whose love for hearty roast beef leads him to steal the parson's Sunday roast. Jobson is described as a man who

THE ENTERTAINING HISTORY OF
JOBSON & NELL.

Near the Sign of the Bell
Liv'd Jobson and Nell
And cobbling of Shoes was his trade
They agreed very well
The neighbours did tell
For he was a funny old blade.

But Jobson loved whiskey
Which made him so friskey
His noddle when once it got in
That frolick he must
And kick up a dust
For his customers car'd not a pin.

CAT. 147. *The Entertaining History of Jobson & Nell*, 1814.

loved whisky so much, "That frolick he must, And kick up a dust, For his customers car'd not a pin." Unlike the subjects of cautionary temperance tract tales, Jobson does not reach a bad end; rather, the parson joins him in feasting upon the stolen roast. The book's metal engravings are probably by publisher William Charles (1776-1820), who had plenty of practice depicting drunken, foolish men in his simultaneous career as a political cartoonist. The illustrations were hand-colored in Charles's shop. *Jobson & Nell* is an excellent example of Charles's brilliance as both a caricaturist and illustrator, from the prominence of the Bell Tavern shingle, to the wobbly pose of the tipsy cobbler.

This is the only known copy of the earliest extant American printing; d'Alté A. Welch located a London edition (probably an antecedent) published by G. Martin. This edition is particularly interesting from a bibliographical standpoint because it contains an advertisement for *Country Scenes Illustrated with Emblematical Prints*, a Charles imprint for which no copy has yet been located. AAS has perhaps the most comprehensive collection of William Charles imprints, numbering well over one hundred items, including many children's picture books.

Helen & Benjamin Tighe Collection of
American Children's Books.
Shaw & Shoemaker 31421; Weiss, p. 7; Welch 357.

148. J. Baker. *My Pony.* Philadelphia: Wm. Charles, 1818.

GIFT OF ELISABETH BALL, 1969.

This is a lovely example of the gentler side of the picture book art of William Charles. The popularity of English poet Ann Taylor's reverential poem *My Mother* spawned a number of similar poems, including *My Father, My Brother,* and *My Sister.* Charles published all of these works in picture book form, as well as *My Daughter, My Son,* and *My Pony,* the only title in his mini-series about a pet. *My Pony,* attributed in an early English edition to a J. Baker, shows in great detail the happy and harmonious relationship between a beloved pet and his young master. Like *Jobson & Nell, My Pony* was likely hand-colored in Charles's shop. According to Charles's bibliographer Henry W. Weiss, he probably executed the engravings as well.

Helen & Benjamin Tighe Collection of
American Children's Books.
Welch 919; Weiss, p. 9.

149. *The Renowned History of Giles Gingerbread, a Little Boy Who Lived upon Learning.* First Worcester ed. Worcester: Isaiah

Thomas, 1786.
GIFT OF ELISABETH BALL, 1969.

This extremely well-used chapbook is the only known copy of the first Isaiah Thomas printing of *Giles Gingerbread*. The work was originally issued in London by famed children's book publisher John Newbery, who probably also wrote the text. Like *Goody Two-Shoes* (another Newbery classic), *Giles Gingerbread* tells the story of a fatherless child who rises up by his own intelligence and honesty. Upon Giles asking his father why Toby Thompson is a wealthy man, Mr. Gingerbread takes a break from teaching young Giles how to read, and chronicles Toby Thompson's rise from a penniless orphan to errand boy for Mr. Goodwill. A boy of unflinching honesty, Toby sends his master a letter exposing a fellow servant's theft. As a result, Toby becomes Goodwill's assistant and eventual business partner. Having delivered his moral tale, Mr. Gingerbread quizzes his son on the alphabet, and Giles delivers a very personal version, ending with: "Z … is a Zany, and a Zany's a Fool, Who don't love his book, or his Master, or School." Like most Isaiah Thomas children's chapbooks in the AAS collection, this one was acquired in the twentieth century.

Helen & Benjamin Tighe Collection of
American Children's Books.
Evans 20675; Welch 452.3.

150. George P. Webster. *Santa Claus and His Works.* New York: McLoughlin Bros., ca. 1875.
GIFT OF HERBERT H. HOSMER, 1978.

McLoughlin Bros. was a major force in the publishing of children's books, games, and paper dolls from 1858 until 1954, when Grosset & Dunlap acquired its book titles. Founded in New York City, the firm moved to Springfield, Massachusetts, in 1920 following its acquisition by Milton Bradley. McLoughlin Bros. played a pivotal role in the application of color printing technology to children's books, particularly during the later nineteenth century. AAS owned few of their imprints until 1978, when Herbert H. Hosmer donated nearly 1,000 picture books and 760 pieces of associated artwork, most formerly part of the firm's business archives.

Illustrated with chromolithographs designed by Thomas Nast, *Santa Claus and his Works* capitalized on McLoughlin Bros.'s successful 1869 picture book version of *The Night before Christmas*, which Nast also illustrated. It is to Nast that we owe the modern image of Santa as a rotund, white-bearded man in a fur suit. Here, Nast takes the Santa image a step further by portraying him as a careful business man, quill pen tucked in his ear, consulting his ledger books for the names of good girls and boys. The accompanying poetry was written by George P. Webster, who also collaborated with Nast on a McLoughlin picture book version of *Rip Van Winkle*.

151. *Kriss Kringle Taking Inventory.* Watercolor on paper, ca. 1897.
GIFT OF HERBERT H. HOSMER, 1978.

This unsigned watercolor of Santa at his desk served as the model for a chromolithographed illustration in the picture book *Kriss Kringle* (New York: McLoughlin Bros., 1897). Here the concept of Santa as businessman is taken a step beyond Thomas Nast's illustration (Cat. 150): now he has an office worthy of a powerful executive! Santa's ledger books recording the good (and bad) deeds of boys and girls are neatly kept on large, deep shelves. Santa himself sits on a cushioned chair at a generously appointed desk, his homely quill replaced by a sleek pen. A telephone, the very latest in nineteenth century technology, sits on the desk. Santa's red felt jacket looks more like business apparel than the traditional fur suit.

This is one of over 700 pieces of artwork assembled by Charles Miller (1869-1951), who started his career at McLoughlin Bros. as a printer's devil and worked his way up to vice-president. When the firm prepared for sale in 1950, books and artwork in the company archives were divided among members of the executive board. Miller took a large cache of picture books and drawings, plus representative samplings of games, paper dolls, and illustration blocks. This important collection was later acquired from Miller's daughter by Herbert Hosmer, who later donated it to AAS.

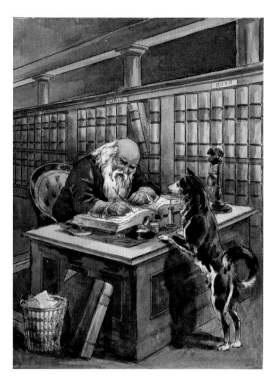

CAT. 151. *Kriss Kringle Taking Inventory,* ca. 1897.

152. Anthony Hochstein. *Crane's Bill.* Watercolor on paper, ca. 1860-1895.

GIFT OF HERBERT H. HOSMER, 1978.

This beautiful watercolor was drawn by Hoboken, New Jersey, artist Anthony Hochstein (1828 or 9 -1911) for a manuscript entitled "Flower Legends." The drawings and manuscript were once in the possession of New York publisher Belford, Clarke & Co., from whom McLoughlin Bros. somehow obtained them, though apparently neither firm ever published the text or illustrations. Eleven of the eighteen original drawings and the manuscript text did survive and are now held at AAS, thanks to the generosity of Herbert Hosmer.

Hochstein specialized in drawing plants and animals, and his eye for detail shines in this whimsical scene of frogs enjoying cocktails while the crane (a natural predator) patiently waits to devour his hors d'oeuvres! Towering over the scene is a crane's bill with flowers in various states of bloom. Hochstein thereby provides the viewer with both a botanical and a tongue-in-cheek definition of "Crane's bill." Art works such as this remind the modern researcher that not all drawings produced for children's books were actually published.

153. *Cinderella.* New York: McLoughlin Bros., 1882.

GIFT OF HERBERT H. HOSMER, 1978.

When publishing editions of popular fairy tales such as *Cinderella,* McLoughlin Bros. experimented with a wide variety of sizes and formats. Particularly successful was its series of *Pantomime Toy Books,* launched in 1882—though admittedly McLoughlin Bros. simply took advantage of vague international copyright laws to pirate the popular *Pantomime Toy Books* issued by London publisher Dean & Son. The series was made up of fairy tales issued in metamorphic picture format, featuring pages of varying sizes that could be flipped to change the entire scene and give the story a greater sense of movement. Each story in the series contains a verse and prose synopsis on

CAT. 154. *Cinderella*, 1891.

the front and end pages, the center leaves being devoted entirely to the lavishly chromolithographed illustrations. A scene of Cinderella being wooed by the prince is told in delightful detail. Both are dressed as luxuriously as their surroundings, and they are oblivious to the time on the clock. The entire scene is framed by a theater proscenium, complete with musicians seated in the pit. Nearly a decade later, McLoughlin Bros. carried the concept a step closer to a genuine toy theater by turning Cinderella into a shaped book (Cat. 154).

154. *Cinderella*. New York: McLoughlin Bros., 1891.

GIFT OF HERBERT H. HOSMER, 1978.

The Herbert Hosmer gift to AAS included a number of McLoughlin Bros. metamorphic picture books, of which this is one of the grandest examples. Employing a newly patented design, the book has a spine on each side, which allows the pages to open in the middle, as if parting a curtain for each new scene. The entire

book is cut in the shape of a theater proscenium, and the side panels feature standing illustrations of families with children watching the show from box seats—reflecting the increasing acceptance of "legitimate" theater as an appropriate middle-class family venue. The proscenium design also reflects the contemporary popularity of toy theaters, consisting of paper cut-outs, which McLoughlin Bros. also printed and sold. In this picture book, the focus is on the chromolithographed scenes portrayed onstage, as in this illustration of Cinderella's marriage to the handsome prince. No extravagance is spared: the wedding takes place in a Gothic cathedral, with an archbishop presiding. The portrayal of such a high church wedding in an American children's book would have been far less likely even a generation before, but the celebrity of Queen Victoria and Prince Albert popularized royalty (and pageantry) on both sides of the Atlantic. Like many McLoughlin picture books, the chromolithographed illustrations are unsigned, but they were undoubtedly executed by a McLoughlin staff artist.

mon House Clocks,

ng Clocks, and Time-p

AAS and the Bibliography of Early American Imprints

A central aspect of Isaiah Thomas's vision for the American Antiquarian Society was that its collections would be formed not only for perpetual preservation, but to serve a purpose. It was not sufficient simply to gather the primary and secondary source materials for American history and to make them accessible. Rather, these materials were to be used to create new knowledge, and AAS members and staff alike bore a special responsibility in this endeavor. Thomas himself served as the exemplar: in building his own library, Thomas had methodically gathered the resources he would need for writing *The History of Printing in America* (1810; Cat. 9), afterwards placing his painstakingly built library at AAS and soliciting donations from others. In essence, Thomas and his fellow donors formed an unwritten compact with AAS: in return for the privilege of possessing these irreplaceable materials, AAS accepted the responsibility for realizing their full scholarly potential.

For Thomas, part of that potential involved describing the entire corpus of early American printing, and AAS has since embraced his dream as one of its principal objectives. It had been Thomas's intention to append a checklist of pre-1776 American imprints to his two-volume history of American printing, but finding that it would extend the work to a third volume, he deferred. Keenly aware of the importance of his labors as America's first imprint bibliographer, Thomas persisted, revising and expanding his checklist for eventual publication. It remained unfinished at his death in 1831, however, and Thomas's notes lay unused at AAS until the late 1850s, when Samuel Foster Haven, Jr. accepted the challenge. The son of AAS librarian Samuel Foster Haven, Samuel, Jr. copied Thomas's entries onto 3 ? x 8 ?-inch slips and identified many new editions by mining bibliographical sources unavailable to Thomas. Haven's checklist was nearly ready for the printer when he was killed in action during the Civil War. After a decade's delay, AAS published this first comprehensive bibliography of early American imprints in a manner that would have pleased Thomas: as a supplement to the 1874 second edition of *The History of Printing in America*.

FIG. 38. Samuel Foster Haven, Jr.

During the 1890s, Charles Evans undertook his monumental project to replace Haven's checklist of pre-1776 imprints with an updated and comprehensive bibliography of all American imprints through the year 1820. Of the many who helped Evans with his project, perhaps none was more valuable than Clarence S. Brigham who, upon arriving at AAS in 1908, promptly made its resources available to the project. For the next twenty-six years, Brigham and his staff compiled lists, provided detailed information on titles unseen by Evans, answered innumerable bibliographical queries, and even shipped

FIG. 39. Clarence S. Brigham.

boxes of AAS books and pamphlets to Chicago for Evans's close inspection. Of equal value to Evans was Brigham's diplomacy in securing the cooperation of other institutions and in finding much-needed funding. When Evans died in 1935, twelve volumes of his *American Bibliography* had been published, bringing the chronological checklist from 1639 up through a portion of 1799. Brigham and his successor Clifford K. Shipton eventually saw the work to completion through the year 1800, with the final two volumes published by AAS in 1955 and 1959.

These projects were in fact only a small portion of the work being performed in AAS's bibliographical hive. By the time of Brigham's appointment as AAS librarian, the semi-annual AAS *Proceedings* had established itself as a prominent forum for bibliographical work, much of it by AAS members, on American history and imprints. This trend only accelerated under Brigham who, being an accomplished bibliographer himself, knew precisely how to encourage and sustain bibliographical scholarship. In addition, during the 1930s while work on the final Evans volumes was underway, AAS librarian R.W.G. Vail, was serving as editor and finishing Joseph Sabin's *Dictionary of Books Relating to America, from its Discovery to the Present Time.*

Meanwhile Brigham was pursuing two innovative projects of his own that would broaden the scope and methodology of American imprint bibliography. The first and most influential was his *History and Bibliography of American Newspapers, 1690-1820*, published in two volumes in 1947 following serialization in draft form in the AAS *Proceedings*. Rather than providing a mere checklist of titles, Brigham offered full publication histories for 2,120 newspapers and a comprehensive census of institutional and private holdings, no matter how slight the file. Brigham estimated that he sent over 15,000 letters to librarians, historians, booksellers, and descendants of newspaper publishers to gather his information, in addition to mining AAS's vast collection of local histories, biographies, genealogies, city directories, and its peerless newspaper holdings. Brigham's vacations were often spent on the road, as he traveled some 10,000 miles visiting over 400 libraries great and small in order to survey their newspaper holdings. A complementary, but no less important, objective was to build AAS's newspaper collection, and in this Brigham was highly successful, rescuing many extremely rare newspaper files. Given the importance of newspapers to the spread of printing throughout the United States—only almanacs were nearly as ubiquitous—Brigham's work was essentially a comprehensive historical survey of early American printers, all the more impressive for the information provided on 194 newspapers for which no copies could be traced (though almost thirty have since been found and acquired for AAS). Though far narrower in scope, Brigham's second project—a bibliography and study of Paul Revere's engravings —also involved years of dogged research. In addition to the better-known prints, Revere had produced much jobbing work which proved elusive to track down. As he pursued leads on Revere bookplates, clock labels, watch papers, trade cards, and other ephemera, Brigham pushed bibliography well beyond its traditional boundaries.

For Clifford K. Shipton, who became the Society's librarian in 1940, there were other bibliographical challenges. Even as he was completing Evans's *American Bibliography* during the 1950s, Shipton well understood its limitations. Not only did it omit thousands of pre-1801 imprints that had since been acquired by AAS or identified at other institutions, but it did little to address the crucial problem of access to these titles, many of which were known in only a handful of copies. In 1954 Shipton and Albert Boni, president of Readex Microprint Corporation, initiated a partner-

FIG. 40. Clifford K. Shipton.

ship between AAS and Readex to address these problems. Readex would offer to subscribing libraries a microprint edition of as many pre-1801 American books, pamphlets, and broadsides as possible, with AAS providing space in Antiquarian Hall for the microfilming and performing editorial work. Completed in 1968, the *Early American Imprints* microprint edition offered over 36,000 conveniently accessible titles to readers at hundreds of subscribing libraries worldwide. The complementary two-volume *National Index of American Imprints through 1800: The Short-title Evans*, prepared by Shipton and James E. Mooney and published by AAS in 1969, greatly expanded Evans's enumerative listing. The AAS-Readex partnership continues to this day, having been broadened to include all pre-1820 American imprints and a substantial selection of pre-1877 newspapers and ephemera. Originally available in microprint and later in microfiche, this corpus of early American printing is now available online with fully searchable texts to subscribing institutions around the world.

Shipton's successor, Marcus A. McCorison, proved equally adept at shepherding bibliographical projects. Following publication by AAS in 1963 of his own *Vermont*

FIG. 41. Marcus A. McCorison.

Imprints, 1778-1820, McCorison significantly expanded the Society's publication program. Over the ensuing four decades, AAS has issued a distinguished series of bibliographical monographs, many of which remain the standard references in their fields. Some have been revised from work originally published in the AAS *Proceedings,* while others have been new publications. The subjects range from specific genres such as book catalogs, songsters, and cookbooks, to ephemeral publications such as carriers' addresses, to catalogs raisonnés of book illustrators such as Alexander Anderson. The most recent bibliography published by AAS, Joseph J. Felcone's *Printing in New Jersey, 1754-1800: a Descriptive Bibliography,* published in 2012, splendidly illustrates how much bibliographical work is still being done on Evans-era imprints.

McCorison seized another opportunity to adapt Isaiah Thomas's original vision for the modern age. The introduction of computers to library cataloguing raised possibilities for storing, manipulating, and sharing bibliographical data in ways print bibliographies could not. With the advent in 1977 of the Eighteenth-Century Short Title Catalogue (ESTC) project (later renamed the English Short Title Catalogue), AAS accepted responsibility for contributing machine-readable records for pre-1801 American imprints, whether owned by AAS or not. The Society's contribution to ESTC was accomplished through the newly established North American Imprints Program (NAIP) and began with the more than fifty percent of Evans titles held by AAS and concluded with titles located elsewhere. In addition, NAIP staff also recorded the locations of more than 120,000 extant copies found in libraries worldwide. Cataloguing as many as 50,000 North American editions would be extremely expensive, hence substantial support was sought from the National Endowment for the Humanities and other national foundations.

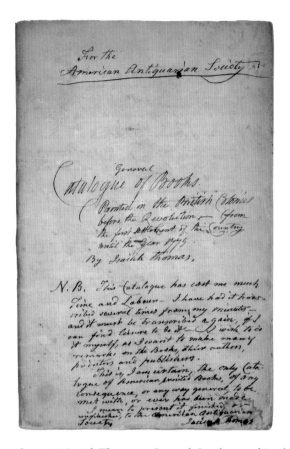

CAT. 155. Isaiah Thomas, "General Catalogue of Books ...," 1800-1810.

155. Isaiah Thomas. "General Catalogue of Books Printed in the British Colonies before the Revolution," compiled 1800-1810.

BEQUEST OF ISAIAH THOMAS, 1831.

It was Isaiah Thomas's long-standing ambition to compile a comprehensive checklist of pre-1776 American imprints. Although he did not complete the project, the extensive notes Thomas made as the first serious bibliographer of American imprints, and the collections and staff of the institution he founded—the American Antiquarian Society—were instrumental in ultimately realizing his dream.

As Thomas compiled information for his 1810 *The History of Printing in America* (Cat. 9), he also gathered notes on the pre-1776 American imprints he had seen or found reference to. Thomas continued the project, re-transcribing the entries into new notebooks as their number grew. Thomas left behind fourteen fascicles . He proudly noted that this foundational work in American imprint bibliography "is, I am certain, the only Catalogue of American printed Books, of any consequence, or any way general, to be met with, or ever has been made."

Thomas first arranged his notes by place of publication, then listed imprints in alphabetical order by author or title, with new additions placed wherever they fit, ready for later recopying in correct order. The information supplied was brief, though Thomas intended at some point "to make many remarks, on the books, their authors, printers and publishers."

Isaiah Thomas Papers.

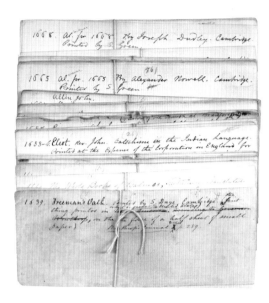

CAT. 156. Samuel Foster Haven, Jr. Working slips for a bibliography of books published in America before the Revolution, 1858-1861.

156. Samuel F. Haven, Jr. Working slips for a bibliography of books published in America before the Revolution, 1858-1861.

BEQUEST OF SAMUEL F. HAVEN.

Isaiah Thomas's unfinished checklist of early American imprints (Cat. 155) lay untouched until the late 1850s, when Samuel F. Haven, Jr. revisited it. Samuel, Jr. (1831-1862) earned his medical degree in Boston, then journeyed to Europe for two years of postgraduate training in ophthalmology before establishing a medical practice in Worcester, Massachusetts, in 1858. Haven devoted his leisure hours to revising and expanding Thomas's notes. Haven added more titles culled from library catalogs and contemporary advertisements, and inspected at AAS and other libraries. Crucial to Haven's project was the liberal access granted by George Brinley (Cats. 34-37) to his superlative library. Haven provided author, title transcriptions, place of publication, and often pagination and brief notes.

Haven's chronological checklist through 1775 was well advanced when, in 1861, he volunteered for duty as an army surgeon. On December 13, 1862, he was killed at Fredericksburg, Virginia. With a shortening of titles to save space and the addition of pagination to many entries, Haven's slips were published by AAS in 1874, fittingly as a 358-page appendix to the second edition of Isaiah Thomas's *The History of Printing in America*. This first attempt to publish a comprehensive bibliography of early American imprints was not superseded until Charles Evans began issuing his *American Bibliography* in 1903.

AAS Archives.

157. Titan Leeds. *The American Almanack for the Year of Christian Account, 1740 ....* Second edition. Philadelphia: Andrew Bradford, 1739.

ACQUIRED BEFORE 1861; SOURCE UNKNOWN.

This well-used Pennsylvania almanac is an example of a publication carefully listed by Haven on his slips. Haven typically listed all almanacs for the same year on a single slip. The penciled additions were likely made when Haven's catalog was being prepared for its 1874 publication.

CAT. 158. Charles Evans, Working slips for *American Bibliography.*

Titan Leeds's (1699-1738) *American Almanack* first appeared with an almanac for 1714. Benjamin Franklin commenced publishing a competitor, *Poor Richard's Almanack*, in 1733. In order to raise the public's interest in his almanac, Franklin predicted Leeds's death at 3:29 pm on October 17, 1733. Leeds responded with an assurance that he was still alive in the *American Almanack* for 1734, but Franklin's almanac for that year claimed that Leeds was in fact dead and suggesting that the Leeds almanac was "only a contrivance of somebody or other, who hopes perhaps to sell two or three years' almanacks still, by the sole force and virtue of Mr. Leeds's name." After Leeds actually died in 1738, the almanac continued to be published with him listed as author until 1745. In this almanac the publishers explain that in 1738 Leeds had given them seven years' worth of almanacs. Thus Franklin's hoax had an odd parallel in what actually later occurred.

Drake 9613; Evans 4374.

158. Charles Evans. Working slips for *American Bibliography,* housed in a corset box.

BEQUEST OF CHARLES EVANS, 1935.

The vision of Isaiah Thomas and Samuel F. Haven, Jr. for a comprehensive bibliography of early Americans imprints was magnificently, if imperfectly, realized in Charles Evans's monumental fourteen-volume *American Bibliography* (1903-1959). Evans (1850-1935) probably began the project around 1892 while on the staff of the Newberry Library. Originally Evans intended to describe, in chronological order, all American imprints through 1820. Evans died before the project was complete, midway through the year 1799. Four decades of his laborious work yielded twelve volumes containing 35,854 entries.

AAS has retained Evans's slips for the period after 1800, which he originally housed in repurposed corset boxes. When making research trips, Evans would carry with him the relevant working slips, arranged in chronological order inside one or more of these ideally-sized long, narrow boxes. The parsimonious Evans would also reuse the slips' blank versos whenever possible, hence the slips for 1801-1820 preserved at AAS also retain on their versos many of Evans's draft entries for 1639-1800.

159. Mason Locke Weems. *The Life and Memorable Actions of*

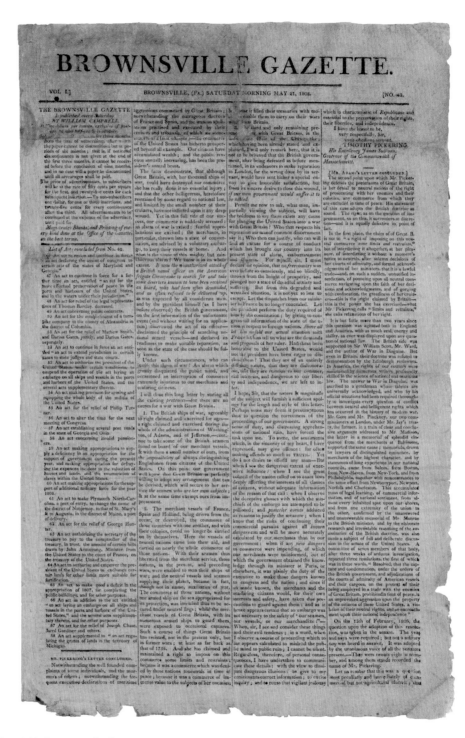

Cat. 161. *Brownsville Gazette*, 1808.

George Washington, General and Commander of the Armies of America, a New Edition, Corrected. Frederick-Town, Maryland: Matthias Bartgis, 1801.

This edition of Weems's popular essay on the life of George Washington is an example of a book noted by Evans while working on his bibliography. AAS retains Evans's draft slips for the years 1801-1820; they illustrate his working method. Using 3 x 5-inch slips or cards cut in half vertically, Evans neatly transcribed the title, imprint, pagination, and format of each work on a separate slip, sometimes adding library locations and other notes. These he sorted, edited, and rewrote if need be prior to publication. Because Evans relied heavily on advertisements, bibliographies, and other sources for titles he could not examine personally, the *American Bibliography* unfortunately contains many inaccuracies and bibliographical "ghosts."

AAS Dated Pamphlets.

Shaw & Shoemaker 1638; Welch 755.

160. Letter, Charles Evans to Clarence S. Brigham, October 4, 1912.

A difficult personality, Charles Evans was fortunate in finding several patient, generous benefactors for his *American Bibliography.* Perhaps none was more crucial for, and committed to, the project's success than Clarence S. Brigham. In 1903, while still at the Rhode Island Historical Society, Brigham wrote Evans to praise the newly-published first volume and to offer his help. Their collaboration deepened after Brigham moved to AAS in 1908. Evans had first visited AAS in 1904, and already he considered it his favorite place to work. Henceforth Brigham and other AAS staff labored assiduously on Evans's behalf. When the Depression strained Evans's finances, Brigham secured from the American Council of Learned Societies a series of grants to keep the project going.

Evans was deeply grateful to AAS for its

assistance, and for his election to membership in 1910. In 1912, Evans presented AAS with a centennial gift: a specially bound, interleaved set of the first six volumes of *American Bibliography,* to which he added later volumes as published. Shown here is the letter Evans sent with the gift. Evans's wish that AAS would "note [in this copy] the additions made to the Society, and correct any faults of omission, or commission," and that it would "become a complete index to the American printed books belonging to the Society" has been honored by staff to this day.

AAS Archives.

161. *Brownsville Gazette.* Brownsville, Pennsylvania, May 21, 1808.

PURCHASE, DUPLICATES FUND, 2004.

Clarence S. Brigham's two-volume *History and Bibliography of American Newspapers, 1690-1820,* published by AAS in 1947, was a landmark in newspaper bibliography. The fruits of thirty-six years of painstaking research are amply displayed in the detailed publishing histories and comprehensive censuses of institutional holdings. For fully 194 (nine percent) of the 2,120 titles included, Brigham was unable to locate any extant issues, though he could document the newspapers' existence from other sources.

Since Brigham's day it has been an AAS priority to locate and acquire issues of these "lost" newspapers. Many have been found, and much new information has been gathered towards a supplement to Brigham's bibliography. Here is one such "discovery issue," for the *Brownsville Gazette,* which turned up on eBay in 2004. The accompanying page from the manuscript to Brigham's bibliography shows his draft entry for this title, clipped from the April 1920 number of the AAS *Proceedings,* where it was originally printed: from Isaiah Thomas's 1810 *The History of Printing in America* (Cat. 9), Brigham knew that the *Brownsville Gazette* was being published early in 1810; and an 1882 county history citation indicated that it began publication no later than January 14, 1809. But no new information had

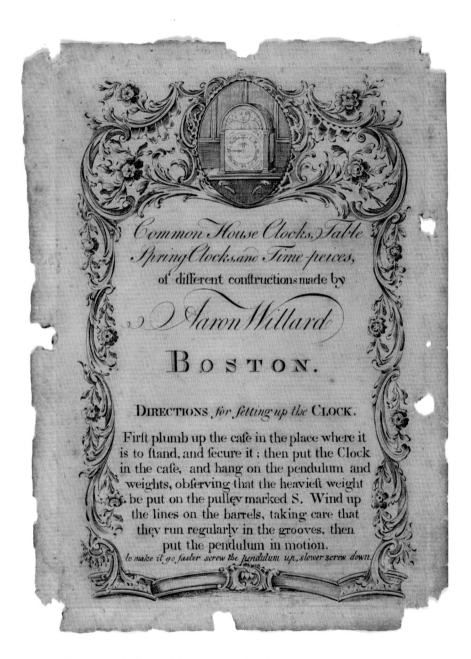

Common House Clocks, Table Spring Clocks, and Time-peices,

of different constructions made by

Aaron Willard

BOSTON.

DIRECTIONS *for setting up the* CLOCK.

First plumb up the case in the place where it is to stand, and secure it; then put the Clock in the case, and hang on the pendulum and weights, observing that the heaviest weight be put on the pulley marked S. Wind up the lines on the barrels, taking care that they run regularly in the grooves, then put the pendulum in motion. *to make it go faster screw the pendulum up, slower screw down.*

CAT. 162. Paul Revere, Clock Label for Aaron Willard, 1781.

come Brigham's way between 1920 and 1947. Based on the discovery issue's date and numbering, however, it is now known that William Campbell launched the *Brownsville Gazette* sometime in 1807.

162. Paul Revere. Clock Label for Aaron Willard. Boston, July 1781.

GIFT OF THE WELLS HISTORICAL MUSEUM, 1954.

Clarence S. Brigham's passion for American imprint bibliography extended beyond books, pamphlets, and newspapers to the graphic arts. While researching his book, *Paul Revere's Engravings,* he went to great lengths to identify and locate examples of every known engraving by the American silversmith and patriot. Once he found an impression in a private collection or dealer's shop, Brigham would often engage the owner in a dialogue about selling or donating the piece to AAS. Thanks to Brigham's diligence and persuasive personality, the Society holds a nearly complete set of Revere's engravings, including prints, paper currency, advertisements, and trade cards.

Brigham's quest for this Chippendale-style advertising label made for clockmaker Aaron Willard offers a fine example of his tenacity and patience. Brigham knew of the label's existence by 1915, when he took careful notes from Revere's daybooks, which showed charges to Simon and Aaron Willard for clock labels. But where to find such labels? In antique clocks, of course. In 1938, Brigham placed an advertisement in the *Boston Transcript* seeking the public's help in locating Revere material. This large Willard clock label, with its depiction of a shelf clock and instructions for setting it up properly, was one of the last Revere acquisitions made by Brigham for AAS before his book went to press. By then he had identified over twenty examples of the label, in three variant printings, inside clocks scattered around New England.

AAS Chief Joys 269, Brigham 57.

163. Sample record from Clarence, the AAS newspaper holdings

database, for the *Massachusetts Spy,* 1775-1778.

AAS is marking the start of its third century with a new, innovative bibliographical initiative which would have greatly impressed Clarence S. Brigham: a searchable online index of the more than two million newspaper issues in its collections. Named for Brigham, the Clarence database of the Society's newspaper holdings was developed entirely in-house over the past five years. It is unique among research library online databases, and it solves the previously intractable problem of determining which newspaper issues the Society holds.

Clarence can be accessed freely over the Internet, either directly or via a link from newspaper records in the AAS online library catalog. A search for a specific newspaper title retrieves a complete, easily read listing of AAS holdings displayed in calendar form. Clarence's powerful capabilities also permit researchers to search across the entire collection by title, city, state, county, or state; by language, frequency of publication, genre, and political affiliation; by printer, publisher, and editor; and, of course, by date. It is even possible to identify all newspaper issues at the Society published at the time of a specific historical event. The development of Clarence has been funded in part by support from the Center for Research Libraries.

164. Clifford K. Shipton, shown promoting the *Early American Imprints, 1639-1800* microprint, Worcester: photographed for the *Telegram & Gazette,* 1957.

[See page 175]

165. *Early American Imprints 1639-1800.* Box 1. Worcester: American Antiquarian Society and Readex Microprint Corporation, 1955.

READEX MICROPRINT CORP., 1955.

Concerned that early American history was declining as a discipline due to the difficulty of accessing the primary sources, AAS librarian Clifford K. Shipton saw the research value of placing surrogate copies in as many libraries as possible. He found a kindred spirit in Albert Boni who, after a distinguished publishing career, was now involved in micropublishing as president of Readex Microprint Corporation. In 1954, the Society and Readex established a partnership which continues to this day.

The concept was simple: produce a microprint edition of every pre-1801 book, pamphlet, and broadside printed in what is now the United States at a price that would be affordable to larger libraries. Its execution, however, was complex and highly demanding. Shipton and other AAS staff undertook the editorial work: completing the final volume of Charles Evans's *American Bibliography,* making AAS's originals available for microfilming, ordering microfilm from other libraries for Evans titles not held by AAS, and preparing target cards for each title. Finished not in the promised ten, but in thirteen years, the *Early American Imprints* microprint edition brilliantly realized Shipton's vision, making over 36,000 titles fully accessible to patrons at hundreds of institutions worldwide.

166. Cotton Mather. *Rules for the Society of Negroes. 1693.* Boston: probably Bartholomew Green, ca. 1714.

The content of this early broadside (which reprints the 1693 rules for the Society of Negroes in Boston) was written by Cotton Mather. It is inscribed in manuscript on the verso by Boston judge Samuel Sewall, author of the anti-slavery text *The Selling of Joseph* (1700). His inscription helps to date the sheet: "Left at my house for me, when I was not at home, by Spaniard Dr. Mather's Negro; March 23, 1713-14." This broadside is an example of a rare printing made widely available via microprint. The *Early American Imprints* microprint edition employed proprietary Readex technology: microfilmed page images were reduced in size, then photographically transferred to a lithographic plate. Each plate contained one hundred images (in ten rows of ten), which were

carefully printed on coated card stock. When viewed on the special reader supplied with each set, even the smallest type appeared sharp and fully legible. During the 1970s, the microprint edition was replaced by a more convenient microfiche edition, which more recently has been superseded by a digital edition with full-text search capabilities.

AAS Broadsides Collection.

Evans 653.

167. Joseph Green, *Entertainment for a Winter's Evening: Being a Full and True Account of a Very Strange and Wonderful Sight in Boston on the Twenty-Seventh of December, 1749.* Boston: Gamaliel Rogers, 1750.

GIFT OF THOMAS WALLCUT, 1834.

Among the thousands of titles catalogued as part of the North American Imprints Program (NAIP) is this mock-epic poem satirizing the first public Masonic procession in Boston. A Latin quotation on the title page is translated in manuscript "First march the Geese, then the Calves, then a troop of Asses. They enter the Temple. A holy man preaches to them surrounded by a mighty crowd of people."

On the title page the author is listed as "Honorable B.B. Esq." but a 1795 edition (also at AAS) identifies the author as Joseph Green (1706-1780), a Boston merchant and distiller identified in *Sibley's Harvard Graduates* as "the most famous wit of that generation of New Englanders." This pamphlet was part of the two tons of books, pamphlets and manuscripts given to AAS by Thomas Wallcut and retrieved from a hot Boston attic in the summer of 1834 by AAS librarian Christopher Columbus Baldwin.

The NAIP record created at AAS for Green's poem is in the MARC format originally developed by the Library of Congress in the 1960s and still a standard format for machine-readable cataloging in libraries throughout the world. Each aspect of a work (for example, author, title, imprint, multiple subjects, and even size and notes on provenance) is entered into a numbered field to allow users to do sophisticated searching.)

CAT. 168. Selected bibliographies published by AAS.

The AAS copy of *Entertainment for a Winter's Evening* was microfilmed by Readex in the 1950s for inclusion in the microprint version of *Early American Imprints*. Since 2004 subscribing libraries worldwide have had access to a digital version of the Readex collection. Texts in the new version fully searchable by word or phrase; AAS's NAIP cataloging underlies the images allowing additional searching options—for example for poetry as a genre.

Evans 6511; Wegelin 185.

168. Bibliographies of American imprints published by AAS.

Isaiah Thomas's vision of a comprehensive early American imprints checklist has been realized, not only through AAS's contributions to Charles Evans's *American Bibliography* and its work on the North American Imprints Program, but also through the Society's publications. Many of the Society's bibliographical publications—covering books, broadsides, periodicals, newspapers, prints, and other genres—are standard references in their specialized fields. Some are shown here, defining such areas as pre-1801 book catalogs and New Jersey imprints; pre-1811 sacred music imprints; pre-1821 American newspapers, carriers' addresses, children's books, songsters, and Vermont imprints; pre-1831 religious periodicals and newspapers; pre-1851 Masonic publications and writing books; pre-1861 city directories and cookery books; and the engravings of Alexander Anderson and Paul Revere.

AAS staff has also compiled other essential bibliographical tools. Among these are two online databases: Catalog of American Engravings, describing nearly 17,000 intaglio images in pre-1821 American books, almanacs, periodicals, as well as separately published broadsides and prints; and the Nineteenth Century American Children's Book Trade Directory, documenting 2,600 individuals and firms. Still unpublished, but accessible at AAS, is the incomparable Printers' File, compiled primarily by AAS cataloguer Avis G. Clarke, an unrivalled source of biographical information on several thousand pre-1821 American printers, publishers, and booksellers.

Collection Development and Responsible Stewardship

Isaiah Thomas's expectation that the collections he and others donated to the American Antiquarian Society would be used to the fullest in illuminating America's early history and culture has long presented the Society with a welcome challenge: that of providing as supportive an environment as possible for scholarship and access. A century ago the bibliographer Charles Evans proclaimed AAS his favorite place to work, and many subsequent testimonials demonstrate how seriously and successfully the Society has embraced that challenge. And as the nature of scholarly research has changed in recent decades, AAS has continually reassessed its activities, adapting them to better address the needs of its constituencies.

One significant change has been the increasingly collaborative character of the research process. As researchers work more frequently in teams to conduct research beyond the capabilities of a single scholar, AAS has tried to accommodate such efforts. Such was the case in 1967, when the Society and Clark University formed a partnership to support a new critical edition of the works of James Fenimore Cooper. Clark faculty supplied the editorial leadership, while AAS proceeded to build the most complete collection anywhere of pre-1877 editions of Cooper's many works, soon augmented by an important group of Cooper's literary manuscripts and a Hinman Collator on which to compare the various texts. These have been placed at the service of the project's editorial teams, which to date have published authoritative texts for the majority of Cooper's works.

Another change has been the rise of new scholarly disciplines, often with an interdisciplinary focus. When, in the early 1980s, American scholars began to study American history and culture through the new perspective of book history, AAS seized the opportunity to nurture their work. Since 1983 the Society's Program in the History of the Book in American Culture has been successful in advancing this scholarly discipline through such activities as the Summer Seminar in the History of the Book, occasional conferences, the Program's widely disseminated newsletter, scholarship published in the Society's *Proceedings,* and the annual James Russell Wiggins Lecture. Most ambitious of all was the Society's support of a multi-volume history written by a team of scholars under the direction of David D. Hall. The two-volume work envisioned in 1982 eventually grew into the five-volume *A History of the Book in America* (2000-2010, Cat. 185), an innovative work of scholarship published to international acclaim. Fittingly, its final volume was issued exactly two hundred years after the appearance of its distinguished precursor, Isaiah Thomas's *The History of Printing in America* (Cat. 9).

More recently, AAS established the Center for Historic American Visual Culture (CHAViC) to advance the interdisciplinary study of the graphic arts in American print culture. Modeled on the Program in the History of the Book, CHAViC has organized conferences, summer seminars, and programs for scholars in the emerging discipline of visual culture. The center also supports the creation of descriptive catalog records and

FIG. 42. Ellen S. Dunlap.

online resources exploring the Society's outstanding holdings of visual material. The primary goal of the center is to create connections between scholars and the visual record that will allow the expansion of our understanding of American history and culture.

AAS has always worked to foster a local community of scholars, and many are the stories of collections formed, books written, and questions resolved based on serendipitous interactions between readers and staff. To further that end, and in recognition of potential economic barriers to the research process, especially for graduate students and junior faculty, in recent years the Society has raised sufficient endowment funding to award over forty long- and short-term fellowships annually. These bring to AAS a lively mix of graduate students, junior and senior faculty, independent scholars, authors, and artists, many of whom elect to stay at the Society's fellows' residence, located next door to the library. In this way the intellectual community formed at AAS extends far beyond the reading room.

There have also been profound changes in the ways in which scholars access primary and secondary source materials. Since the days of Clifford K. Shipton and his partnering with Readex Microprint Corporation, AAS has been a pioneer in broadening access to its collections. In the current digital era, the Society, under the leadership of president Ellen S. Dunlap (1992-), has forged new commercial partnerships through which some fifteen million additional pages from the AAS collections have been made available online in digital form with full-text search capabilities. In addition to pre-1821 imprints, the newly available texts include nineteenth-century newspapers; nearly 6,500 pre-1900 periodical titles; thousands of items listed in Joseph Sabin's *A Dictionary of Books Relating to America, from its Discovery to the Present Time;* and specialized collections of genealogies, local histories, American literature, manuscripts, and many other resources.

These changes also have had implications for the AAS collections. Since Marcus A. McCorison's retirement in 1992, Society Librarians Nancy H. Burkett (1991-2006) and Thomas Knoles (2006-) have encouraged individual curators to take the lead in expanding the portions of the collections for which they are responsible. They have collected broadly, without limiting themselves to current trends. Time and again researchers exploring new avenues of scholarly inquiry have found at the Society precisely those primary source materials essential for their research. Some of the areas in which curators are presently acquiring include periodical issues in original printed wrappers; imprints from the period ca. 1855-1880 illustrated with original mounted photographs; examples of fine and publishers' bookbindings, especially unusual styles, those signed by the binder, and those still in fine condition; examples of transatlantic publishing, that is, publications or prints issued for the American market which reflect some degree of collaboration among authors, illustrators, printers, publishers, distributors, and binders on both sides of the Atlantic; publications, especially newspapers, printed by hobbyist printers on "amateur" presses; periodicals issued in manuscript; and partly printed volumes sold by stationers for the purposes of customized record-keeping.

These initiatives would not have been possible without the continued support, both financial and in-kind, of many generous AAS donors. As this exhibition makes clear, until the mid-twentieth century the Society's collections earned their distinction primarily through gift rather than by purchase. But beginning in the 1960s, AAS initiated a concerted effort to build its endowment, striving not only to develop a stable funding base, but to fund new programmatic activities. This effort has succeeded admirably, having encouraged many gifts that are of considerable importance to the Society's collection. The fourteen endowed acquisitions funds in existence in 1967 have since grown to ninety-two funds, ensuring that the Society will have the means to continue building all of its many collections. Of special note are the Harry G. Stoddard Memorial Fund, AAS's largest acquisitions endowment, established in 1982 by the Stoddard Charitable Trust of Worcester, and the Linda F. and Julian L. Lapides Fund, which since 1986 has enabled AAS to develop its children's literature holdings in more considered fashion. More recently, the graphic arts collections have benefited from transformational gifts from AAS member and semiconductor pioneer Jay Last which have funded acquisitions, fellowships, and start-up costs for the Center for Historic American Visual Culture (CHAViC). Perhaps the most valuable commodity for an institution such as AAS is space to shelve new acquisitions, and generous gifts from many sources enabled the Society in 2001 to add its fourth addition to Antiquarian Hall: a state-of-the art book stack providing ample room for collection growth well into AAS's third century.

CAT. 169. Samuel Richardson. *Pamela: Or, Virtue Rewarded*, 1742-1743.

169. Samuel Richardson. *Pamela: Or, Virtue Rewarded* ... Fifth edition. Philadelphia: B. Franklin, 1742-1743.

GIFT OF THE STODDARD CHARITABLE TRUST, 1968.

Of the several dozen endowed acquisitions funds established at AAS over the past five decades, none has been more significant than the Harry G. Stoddard Memorial Fund, which honors Harry G. Stoddard (1873-1969), a Worcester industrialist and newspaper publisher who very generously supported AAS. Indeed, prior to the Fund's establishment, Stoddard (and later the Stoddard Charitable Trust) regularly made special acquisitions grants to AAS. Today the fund accounts for fully one-fifth of the Society's annual acquisition budget.

One of the most significant Stoddard-funded acquisitions was this unique copy of the first modern novel to be published in America. Intending to capitalize on the popularity of Samuel Richardson's *Pamela* (1740), Benjamin Franklin resolved in 1742 to print an edition for sale in the American colonies. However, Franklin's edition was not placed on sale until late 1744, having been delayed by other work. By then imported copies had satisfied much of the demand, and never again did Franklin reprint a novel. This copy was among those shipped to Boston bookseller Charles Harrison and bound in his bindery (see also Cat. 37). Eventually this copy found its way to the library of Simmons College, where it was rediscovered in the 1960s and, with Stoddard funding, soon relocated to AAS.

AAS Chief Joys 140; Evans 5486; Miller 293, 338.

170. *Harry; The Boy That Did Not Own Himself.* Boston: American Tract Society, ca. 1863.

PURCHASE, LINDA F. AND JULIAN L. LAPIDES FUND, 2009.

This fine example of an antislavery children's book was published by the American Tract Society of Boston, which in 1859 split from the national office in New York because of that organization's reluctance to address the evil of slavery in its publications. It is a fictional chronicle of Harry's perilous journey to manhood, from his abduction by slave traders as a baby to his escape to Canada as a young man. One illustration portrays the pivotal moment when young Harry asks a white schoolboy to teach him to read a store sign, thus launching the slave into the world of literacy and, ultimately, freedom. The image was executed by John N. Hyde (1837-1895), who worked as a staff artist for the American Tract Society and as art director for magazine publisher Frank Leslie.

This copy of *Harry* was acquired in 2009 using the Linda F. and Julian L. Lapides Fund. The Lapides endowment was AAS's first acquisition fund devoted exclusively to children's literature, and for the past twenty-five years it has provided crucial support for building the Society's comprehensive collection of pre-1877 American children's literature. Within the last decade alone, AAS has added over 700 juvenile titles with the support of this important fund.

171. David Claypoole Johnston. *Early Development of Southern Chivalry.* India ink and watercolor on paper, ca. 1864.

PURCHASE, ADOPT-A-BOOK FUNDS, 2009.

This provocative sketch by artist and satirist David Claypoole Johnston (1799-1865) (see also Cats. 61-62) was created shortly before his death, as the Civil War was drawing to a close. It depicts two Southern children in a parlor whipping an African-American doll, which has been tied to a chair. Portraits of Confederate General P. G. T. Beauregard and Jefferson Davis hang on the walls. The girl's cruel smile and the boy's manly stance are depicted with a brutality that Johnston usually reserved for such targets as politicians and social reformers. The sketch was probably intended to

CAT. 171. David Claypoole Johnston. *Early Development of Southern Chivalry,* ca. 1864.

become a lithograph or book illustration, though no evidence has been found that it was ever reproduced. Johnston frequently ridiculed both sides of the era's various reform movements, including temperance, dress reform and anti-slavery, often casting children in adult roles. Other Johnston cartoons show little boys as incompetent soldiers, or gathering in social groups, gambling and smoking.

AAS acquired the sketch with funds raised during its first Adopt-a-Book event, held in 2008. This annual acquisitions fundraiser, in which AAS supporters may "adopt" a recent acquisition by donating its purchase price, has raised nearly $100,000 to date. *Southern Chivalry* was also one of the first images to be digitized and made available online under the auspices of the Center for Historic American Visual Culture (CHAViC), established by AAS in 2005 to promote awareness of AAS collections and to stimulate research and intellectual inquiry into American visual materials. Over a dozen online illustrated collection inventories and multiple digital exhibitions featuring AAS materials have been produced with CHAViC support, significantly broadening global access to AAS holdings.

172. *The Chess Monthly.* New York, Vol. 3, No. 2, February 1859.

It has long been common practice when

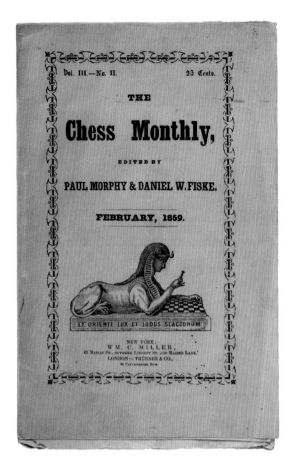

CAT. 172. *The Chess Monthly,* 1859.

binding periodicals—whether by publishers in order to sell cumulative volumes, or by libraries and private owners for purposes of convenience and preservation—to remove the outer wrappers and advertisement leaves from individual issues, leaving only the main body of text. However, periodical wrappers and advertisement leaves often contain important material which scholars (and bibliographers) are increasingly finding vital to their research. In recent years AAS has made it a priority to collect early American periodical issues with wrappers intact, even going so far as to acquire second, wrappered copies to complement a set bound without wrappers. In many instances, wrappered copies prove to be exceptionally rare survivals.

This issue of *The Chess Monthly* is a good example. The journal's editor was Daniel W. Fiske (1831-1904), then champion of the New York Chess Club and later Cornell University's first librarian. For a time, American chess prodigy and unofficial world champion Paul Morphy (1837-1884) held the title of co-editor, lending the magazine his marquee name. Only on the wrappers, however, are their editorial roles mentioned. The wrappers also contain publication information not available elsewhere, an advertisement for a set of Morphy-endorsed chessmen made of cast iron and—perhaps most important of all—the answers to chess problems published in the previous issue.

AAS Periodical Collection.

CAT. 174. Susan Pindar, *Fireside Fairies*, 1849.

173. James Porter. *Clergyman's Pocket Diary and Visiting Book. 186__*. New York: Carlton and Porter, 1860.

PURCHASE, JOHN THOMAS LEE FUND, 2008.

In recent years AAS has been actively acquiring partly printed volumes intended to be written in by the user. These volumes falling at the intersection of manuscript and print include albums, composition books, lawyers' commonplace books, ship's logs, diaries, and volumes prepared for customized record-keeping of all kinds. With the increasing availability of print and expanding markets during the nineteenth century, such volumes became highly specialized; diaries, for example, were available in a wide range of sizes, from small pocket volumes to large quartos. Partly printed volumes have long been overlooked by curators and book historians alike, in part because they present challenges to catalogers, being both book and manuscript. Although such volumes have been preserved in manuscript collections, they have yet to be appreciated for what they reveal about the very considerable market for job printing, stationers' supplies, and specialty publishing.

This pocket diary was prepared for use by Methodist ministers. Publishers Carlton and Porter were agents for the Methodist Book Concern and the Sunday School Union of the Methodist Episcopal Church. A calendar for 1861 is included, though years and days of the week are otherwise omitted for ease of updating and annual republication. In addition to the diary, the volume provides sections for keeping accounts, records of baptisms, marriages and funerals, and membership lists. There is also provision for recording the owner's actions "as agents for books and periodicals, and the benevolent societies of the Church."

CAT. 175. *Our Choir,* 1861.

174. Publisher's Binding on: Susan Pindar. *Fireside Fairies: Or Christmas at Aunt Elsie's.* New York: D. Appleton; Philadelphia: Geo. S. Appleton, ca. 1849.

GIFT OF JOHN AND CAROLYN GROSSMAN, 2006.

Acquiring particularly fine or notable pre-1877 American bookbindings is an ongoing priority for AAS, an initiative supported in part by an endowed acquisitions fund established by Michael Papantonio's friends following his death. One recent acquisition is this copy of *Fireside Fairies,* in a highly unusual publisher's binding of fine white cloth with an elaborate cover design printed in five colors. The late 1840s was a time of much innovation and creativity in the design of American publishers' bindings. D. Appleton and Leavitt & Co. were among those who experimented briefly with these attractive printed cloth bindings. Today, examples are rarely encountered, especially in such fine condition.

175. *Our Choir, in 1860-61.* By You Know Who. Illustrated by Phiz. New York, 1861.

PURCHASE, HARRY G. STODDARD MEMORIAL FUND, 2008.

From the 1850s to the 1880s, several thousand American publications were illustrated with original mounted photographs. Many are quite rare and, because there is no comprehensive checklist of these publications, remain little known. AAS has been actively acquiring new titles and identifying the approximately one thousand already on its shelves, which constitute perhaps the best extant collection of American imprints illustrated with original mounted photographs.

One recent acquisition is this American photographically illustrated book, of which only one other copy has been recorded. During the winter of 1860-1861, choristers of New York's Eleventh Presbyterian Church (then at Fourth Street and Avenue C) formed an especially strong social bond by rehearsing in one another's homes. This privately printed volume served as a keepsake of their friendship. Eight-

CAT. 176. *Politics in an Oyster House*, 1851.

een choir members are profiled in light verse, with their oval albumen photographic portraits mounted on the facing pages, save for two men whose portraits, a penciled caption states, "would be obtained on [their] return from the war." The choir's female members come first, followed gallantly by the men, one of whom—T. B. Van Amringe—may be the versifier "You Know Who;" "Phiz" the photographer has yet to be identified.

176. Michele Fanoli, after Richard Canton Woodville. *Politics in an Oyster House.* Paris and New York: Lemercier for Goupil & Co., 1851.

GIFT OF JAY LAST, 2005.

This lithograph with added watercolor of two men seated in an oyster house debating the day's news is an excellent example of the intricacies of transatlantic publishing. American artist Richard Canton Woodville, known for his genre scenes of Baltimore life, painted this image in 1848 while studying in Düsseldorf, later selling the painting to a Baltimore patron. The French firm Goupil & Co. reproduced Woodville's painting as part of its strategy to develop an American market for fine prints. Produced in Paris by Lemercier, then one of the world's largest lithographic companies, the sheets were sold internationally through Goupil's network of shops in New York, London, Berlin and Paris. French lithographers, artists, and pressmen were instrumental to the rise of American lithography, a topic explored in a 2012 exhibition curated by AAS staff, *With a French Accent: French and American Lithography before 1860.*

This impression was acquired as part of a gift made to AAS by member Jay Last. Over the last two decades, Last has provided generous financial support for stack and building expansion, fellowships in visual culture, and graphic arts acquisitions. As a collector and scholar of American lithography, Last has worked with AAS curators to add some 550 prints to the collection, enabling AAS to fill significant gaps and to expand in areas previously beyond the Society's financial reach.

177. *The Life of Philip Quarll, Giving an Account of his Surprising Adventures on an Inunhabited* [sic] *Island.* Baltimore: C. Scheld and Co., 1833.

PURCHASE, RUTH E. ADOMEIT BOOK FUND, 2004.

Over the past two decades, collecting transatlantic children's books—that is, those reflecting a transatlantic collaboration among printer, publisher, and distributor—has become a priority for AAS. Such imprints reveal the extent to which children's book publishing became an international activity during the nineteenth century.

Take, for instance, this edition of *The Life of Philip Quarll*, an adaptation for children of Peter Longueville's *The Unparalleled Sufferings and Surprising Adventures of Philip Quarll*. It was probably printed in Paris as part of the series *Truchy's French and English Library*—the footnotes provide French translations for some words and phrases in the English text. The portion of the edition intended for sale in the United States received a Baltimore imprint. This robinsonade sports a brilliantly hand-colored lithographed frontispiece of *Quarll* discovering a monkey in his hut. This unusual example was acquired on the Ruth E. Adomeit Book Fund, established in 1992 through Adomeit's generous bequest to support the acquisition of American children's books printed before 1851.

178. Johann Hübner. *Hübners Biblische Historien als dem Alten und Neuen Testamente ...* Cornersburg, Ohio: Augustus Gräter, 1835.

PURCHASE, HARRY G. STODDARD MEMORIAL FUND, 2008.

European printers began to produce books for American publishers as far back as 1658, when Hezekiah Usher commissioned from an unidentified printer in Cambridge, England, an edition of the Bay Psalm Book bearing his imprint, for importation and sale in his Boston bookshop. Such transatlantic imprints were rare until the nineteenth century when, despite rampant piracy, the European and American book trades forged closer ties.

AAS actively seeks interesting examples of transatlantic publishing, and this recent acquisition is one of the more unusual. Although the title page bears a Cornersburg, Ohio, imprint this 376-page volume with over fifty finely executed wood engravings was clearly printed and bound in Germany for export. First published in 1714, Hübner's popular *Biblische Historien* became a specialty of the Reutlingen book trade, and this volume has title wording, pagination, and illustrations identical to those of several 1830's Reutlingen editions. Indeed, careful examination reveals the Cornersburg imprint to be a cancel slip pasted over the original Reutlingen imprint. Augustus Gräter published several other works for the German-American market, all being substantial illustrated volumes printed in Germany, where such technically demanding work could be executed more competently and economically. Through enterprising distributors such as Gräter, the German book trade was able to disseminate its products throughout the United States.

179. Edward C. Gay. *The Boy Smuggler.* Farmer City, Illinois: Ed. C. Gay, 1876.

PURCHASE, HARRY G. STODDARD MEMORIAL FUND, 2007.

With the advent of the parlor press in the 1860s came not only thousands of amateur newspapers, but many full-blown amateur books. Over the past two decades, developing AAS's amateur book collection has become a high priority, as these homespun imprints serve to complement the Society's unrivalled collection of amateur newspapers.

The Boy Smuggler is an adventure story about smuggling, shipwrecks, and courtship—all topics of no little interest to teenage boys! Although published in Farmer City, Illinois, the book was actually printed by Thomas G. Har-

rison in Lafayette, Indiana, some seventy-five miles distant. Seven years later Harrison (b. 1860) published an extensive history of amateur journalism, with reminiscences of his own career as an amateur printer and president of the National Amateur Press Association. About this title Harrison wrote, "Gay sent me the mss. for a book, entitled 'The Boy Smuggler,' which I was to print for him. Upon the receipt of fifty pounds of new brevier type ... I printed and bound 300 copies for him, using blue ink." The book's advertisements are particularly interesting: they include ads for amateur printers operating in Otterville, Iowa and in Indianapolis; and the book's author, Edward C. Gay (b. 1859 or 60), advertises printing equipment for sale, including a "good new octavo novelty press."

180. *Le Bijou.* Cincinnati, Vol. 3, No. 2, September 1879.

A hobby practiced especially by teenagers, amateur journalism exploded in popularity in the United States following the invention of an inexpensive table-top printing press in 1867. During the 1870s and 1880s, thousands of amateur newspapers were published and liberally exchanged with other amateur journalists around the country. Because of the circumstances under which they were produced, amateur newspapers are becoming of increasing interest to historians, and AAS actively adds to its large collection.

One of the most interesting amateur newspapers at AAS is *Le Bijou*, edited and published by Herbert A. Clark (ca. 1860-ca. 1924). A great-grandson of Lewis and Clark Expedition leader William Clark, Herbert was born into one of Cincinnati's leading African-American families. His father Peter, an associate of Frederick Douglass, was politically active and instrumental in establishing free public schools for Ohio African-Americans. *Le Bijou* is notable for its prominent and forthright advocacy of civil rights, a fight carried over to the Amateur Press Association, which in 1879 elected Clark its third vice-president over the heated objections of its Southern members. Many withdrew, forming in its stead the secret Ama-

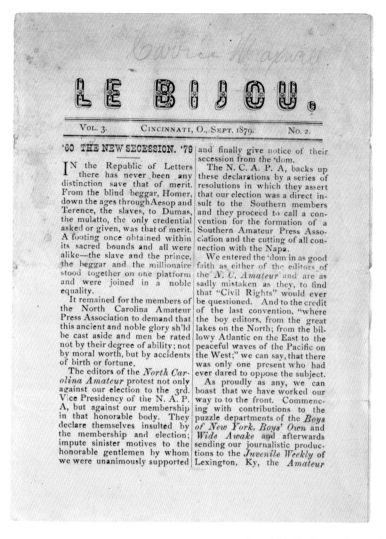

CAT. 180. *Le Bijou*, September 1879.

teur Anti-Negro Admission Association. Clark delightedly reported on the controversy in the pages of *Le Bijou*, which he published from 1878 to 1880. He then moved on to a career as a journalist and publisher of African-American newspapers.

AAS Amateur Newspaper Collection.

181. "The Kentucky Spy and Porcupine Quill." Frankfort, Kentucky, Vol. 6, No. 1, January 25, 1849.

In recent years AAS has actively collected

issues of pre-1877 American manuscript periodicals. These handwritten examples mimic printed periodicals in format and content, containing stories, news, and advertisements. Sometimes they were produced by individuals, serving as the manuscript equivalent of amateur newspapers, and sometimes they were issued by small groups. Others were produced as an activity of a school or lyceum.

AAS has held manuscript periodicals since the nineteenth century; but because these were long shelved alongside printed periodicals, they were easily overlooked. In the 1990s AAS staff began to pull them together into a separate collection, in the process discovering not only how

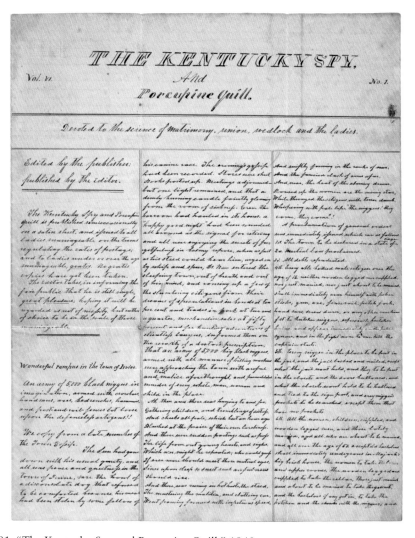

CAT. 181. "The Kentucky Spy and Porcupine Quill," 1849.

many titles were already at AAS, but also the frequency with which they were produced. As it became apparent that the more specimens AAS had, the more they collectively revealed about early American scribal culture, AAS began to seek them actively. The collection now numbers more than sixty titles.

One of the more unusual is "The Kentucky Spy and Porcupine Quill." The masthead claims that it is "Devoted to the science of matrimony, union, wedlock and the ladies." However, the chief story, entitled "Wonderful rumpus in the town of Irvine," is a fictional account, humorous in tone, of a revolt by 5,000 heavily armed slaves which in the story turns out to be a hoax. The editor and contributor(s) are unnamed.

AAS Manuscript Periodical Collection.

182. James Fenimore Cooper. *The Last of the Mohicans; A Narrative of 1757.* **Philadelphia: H.C. Carey & I. Lea, 1826.**

GIFT OF THE FAMILY OF
JAMES F. BEARD, JR., 1990.

183. James Fenimore Cooper. *The Last of the Mohicans; A Narrative of 1757.* **Albany: State University of New York Press, 1983.**

GIFT OF THE PUBLISHER, 1982.

CAT. 185. *A History of the Book in America*, 2000-2010.

The longest running scholarly initiative based on AAS collections has been *The Writings of James Fenimore Cooper*. Conceived by Cooper scholar James Franklin Beard, Jr. of Clark University in Worcester, the project was established in 1967 as the joint undertaking of AAS and Clark University, with funding from the American Philosophical Society, the National Endowment for the Humanities, and other sources. Over the past forty-five years, teams of scholars have established definitive, critically edited texts for twenty-two of Cooper's works.

AAS's contribution to the project has been to asssemble as complete a collection as possible of all editions of Cooper's works, in any language, published up to 1877. Many are present in multiple copies acquired either by AAS, or from the collection of Cooper's works assembled by Beard for the use of the Edition's editors. To these have been added a substantial group of Cooper's letters and literary manuscripts, bequeathed to AAS in 1988 by Cooper's great-great-grandson, Paul Fenimore Cooper, Jr. Cooper Edition editors have employed these resources to trace the textual history of each work, and then to establish a definitive text by collating multiple copies,

often using the Hinman Collator acquired by AAS for the project.

This well-used first edition copy of *The Last of the Mohicans*, collated on AAS's Hinman Collator, served as the copy-text and printer's copy for the 1983 critical edition. Although in far from "collector's condition," this copy will be retained for permanent reference in AAS's Cooper collecton.

184-185. Letter. David D. Hall to Marcus A. McCorison, July 14, 1982.

A History of the Book in America. Cambridge, England: Cambridge University Press & American Antiquarian Society, 2000; Chapel Hill, North Carolina: University of North Carolina Press & American Antiquarian Society, 5 Vols., 2007-2010.

Of the many scholarly activities sponsored by AAS over the past four decades, perhaps the most influential has been the Program in the History of the Book in American Culture (PHBAC). Established in 1983, PHBAC sought to forge enduring and productive bonds between the AAS collections and staff, and scholars active in the burgeoning academic field of book history. Under the initial chairmanship of David D. Hall, then of Boston University, PHBAC convened conferences on the book in early America, inaugurated the annual James Russell Wiggins Lecture in the History of the Book in American Culture, instituted an annual Summer Seminar in the History of the Book, and launched *The Book,* a newsletter disseminating news on American book history to an international forum.

PHBAC's most ambitious endeavor, however, has been the five-volume *A History of the Book in America.* It was conceived by David Hall as an American response to the path breaking, four-volume *Histoire de l' Édition française* (1983-1986), which attempted the "synthesis of 'book and society'" advocated by practitioners of the new histoire du livre. Hall broached the idea to AAS in a July 1982 letter, and AAS enthusiastically agreed to serve as sponsor. Initially scheduled to be completed in 1990 in two volumes, the project simultaneously expanded and slowed as it tried to keep pace with an outpouring of PHBAC-sponsored scholarship. Eventually completed in five volumes to international acclaim, *A History of the Book in America* contains over 3,250 pages written by over a hundred contributors.

AAS Archives; AAS Collections.

186. Bookplates for selected AAS endowed acquisitions funds, various designers, 1965-2010.

As *In Pursuit of a Vision* so richly demonstrates, AAS has built its collections primarily through the generosity of thousands of donors. Indeed, until the mid-1960s, donations in kind or in cash, supplemented by occasional extraordinary one-time benefactions such as the Brinley, Cooke, and Streeter bequests, were the principal engines of AAS collection growth.

The Society established its first permanent endowed acquisitions fund in 1858, but the effort grew slowly. When Marcus A. McCorison assumed the AAS directorship over a hundred years later in 1967, there were just fourteen funds supplying nearly sixty percent of the annual acquisitions budget.

Realizing that changes to the Society's funding model were necessary, McCorison and the AAS Council built up the AAS endowment through fundraising and a series of capital campaigns. McCorison's successor Ellen S. Dunlap has done much to encourage the continued creation of book funds. Today the AAS acquisitions program is fully funded through ninety-two endowed funds, supplemented by gifts and an annual Adopt-a-Book fundraising event. Items purchased on the endowed funds are marked with special bookplates, a selection of which is shown here. While these individual funds allow great flexibility in acquisitions, it is hoped that expansion of the collection through generous bequests and gifts (like many of those included in the exhibition) continues, as well. The enthusiasm of book, newspaper, manuscript, and art collectors, and their continued support, will remain essential as the Society moves forward into its third century.

FIG. 43

CAT. 186. A selection of AAS bookplates for endowed funds.

Hand List for the Exhibition

Case 1 – Isaiah Thomas

The Lawer's Pedigree. Boston: Zechariah Fowle, 1755. (Cat. 1; plate).

Tom Thumb's Play-Book; to Teach Children Their Letters as Soon as They Can Speak. Boston: Printed by Isaiah Thomas and sold by A. Barclay, 1764. (Cat. 2).

A Narrative, of the Excursion and Ravages of the King's Troops under the Command of General Gage, on the Nineteenth of April, 1775 ... Worcester: Isaiah Thomas, 1775. (Cat. 5).

Isaiah Thomas. "Catalogue of The Private Library of Isaiah Thomas, Senior, of Worcester, Massachusetts." March-July 1812. (Cat. 11; plate).

Phillis Wheatley. *Phillis's Poem on the Death of Mr. Whitefield.* On a sheet with *Bedlam Garland. Together with the Spinning Wheel.* Boston: Isaiah Thomas, 1770. (Cat. 3; plate).

A Monumental Inscription on the Fifth of March. Together with a Few Lines on the Enlargement of Ebenezer Richardson, Convicted of Murder. Boston: Isaiah Thomas, 1772. (Cat. 4).

William M. S. Doyle. *Isaiah Thomas.* Watercolor on ivory, ca. 1805. (Cat. 8; plate).

Tommy Trapwit. *Be Merry and Wise; or, the Cream of the Jests, and Marrow of Maxims, for the Conduct of Life. Published for the Use of all Good Little Boys and Girls.* First edition. Worcester: Isaiah Thomas and E. Battelle, 1786. (Cat. 7; plate).

"Songs, Ballads, &c. In Three Volumes. Purchased from a Ballad Printer and Seller in Boston." Volume 1 of 3. Boston: Various printers, 1811-1814. (Cat. 12).

Isaiah Thomas. *The History of Printing in America. With a Biography of Printers, and an Account of Newspapers ...* Worcester: Isaiah Thomas, Jr., 1810. (Cat. 9).

Michigan Essay; Or, the Impartial Observer. Detroit, Michigan, August 31, 1809. (Cat. 10; plate).

John Baine & Grandson. *A Specimen of Printing Types by John Baine & Grandson in Co., Letter-Founders.* Edinburgh, 1787. (Cat. 6; plate).

Case 1 – Hannah Mather Crocker

"Donors and Donations to the Amer. Antiquarian Society." Vol. 1, 1813-1829. (Cat. 13; plate).

Richard Mather. "A Platforme of Church-discipline, Gathered out of ye Word of God, and Agreed upon by ye Elders and Messengers of ye Churches, Assembled in the Synod at Cambridge in New England, ye 6th month, 1648." (Cat. 14; plate).

Letter, Cotton Mather to Increase Mather, May 17, 1690. (Cat. 15).

Thomas Johnston, attributed. *Mather Family Coat of Arms.* Watercolor and ink on paper, before 1767. (Cat. 16; plate).

Archibald Simson. *Hieroglyphica Animalium Terrestrium, Natatilium, Reptilium, Insectorum ... quæ in Scripturis Sacris Inveniuntur ...* Edinburgh: Thomas Finlayson, 1622 [i.e. 1624]. (Cat. 17; plate).

Case 2 – William Bentley

William Bentley Fowle. Inventory of the Library of William Bentley, 1820. (Cat. 18).

William Bentley. Diary, October 9, 1815-March 15, 1818. (Cat. 19).

William Bentley Fowle. "An Abridgement of Dibdin's Classics to Which Are Added Useful Notes and Remarks," ca. 1813. (Cat. 20; plate).

Samuel McIntire. *John Winthrop.* Carved and painted pine, 1798. (Cat. 22).

Samuel Harris. *Portrait of Elisha Cooke, the Son.* Red chalk on paper, ca. 1805-1807. (Cat. 23; plate).

John Foster. *Mr. Richard Mather.* Woodcut, second state, ca. 1670. (Cat. 21; plate).

Case 2 – Christopher Columbus Baldwin

Christopher Columbus Baldwin. Diary, September 15, 1833-July 15, 1835. (Cat. 25).

Sarah Goodridge. *Christopher Columbus Baldwin.* Watercolor on ivory, 1835. (Cat. 24; plate).

Several Rules, Orders, and By-Laws ... Made and Agreed upon ... May, 12. and September 22. 1701 ... Boston: Bartholomew Green and John Allen, for Benjamin Eliot, 1702. (Cat. 29; plate).

First Church, Salem, Massachusetts. *A Copy of the Church-Covenants Which Have Been Used in the Church of Salem ...* Boston: John Foster, 1680. (Cat. 28; plate).

The Sons of Africans: an Essay on Freedom, with Observations on the Origin of Slavery. Boston: African Society, 1808. (Cat. 27; plate).

Christopher Columbus Baldwin, "Catalogue of Pamphlets Received of the Boston Atheneum [sic] by the American Antiquarian Society." January 23, 1834. (Cat. 26).

Case 2 – Lucy Chase and Sarah E. Chase

Confederate States of America. *Public Laws of the Confederate States of America, Passed at the First Session of the Second Congress; 1864 ...* Richmond: R.M. Smith, 1864. (Cat. 32; plate).

Dickinson, Hill & Co. Account Book of Slave Auctions, Richmond, Virginia, 1846 to 1849. (Cat. 30; plate).

Coffee beans from General U.S. Grant's headquarters at City Point, Virginia, April 1865. (Cat. 31).

Case 3 – Joseph J. Cooke

John Smith. *The Generall Historie of Virginia, New-England, and the Summer Isles ...* London: John Dawson and John Haviland for Edward Blackmore, 1632. (Cat. 39; plate).

Roger Williams. *The Bloudy Tenent, of Persecution, for Cause of Conscience, Discussed, in a Conference between Truth and Peace ...* London, 1644. (Cat. 38).

Charles John Ann Hereford. *The History of Spain ...* Dublin: J. Exshaw, L. White, and Wm. Jones, 1793. (Cat. 41; plates).

Henry Clinton. *Correspondence between His Excellency General Sir Henry Clinton and Lieutenant General Earl Cornwallis.* Probably New York: James Rivington, 1781. (Cat. 40).

Case 3 – George Brinley

Letter, George P. Brinley and J. Hammond Trumbull to Stephen Salisbury II, February 24, 1879. (Cat. 33).

Richard Mather. A Defence of the Answer and Arguments of the Synod Met in Boston in the Year 1662 ... Cambridge, Massachusetts: S. Green and M. Johnson for Hezekiah Usher, 1664. (Cat. 34).

James Janeway. *A Token for Children. ... to Which is Added, A Token for the Children of New England.* Boston: Nicholas Boone and Benjamin Eliot for Timothy Green, 1700. (Cat. 36).

Increase Mather. *Wo to Drunkards. Two Sermons Testifying against the Sin of Drunkenness* ... Cambridge, Massachusetts: Marmaduke Johnson for Edmund Ranger, 1673. (Cat. 35; plate).

Marcus Tullius Cicero. *M. T. Cicero's Cato Major, or his Discourse of Old-Age: with Explanatory Notes.* Philadelphia: Benjamin Franklin, 1744. (Cat. 37; plate).

Case 3 – George Frisbee Hoar

Leonard Hoar. *The Sting of Death and Death Unstung, Delivered in Two Sermons* ... Boston: John Foster, 1680. (Cat. 51).

Samuel Cheever. *An Almanac for the Year of Our Lord 1661* ... Cambridge, Massachusetts: Samuel Green and Marmaduke Johnson, 1661. (Cat. 50; plate).

Jonas Clark. *The Fate of Blood-Thirsty Oppressors, and God's Tender Care of His Distressed People. A Sermon, Preached at Lexington, April 19, 1776* ... Boston: Powars and Willis, 1776. (Cat. 52; plate).

Case 3 – Stephen Salisbury III

The Atlantic Souvenir, A Christmas and New Year's Offering. 1826. Philadelphia: H.C. Carey & I. Lea, 1825. (Cat. 43; plate).

The Children's Friend. Number III. A New-Year's Present, to the Little Ones from Five to Twelve. New York: William B. Gilley, 1821. (Cat. 42; plate).

Case 3 – Nathaniel Paine

Nathaniel Paine. *Isaiah Thomas House.* 1887; *The Worcester Camera Club at Merriam's Corner, Concord Mass.* 1892; and *White Birch Tree, Intervale, N.H.* 1892. (Cats. 44-46).

Nathaniel Paine, compiler, *Freaks of Nature Illustrated.* 1891. (Cat. 48; plate).

Charleston Mercury Extra ... The Union is Dissolved! December 20, 1860. Charleston, South Carolina: Mercury Office, 1860. (Cat. 47; plate).

The Charter of the City of Saint John, in the Province of New-Brunswick. St. John: Lewis and Ryan, 1785. (Cat. 49).

Case 4 – Charles Henry Taylor

Bass Otis. *Self-Portrait.* Oil on tin, 1860. (Cat. 54).

Bass Otis. Account Book, 1815-1854. (Cat. 53; plate).

Nicolas-Eustache Maurin, after Gilbert Stuart. *George Washington, First President of the United States.* Boston: Pendleton, 1825-1828. (Cat. 55).

M.E.D. Brown, after John Neagle. *Wm. P. Dewees, M.D.* Philadelphia: N. Currier for M.E.D. Brown, 1834. (Cat. 56; plate).

Frances Sargent Locke Osgood. *The Cries of New-York.* New York: John Doggett, Jr., 1846. (Cat. 65; plate).

David Claypoole Johnston. *Taproom.* Watercolor on paper, ca. 1858. (Cat. 61; plate).

David Claypoole Johnston. Assorted ephemera and lens, ca. 1815-1850. (Cat. 62).

Moritz Furst, designer. American Institute Premium Medal. Struck by William and John Mott, Philadelphia, 1831. (Cat. 60).

The New-England Courant. Boston, February 5, 1722. (Cat. 63; plate).

Stephen H. Branch's Alligator. New York, September 11, 1858. (Cat. 64; plate).

Henry M. Johnson. Iron, Steel & Metals. 36 India Street, Boston, Mass. Boston: Ch. H. Crosby, 1870-1872. (Cat. 57).

Louis Prang & Co. *Cloisonné Vase.* New York: D. Appleton & Co., 1896-1897. (Cat. 58; plate).

F. Mayer & Co. Specimen Book. 1863. New York, 1863. (Cat. 59).

Case 5 – Herbert E. Lombard

John Greenleaf Whittier. *Poems Written During the Progress of the Abolition Question in the United States, between the Years 1830 and 1838.* Boston: Isaac Knapp, 1837. (Cat. 67; plate).

William Lloyd Garrison. *Selections from the Writings and Speeches of William Lloyd Garrison.* Boston: R. F. Wallcut, 1852. (Cat. 66).

Case 5 – Matt B. Jones

Michael Wigglesworth. *The Day of Doom, or, a Poetical Description of the Great and Last Judgment.* Cambridge, Massachusetts: Samuel Green, 1666. (Cat. 68).

Elisha Rich. *A Poem on the Late Distress of the Town of Boston ...* Chelmsford Massachusetts: Nathaniel Coverly, 1776. (Cat. 70; plate).

Job Weeden. *Job Weeden, Salem News-Boy, Begs Leave to Present the Following Lines ...* Salem, Massachusetts: Samuel Hall, 1771. (Cat. 69).

Case 5 – Frank Brewer Bemis

Nathaniel Hawthorne. *Fanshawe, a Tale*. Boston: Marsh & Capen, 1828. (Cat. 71).

Ralph Waldo Emerson. *Letter from the Rev. R.W. Emerson, to the Second Church and Society*. Boston: I.R. Butts, 1832. (Cat. 73).

Bret Harte. *The Pliocene Skull*. Washington, D.C.: Peters & Rehn, ca. 1871. (Cat. 72; plate).

Case 5 – Charles Henry Taylor

Herman Melville. *John Marr and Other Sailors, with Some Sea-Pieces*. New York: The De Vinne Press, 1888. (Cat. 75).

William Cook, author and illustrator. Five poetry booklets and broadsides. Salem, Massachusetts, 1852-1876. (Cat. 74; plate).

Case 5 – The Book Trades: Arthur Swann & William J. Campbell

American Art Association. *Illustrated Catalogue of New Jersey Memorabilia ... Comprising the Extensive Library of the Late William Nelson ... to be Sold on November 22-23, 1915 ...* New York: American Art Association, 1915. (Cat. 100).

Stan. V. Henkels. *Catalogue no. 1116. Valuable Americana ... of the Late Hon. Garret D. W. Vroom ... to be Sold ... Oct. 15 & 16, 1914 ...* Philadelphia: Stan. V. Henkels, 1914. (Cat. 101).

Case 5 – John W. Farwell

Edmond Halley. *A New Plan of the Harbour of Boston in New England ...* Watercolor and ink on paper, 1702. (Cat. 76; plate).

Council for Virginia. *A Declaration of the State of the Colony and Affaires in Virginia. With the Names of the Aduenturors, and Summes Aduentured in that Action*. London: Thomas Snodham, 1620. (Cat. 77).

John Norton. *The Redeemed Captive. Being a Narrative of the Taking and Carrying into Captivity the Reverend Mr. John Norton ...* Boston: Samuel Kneeland and Timothy Green, 1748. (Cat. 79).

The Death of the Brave General Wolf. Massachusetts: Ezekiel Russell, between 1775 and 1797. (Cat. 80; plate).

Library Company of Philadelphia. *A Catalogue of Books Belonging to the Library Company of Philadelphia*. Philadelphia: Benjamin Franklin, 1741. (Cat. 78).

Floor Case – Frederick Lewis Gay

Interesting Tracts, Relating to the Island of Jamaica, Consisting of Curious State-Papers, Councils of War, Letters ... Down to the Year 1702. St. Jago de la Vega: Lewis, Lunan, and Jones, 1800. (Cat. 82).

Judah Monis. *Dickdook Leshon Gnebreet. A Grammar of the Hebrew Tongue* ... Boston: Jonas Green, 1735. (Cat. 81; plate).

Floor Case – James Melville Hunnewell

James Frothingham Hunnewell. *A Catalogue of Books Belonging to James F. Hunnewell, of Charlestown, Mass.* Cambridge, Massachusetts: The Riverside Press, April 1873. (Cat. 83).

John Rocque. *A Set of Plans and Forts in America. Reduced from Actual Surveys.* London: Mary Ann Rocque, 1765. (Cat. 85; plate).

Urian Oakes. *New-England Pleaded with, and Pressed to Consider the Things which Concern Her Peace* ... Cambridge, Massachusetts: Samuel Green, 1673. (Cat. 84).

Sandwich Island Gazette and Journal of Commerce. Honolulu, July 30, 1836. (Cat. 86).

John Smith Emerson. *O ke kumumua na na kamalii: he palapala e ao aku ai i na kamalii ike ole i ka heluhelu palapala. [First Lessons for Children; A Book Teaching the Children Who Do Not Know How to Read Books.]* Second edition. Oahu: Mission Press, 1837. (Cat. 87; plate).

Floor Case – Samuel L. Munson

Davy Crockett's Almanack, of Wild Sports of the West, and Life in the Backwoods ... 1835. Nashville: Snag & Sawyer, 1834. (Cat. 90; plate).

Caleb Gibbs. Diary, 1778. In: *Poor Will's Pocket Almanack, for the Year 1778; Fitted to the Use of Pennsylvania* ... Philadelphia: J. Crukshank, 1777. (Cat. 91).

Benjamin Banneker. Holographic manuscript of his 1792 almanac and ephemeris. (Cat. 88).

Benjamin Banneker's Pennsylvania, Delaware, Maryland and Virginia Almanack and Ephemeris, for the Year of Our Lord, 1792 ... Baltimore: William Goddard and James Angell ..., both 1791. (Cat. 89; plate).

Case 6 – Edward Larocque Tinker

William Rollinson, after Jacques Tanesse. *Plan of the City and Suburbs of New Orleans from an Actual Survey Made in 1815* .... New York: Charles del Vecchio; New Orleans: Pierre Maspero, 1817. (Cat. 94; plate).

Laussat, Préfet colonial, Commissaire du Gouvernement français, ... 30 novembre 1803 ... New Orleans: Jean Baptiste Le Seur Fontaine, 1803. (Cat. 92).

Moniteur de la Louisiane. New Orleans, February 21, 1810. (Cat. 93; plate).

Félix de Courmont. *Le Capitaine May et le General de la Vega sur les Bords du Rio Grande, Opera comique en un Acte* ... Nouvelle Orléans: J. L. Sollée, 1847. (Cat. 96).

Les Cenelles. Choix de Poesies indigenes. Nouvelle Orléans: H. Lauve et cie., 1845. (Cat. 95).

Case 6 – Waldo Lincoln

The Royal Danish American Gazette. Christiansted, St. Croix, Vol. VII, No. 911, September 11, 1776. (Cat. 104; plate).

Sidney Smith. *Smith's Universal Receipt Book of Culinary Arts, ...* New York, 1842. (Cat. 105; plate).

Louise-Béate-Augustine Friedel. *The French Cook: A Full and Literal Translation of "La petite Cuisinière habile"* ... New York: Wm. H. Graham, 1846. (Cat. 106).

Case 6 – Thomas O. Mabbott

The Weekly Rake. New York, July 9, 1842. (Cat. 99).

Case 6 – Michael Papantonio

John Ratcliff. Bookbinding, Boston, ca. 1670, on: Nathaniel Morton. *New-Englands Memorial or, a Brief Relation of the Most Memorable and Remarkable Passages of the Providence of God* ... Cambridge, Massachusetts: Samuel Green and Marmaduke Johnson for John Usher, 1669. (Cat. 102; plate).

Francis Skinner. Bookbinding, Newport, Rhode Island, ca. 1750, on: Jeremiah Burroughs. *Two Treatises of Mr. Jeremiah Burroughs. The First of Earthly Mindedness* ... London: Peter Cole, 1649. (Cat. 103; plate).

Case 6 – Frank J. Metcalf

James Lyon. *Urania, or a Choice Collection of Psalm-Tunes, Anthems, and Hymns* ... Philadelphia: possibly William Bradford, 1761. (Cat. 97).

Frank J. Metcalf. *American Psalmody, or, Titles of Books, Containing Tunes Printed in America from 1721-1820.* New York: C. F. Heartman, 1917. (Cat. 98).

Case 6 – Charles Lemuel Nichols

Thomas White. *A Little Book for Little Children.* Boston: Timothy Green for Nicholas Buttolph, 1702. (Cat. 108).

Isaiah Thomas. *Catalogue of Books to be Sold by Isaiah Thomas, at His Book-Store in Worcester* ... Worcester: Isaiah Thomas, 1787. (Cat. 107; plate).

Mother Goose's Melody: or Sonnets for the Cradle ... Worcester: Isaiah Thomas, Jun., 1799. (Cat. 109; plate).

Mother Goose's Quarto: or Melodies Complete. Boston: Munroe & Francis, ca. 1824-1827. (Cat. 110; plate).

Case 7 – Donald McKay Frost

Henry James Warre. *Breakfast, July 19, 1845, Our First View of the Rocky Mountains.* Watercolor on paper, 1845. (Cat. 111).

Henry James Warre. *Camp in the Mountains, July 24, 1845.* Watercolor on paper, 1845. (Cat. 112; plate).

Frontier Scout. Fort Rice, Dakota Territory, June 15, 1865. (Cat. 117; plate).

American Society for Encouraging the Settlement of the Oregon Territory. *A General Circular to All Persons of Good Character, Who Wish to Emigrate to the Oregon Territory* ... Charlestown, Massachusetts: William W. Wheildon, R.P. & C. Williams, 1831. (Cat. 113).

John Ross Dix. *Amusing and Thrilling Adventures of a California Artist, while Daguerreotyping a Continent* ... Boston: Geo. K. Snow for John Ross Dix, 1854. (Cat. 116).

Zenas Leonard. *Narrative of the Adventures of Zenas Leonard ... Who Spent Five Years in Trapping for Furs, Trading with the Indians* ... Clearfield, Pennsylvania: D.W. Moore, 1839. (Cat. 115).

James Harvey Barnum. *The Traveller's Guide, or, the Life of James H. Barnum.* Great Barrington, Massachusetts: James H. Barnum, 1847. (Cat. 114).

Thomas J. Dimsdale. *The Vigilantes of Montana, or Popular Justice in the Rocky Mountains* ... Virginia City, Montana Territory: Montana Post Press, D.W. Tilton & Co., 1866. (Cat. 118).

Now Completed and for Sale! An Impartial and Correct History of the Vigilantes of Montana Territory! ... D.W. Tilton & Co., 1866. (Cat. 119; plate).

Case 7 – Thomas W. Streeter

Denver City and Auraria, the Commercial Emporium of the Pike's Peak Gold Regions, in 1859. Possibly St. Louis, 1860. (Cat. 128; plate).

Holisso hushi holhtena isht anoli. Chahta Almanac for the Year of our Lord 1836: Adapted to the Latitude of the Choctaw Country. Union, Oklahoma: Mission Press, John F. Wheeler, 1836. (Cat. 123; plate).

Knox & M'Kee. *Transportation to the West. Wheeling, May 20, 1834* ... Wheeling, West Virginia: Times Press, 1834. (Cat. 121).

Indignation Meeting! Down with All Monopolies! ... Wooster, Ohio: 1853. (Cat. 122; plate).

Madison, Indianapolis, and Lafayette Rail-Road Company. *An Act to Incorporate the Madison, Indianapolis and Lafayette Rail-Road Company, Passed ... February 2, 1832.* Madison, Indiana: Arion & Lodge, 1832. (Cat. 120).

Northwest Territory. *Laws of the Territory of the United States North-West of the Ohio* ... Cincinnati: W. Maxwell, 1796. (Cat. 125).

Florida General Assembly. *Report of the Committee Appointed to Frame the Plan of Provisional Government for the Republic of Floridas* ... Fernandina, Florida: R. Findley, December 9, 1817. (Cat. 126).

José Mariano Romero. *Catecismo de Ortologia. Dedicado á los Alumnos de la Escuela normal de Monterrey.* Monterey, California: Agust. V. Zamorano, 1836. (Cat. 127).

David Rice. *A Lecture on the Divine Decrees, to Which is Annexed a Few Observations on a Piece lately printed in Lexington* ... Lexington, Kentucky: John Bradford, 1791. (Cat. 124).

Thomas W. Streeter. "Catalogue of the American Library of Thomas W. Streeter," vol. 3 (of 87), ca. 1941-1965. (Cat. 129).

Case 8 – Wilbur Macey Stone

Isaac Watts. *Divine Songs, Attempted in Easy Language, for the Use of Children.* Boston: N. Coverly, 1775. (Cat. 130).

Isaac Watts. *Watts Divine Songs for the Use of Children.* Philadelphia: J. Johnson, 1807. (Cat. 131; plate).

Isaac Watts. *Divine Songs, Attempted in Easy Language, for the Use of Children.* Boston: Samuel T. Armstrong, 1819. (Cat. 132).

Isaac Watts. *Watts' Divine and Moral Songs. For the Use of Children.* New York: Mahlon Day, 1829. (Cat. 133).

Case 8 – James d'Alté A. Welch

The Book of Nouns, or, Things Which May Be Seen. Philadelphia: J. Johnson, 1802. (Cat. 134).

Alfred Mills. *Pictures of English History, in Miniature, from the Reign of Henry VI to the Death of Lord Nelson.* Philadelphia: Johnson and Warner, 1815. (Cat. 138; plate).

The Affecting History of the Children in the Wood. Newport, Rhode Island: H. & O. Farnsworth, 1799. (Cat. 135).

The Courtship, Marriage, and Pic-nic Dinner of Cock Robin & Jenny Wren, with the Death and Burial of Poor Cock Robin. Harrisburg, Pennsylvania: G.S. Peters, 1837. (Cat. 136).

The Mother's Remarks on a Set of Cuts for Children. Parts I-II. Philadelphia: T. S. Manning for Jacob Johnson, 1803. (Cat. 137; plate).

Case 8 – Ruth E. Adomeit

Bible History. New York: S. Wood, 1814. (Cat. 139).

A Short History of the Holy Bible. Harrisburg, Pennsylvania: G. S. Peters, 1840. (Cat. 140).

Joseph Wetherbee Carpenter, ed. *The St. George Juvenile.* St. George, Utah Territory, December 15, 1868. (Cat. 141).

J. J. Jackson. *Nonsense for Girls.* New York: McLoughlin Bros., ca. 1874. (Cat. 142; plate).

Case 8 – Benjamin Tighe / Elisabeth Ball

People of All Nations: An Useful Toy for Girl or Boy. Albany, New York: H. C. Southwick, ca. 1812. (Cat. 145; plate).

Charles Perrault. *Contes du Tems passé de Ma Mere l'Oye … Tales of Passed Times by Mother Goose … Septieme ed.* New York: J. Rivington, 1795. (Cat. 146).

The Renowned History of Giles Gingerbread, a Little Boy Who Lived upon Learning. First Worcester ed. Worcester: Isaiah Thomas, 1786. (Cat. 149).

The Entertaining History of Jobson & Nell: Illustrated with Humorous Engravings. Philadelphia: Wm. Charles, 1814. (Cat. 147; plate).

J. Baker. *My Pony.* Philadelphia: Wm. Charles, 1818. (Cat. 148).

Case 8 – Benjamin Tighe

John Greene Chandler. *Remarkable Story of Chicken Little.* Roxbury, Massachusetts: J. G. Chandler, 1840. (Cat. 143; plate).

Hans Christian Andersen. *Good Wishes for the Children.* Cambridge, Massachusetts: The Riverside Press, 1873. (Cat. 144; plate).

Case 8 – Herbert H. Hosmer

Anthony Hochstein. *Crane's Bill.* Watercolor on paper, ca. 1860-1895. (Cat. 152).

George P. Webster. *Santa Claus and His Works.* New York: McLoughlin Bros., ca. 1875. (Cat. 150).

Kriss Kringle Taking Inventory. Watercolor on paper, ca. 1897. (Cat. 151; plate).

Cinderella. New York: McLoughlin Bros., 1882. (Cat. 153).

Cinderella. New York: McLoughlin Bros., 1891. (Cat. 154; plate).

Case 9 – Bibliography / Isaiah Thomas

Isaiah Thomas. "General Catalogue of books Printed in the British Colonies before the Revolution," fascicles 3 & 5, compiled 1800 1810. (Cat. 155; plate).

Case 9 – Bibliography / Samuel Foster Haven, Jr.

Samuel F. Haven, Jr. Working slips for a bibliography of books published in America before the Revolution, compiled 1858-1861. (Cat. 156; plate).

Titan Leeds. *The American Almanack for the Year of Christian Account, 1740 ...* Second edition. Philadelphia: Andrew Bradford, 1739. (Cat. 157).

Case 9 – Bibliography / Charles Evans

Charles Evans. Working slips for *American Bibliography,* housed in a corset box. (Cat. 158; plate).

Letter, Charles Evans to Clarence S. Brigham, October 4, 1912. (Cat. 160).

Mason Locke Weems. *The Life and Memorable Actions of George Washington, General and Commander of the Armies of America, a New Edition, Corrected.* Frederick-Town, Maryland: Matthias Bartgis, 1801. (Cat. 159).

Case 9 – Bibliography / Clarence S. Brigham

Brownsville Gazette. Brownsville, Pennsylvania, May 21, 1808. (Cat. 161; plate).

Paul Revere. Clock Label for Aaron Willard. Boston, July 1781. (Cat. 162; plate).

Sample record from Clarence, the AAS newspaper holdings database, for the *Massachusetts Spy*. (Cat. 163).

Case 9 – Bibliography / Clifford K. Shipton

Clifford K. Shipton, shown promoting the *Early American Imprints* microprint, Worcester: photographed for the *Telegram & Gazette*, 1957. (Cat. 164; Fig. 40, p. 175).

Early American Imprints 1639-1800. Box 1. Worcester: American Antiquarian Society and Readex Microprint, 1955. (Cat. 165).

Cotton Mather. *Rules for the Society of Negroes. 1693*. Boston: probably Bartholomew Green, ca. 1714. (Cat. 166).

Case 9 – Bibliography / Computerization

Joseph Green, *Entertainment for a Winter's Evening: Being a Full and True Account of a Very Strange and Wonderful Sight in Boston on the Twenty-Seventh of December, 1749*. Boston: Gamaliel Rogers, 1750. (Cat. 167).

Case 9 – Bibliography / AAS Publications

Selected bibliographies published by the American Antiquarian Society. (Cat. 168; plate).

Case 10 – Endowed Book Funds

Samuel Richardson. *Pamela: Or, Virtue Rewarded ...* Fifth edition. Philadelphia: B. Franklin, 1742-1743. (Cat. 169; plate).

Harry; The Boy That Did Not Own Himself. Boston: American Tract Society, ca. 1863. (Cat. 170).

David Claypoole Johnston. *Early Development of Southern Chivalry*. India ink and watercolor on paper, ca. 1864. (Cat. 171; plate).

Bookplates for selected AAS endowed acquisitions funds, various designers, 1965-2012. (Cat. 186; plate).

Case 10 – Collecting Transatlantic Printing

Michele Fanoli, after Richard Canton Woodville. *Politics in an Oyster House*. Paris and New York: Lemercier for Goupil & Co., 1851. (Cat. 176; plate).

Johann Hübner. *Hübners Biblische Historien als dem Alten und Neuen Testamente ...* Cornersburg, Ohio: Augustus Gräter, 1835. (Cat. 178).

The Life of Philip Quarll, Giving an Account of His Surprising Adventures on an Inunhabited [sic] *Island*. Baltimore: C. Scheld and Co., 1833. (Cat. 177).

Case 10 – Curatorial Collecting Priorities

The Chess Monthly. New York, Vol. 3, No. 2, February 1859. (Cat. 172; plate).

Our Choir, in 1860-61. By You Know Who. Illustrated by Phiz. New York, 1861. (Cat. 175; plate).

Publisher's Binding on: Susan Pindar. *Fireside Fairies: Or Christmas at Aunt Elsie's.* New York: D. Appleton; Philadelphia: Geo. S. Appleton, ca. 1849. (Cat. 174; plate).

Edward C. Gay. *The Boy Smuggler.* Farmer City, Illinois: Ed. C. Gay, 1876. (Cat. 179).

Le Bijou. Cincinnati, Vol. 3, No. 2, September 1879. (Cat. 180; plate).

"The Kentucky Spy and Porcupine Quill." Frankfort, Kentucky, Vol. 6, No. 1, January 25, 1849. (Cat. 181; plate).

James Porter. *Clergyman's Pocket Diary and Visiting Book. 186__.* New York: Carlton and Porter, 1860. (Cat. 173).

Case 10 – Cooperative Projects

James Fenimore Cooper. *The Last of the Mohicans; a Narrative of 1757.* Philadelphia: H.C. Carey & I. Lea, 1826. (Cat. 182).

James Fenimore Cooper. *The Last of the Mohicans; a Narrative of 1757.* Albany: State University of New York Press, 1983. (Cat. 183).

Letter. David D. Hall to Marcus A. McCorison, July 14, 1982. (Cat. 184).

A History of the Book in America. Cambridge, England: Cambridge University Press & American Antiquarian Society, 2000; University of North Carolina Press & American Antiquarian Society, 5 vols., 2007-2010. (Cat. 185; plate).

Figures

Figures, all collection of the American Antiquarian Society.

1. Paul Revere, Bookplate for Isaiah Thomas, first state, 1769.

2. Bookplate for Isaiah Thomas's Gifts to the Society, ca. 1820.

3. Signature of Hannah Mather Crocker, ca. 1820.

4. Bookplate for William Bentley, ca. 1800.

5. Bookplate for Thomas Wallcut, 1774.

6. Signature of Christopher Columbus Baldwin, ca. 1834.

7. Signature of Lucy Chase, ca. 1865-1870.

8. Signature of Sarah E. Chase, ca. 1865-1870.

9. Bookplate for George Brinley, ca. 1860-1870.

10. Adams Gallery, Worcester, *Stephen Salisbury III,* carte-de-visite, 1862-1870.

11. Bookplate for Stephen Salisbury Jr., ca. 1875-1900.

12. Bookplate for Nathaniel Paine, ca. 1875-1900.

13. Bookplate for George F. Hoar, ca. 1875-1900.

14. Edwin D. French after E. B. Bird, Bookplate for Charles Henry Taylor, 1896.

15. Blank & Stoller, New York, *Charles Henry Taylor,* ca. 1937-40.

16. William F. Hopson, Bookplate for Herbert E. Lombard, 1918.

17. Bookplate for Matt B. Jones, n.d.

18. Sidney L. Smith, Bookplate for Frank Brewer Bemis, 1925.

19. Sidney L. Smith, Bookplate for the Frederick Lewis Gay Bequest, 1919.

20. Sidney L. Smith, Bookplate for John Whittemore Farwell, 1908.

21. Sidney L. Smith, Bookplate for James Frothingham Hunnewell, 1902.

22. Signature of Samuel L. Munson, ca. 1920.

23. Bookplate for Edward Larocque Tinker, n.d.

24. Bookplate for Frank J. Metcalf, 1882.

25. Bookplate for the Michael Papantonio Memorial Fund, 1978.

26. Fabian Bachrach, *Waldo Lincoln,* 1922.

27. Bookplate for the Waldo Lincoln Collection of American Cookery Books, 1929.

28. Benson, *Charles L. Nichols,* May 29, 1929.

29. Bookplate for Charles L. Nichols, Jr., n.d.

30.   Alfred J. Downey, Bookplate for Donald McKay Frost, 1934.

31.   Bookplate for Thomas W. Streeter, n.d.

32.   B. Cory Kilvert, Bookplate for Wilbur Macey Stone, 1901.

33.   Business card for Benjamin Tighe, bookseller, n.d.

34.   Bookplate for James d'Alté Welch, n.d.

35.   Bookplate for Ruth Adomeit, n.d.

36.   Bookplate for Elisabeth Ball, n.d.

37.   Bookplate for the Herbert H. Hosmer Donation, American Antiquarian Society, 1978.

38.   *Samuel Foster Haven, Jr.,* tintype, ca. 1860.

39.   Rufus Gould, Worcester, *Clarence S. Brigham,* May 20, 1940.

40.   *Clifford K. Shipton promoting the Early American Imprints microprint, Worcester:* photographed for the *Telegram & Gazette,* 1957.

41.   Marvin Richmond, *Marcus A. McCorison,* photographed for the *Telegram & Gazette,* January 31, 1979.

42.   Frank Armstrong, *Ellen S. Dunlap with the Massachusetts Spy,* 1998

43.   John Kristensen, Firefly Press, Bookplate for the American Antiquarian Society Bicentennial, 2010.

Illustration facing Preface:
   E. B. Luce, *Interior of the Second Antiquarian Hall,* 1910 (detail).

Illustration facing Hand List for the Exhibition:
   Frank Armstrong, *The Reading Room at the American Antiquarian Society,* 2006 (detail).

Detail on the title page is from Archibald Simson. *Hieroglyphica Animalium Terrestrium, Natatilium, Reptilium, Insectorum ... quæ in Scripturis Sacris Inveniuntur ...* Edinburgh: Thomas Finlayson, 1622 [i.e. 1624]. (Cat. 17).

References

AAS Chief Joys   American Antiquarian Society. *A Society's Chief Joys*. Worcester: American Antiquarian Society, 1969.

AAS Wellsprings   American Antiquarian Society, *Wellsprings of a Nation*. Text by Rodger D. Parker. Worcester: American Antiquarian Society, 1977.

Adomeit   Adomeit, Ruth E. *Three Centuries of Thumb Bibles: A Checklist*. New York: Garland Pub., 1980.

American Imprints   *A Checklist of American Imprints: For 1830-1846*. Compiled by Gayle Cooper, Scott Bruntjen, and Carol Rinderknecht. Metuchen, New Jersey: Scarecrow Press, 1972-1997.

BAL   Blanck, Jacob. *Bibliography of American Literature*. Compiled by Jacob Blanck, Virginia L. Smyers, and Michael Winship. New Haven: Yale University Press, 1955-1991.

Bradbury   Bradbury, Robert C. *Antique United States Miniature Books, 1690-1900: Principally from the Collections of the American Antiquarian Society and the Lilly Library, Indiana University*. North Clarendon, Vermont: The Microbibliophile, 2001.

Brigham   Brigham, Clarence S. *Paul Revere's Engravings*. Worcester: American Antiquarian Society, 1954.

Brinley Sale   *Catalogue of the American Library of the Late Mr. George Brinley of Hartford, Conn. ...* Hartford: Case, Lockwood & Brainard Co., 1878-1897.

Bristol   Bristol, Roger P. *Supplement to Charles Evans' American Bibliography*. Charlottesville: Published for the Bibliographical Society of America and the Bibliographical Society of the University of Virginia by University Press of Virginia, 1970.

Britton & Lowens   *American Sacred Music Imprints, 1698-1810: A Bibliography*. By Allen Perdue Britton and Irving Lowens, completed by Richard Crawford. Worcester: American Antiquarian Society, 1990.

Cooke Sale   George A. Leavitt & Co. *Catalogue of the Library of the Late Joseph J. Cooke, of Providence, Rhode Island ...* New York: George A. Leavitt & Co., 1883.

Drake   Drake, Milton. *Almanacs of the United States*. New York: Scarecrow Press, 1962.

Evans   Evans, Charles. *American Bibliography: A Chronological Dictionary of all Books, Pamphlets, and Periodical Publications Printed in the United States of America from the Genesis of Printing in 1639 Down to and Including the Year 1820: With Bibliographical and Biographical Notes*. Chicago: Privately printed for the author, 1903-1934; Worcester: American Antiquarian Society, 1955-1959.

Forbes   Forbes, David W. *Hawaiian National Bibliography, 1780-1900*. Honolulu: University of Hawaii Press, 1998-2003.

Hewes   Hewes, Lauren B. *Portraits in the Collection of the American Antiquarian Society.* Worcester: American Antiquarian Society, 2004.

Holmes, *Cotton Mather*   Holmes, Thomas James. *Cotton Mather: A Bibliography of His Works.* Cambridge, Massachusetts: Harvard University Press, 1940.

Holmes, *Increase Mather* Holmes, Thomas James. *Increase Mather: A Bibliography of His Works.* Cleveland: W. G. Mather, 1931.

Holmes, *Minor Mathers*   Holmes, Thomas James. *Minor Mathers: A List of Their Works.* Cambridge, Massachusetts: Harvard University Press, 1940.

Judd   Judd, Bernice. *Hawaiian Language Imprints, 1822-1899: A Bibliography.* Honolulu: Hawaiian Mission Children's Society, 1978.

Jumonville   Jumonville, Florence M. *Bibliography of New Orleans Imprints, 1764-1864.* New Orleans: Historic New Orleans Collection, 1989.

Lowenstein   Lowenstein, Eleanor. *Bibliography of American Cookery Books, 1742-1860.* Worcester: American Antiquarian Society, 1972.

McDonald   McDonald, Gerald D. *A Checklist of American Newspaper Carriers' Addresses, 1720-1820.* By Gerald D. McDonald, Stuart C. Sherman, and Mary T. Russo. Worcester: American Antiquarian Society, 2000.

McKay   McKay, George L. *American Book Auction Catalogues, 1713-1934: A Union List.* New York: The New York Public Library, 1937.

Miller   Miller, C. William. *Benjamin Franklin's Philadelphia Printing, 1728-1766: A Descriptive Bibliography.* Philadelphia: American Philosophical Society, 1974.

Mosley   Mosley, James. *British Type Specimens before 1831: A Hand-list.* Oxford: Oxford Bibliographical Society, Bodleian Library in association with the Dept. of Typography & Graphic Communication, University of Reading, 1984.

Papantonio   *Early American Bookbindings from the Collection of Michael Papantonio.* Second ed., enl. Worcester: American Antiquarian Society, 1985.

Parrish & Willingham   Parrish, T. Michael. *Confederate Imprints: A Bibliography of Southern Publications from Secession to Surrender.* By T. Michael Parrish & Robert M. Willingham, Jr. Austin: Jenkins Publishing Co., 1987.

Pomeroy   Pomeroy, Jane R. *Alexander Anderson (1775-1870): Wood Engraver and Illustrator: An Annotated Bibliography.* New Castle, Del.: Oak Knoll Press; Worcester: American Antiquarian Society in association with the New York Public Library, 2005.

Rosenbach   Rosenbach, A. S. W. *Early American Children's Books.* Portland, Maine: The Southworth Press, 1933.

Shaw & Shoemaker   Shaw, Ralph R. *American Bibliography: A Preliminary Checklist for 1801-1819.* Compiled by Ralph R. Shaw and Richard H. Shoemaker. New York: Scarecrow Press, 1958-1966.

Shipton & Mooney   Shipton, Clifford K. *National Index of American Imprints through 1800: The Short-Title Evans.* Clifford K. Shipton, James E. Mooney. Worcester: American Antiquarian Society; Barre Publishers, 1969.

Shoemaker — Shoemaker, Richard H. *Checklist of American Imprints for 1820-1829*. New York: Scarecrow Press, 1964-1973.

Spear — Spear, Dorothea N. *Bibliography of American Directories through 1860*. Worcester: American Antiquarian Society, 1961.

STC — Jackson, William A. *A Short-Title Catalogue of Books Printed in England, Scotland, & Ireland, and of English Books Printed Abroad 1475-1640*. Begun by W.A. Jackson and F.S. Ferguson, completed by Katharine F. Pantzer. 2nd ed., rev. and enl. London: The Bibliographical Society, 1976-1991.

Stoddard — Stoddard, Roger E. *A Bibliographical Description of Books and Pamphlets of American Verse Printed from 1610 through 1820*. University Park: The Pennsylvania State University Press for the Bibliographical Society of America, 2012.

Streeter Sale — Parke-Bernet Galleries. *The Celebrated Collection of Americana Formed by the Late Thomas Winthrop Streeter* ... New York: Parke-Bernet Galleries, 1966-1970.

Suzuki & Pulliam — Suzuki, Seiko June. *California Imprints: 1833-1862: A Bibliography*. Compiled by Seiko June Suzuki & Marjorie Pulliam and the Historical Records Survey; edited by Robert Greenwood. Los Gatos, California: Talisman Press, 1961.

Tremaine — Tremaine, Marie. *A Bibliography of Canadian Imprints, 1751-1800*. Toronto: University of Toronto Press, 1952.

Wagner-Camp — Wagner, Henry R. *The Plains and the Rockies: A Critical Bibliography of Exploration, Adventure and Travel in the American West, 1800-1865*. Henry R. Wagner and Charles L. Camp. 4th ed. rev., enl. and ed. by Robert H. Becker. San Francisco: John Howell Books, 1982.

Wegelin — Wegelin, Oscar. *Early American Poetry: A Compilation of the Titles and Volumes of Verse and Broadsides by Writers Born or Residing in North America, North of the Mexican Border*. 2nd ed., rev. and enl. New York: Peter Smith, 1930.

Weis — Weis, Frederick L. *Checklist of the Portraits in the Library of the American Antiquarian Society*. Worcester: American Antiquarian Society, 1947.

Weiss — Weiss, Harry B. *William Charles, Early Caricaturist, Engraver and Publisher of Children's Books: With a List of Works by Him in the New York Public Library and Certain Other Collections*. New York: New York Public Library, 1932.

Welch — Welch, d'Alté A. *A Bibliography of American Children's Books Printed Prior to 1821*. Barre, Massachusetts: American Antiquarian Society and Barre Publishers, 1972.

Winans — Winans, Robert B. *A Descriptive Checklist of Book Catalogues Separately Printed in America, 1693-1800*. Worcester: American Antiquarian Society, 1981.

Wing — Wing, Donald G. *Short-Title Catalogue of Books Printed in England, Scotland, Ireland, Wales, and British America, and of English Books Printed in other Countries, 1641-1700*. 2d ed., rev. and enl. New York: Index Committee of the Modern Language Association of America, 1982-1994.

IN PURSUIT OF A VISION
Two Centuries of Collecting
at the American Antiquarian Society
was published in September 2012
in celebration of the Society's bicentennial.

The text is set in Sabon,
Copperplate Gothic, and Perpetua,
and is printed on Endurance.

Printed by
Capital Offset Company,
Concord, New Hampshire
&
Bound by
Acme Bookbinding Company
Charlestown, Massachusetts